ESSENTIAL
JAPANESE
KANJI

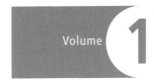

Volume 1

ESSENTIAL
JAPANESE
KANJI

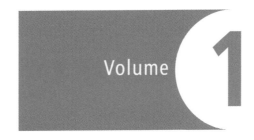

Volume 1

The Kanji Text Research Group, The University of Tokyo

TUTTLE Publishing

Tokyo | Rutland, Vermont | Singapore

Published by Tuttle Publishing, an imprint of Periplus Editions (HK) Ltd.

www.tuttlepublishing.com

Library of Congress Control Number: 2014949127

ISBN 978-4-8053-1340-4

Distributed by

North America, Latin America & Europe
Tuttle Publishing
364 Innovation Drive
North Clarendon,
VT 05759-9436 U.S.A.
Tel: 1 (802) 773-8930
Fax: 1 (802) 773-6993
info@tuttlepublishing.com
www.tuttlepublishing.com

Japan
Tuttle Publishing
Yaekari Building, 3rd Floor,
5-4-12 Osaki, Shinagawa-ku
Tokyo 141 0032
Tel: (81) 3 5437-0171
Fax: (81) 3 5437-0755
sales@tuttle.co.jp
www.tuttle.co.jp

Asia Pacific
Berkeley Books Pte. Ltd.
3 Kallang Sector #04-01
Singapore 349278
Tel: (65) 6741-2178
Fax: (65) 6741-2179
inquiries@periplus.com.sg
www.periplus.com

24 23 22 21 20   10 9 8 7 6 5 4

Printed in Singapore   2005TP

TUTTLE PUBLISHING® is a registered trademark of Tuttle Publishing, a division of Periplus Editions (HK) Ltd.

TO THE LEARNER

Do you like learning kanji? Or do you wish that kanji would disappear from the face of the earth—or at least from the Japanese language? Well, learning kanji can be fun, *if* you are motivated. And this kanji book was created to motivate you, with practical learning methods that really work, and which will enable you to enjoy studying kanji.

The first edition of this book was published in 1993, and a second volume was published in 1997. Since then, they've helped countless learners master kanji. In later editions, we revised the books to include the 410 kanji required for the College Board Advanced Placement Japanese Language and Culture Course Exam.

Taking an Active Approach

An important feature of this book is the active approach it takes to introducing kanji. By using authentic materials, periodic quizzes, and memory aids, it gradually helps learners acquire the ability to understand and use kanji in natural contexts—that is, in everyday life.

Another key aspect of *Essential Japanese Kanji Volume 1* is the presentation of authentic materials, for instance the actual instructions written on the medicine envelopes you might receive from the doctor in Japan. We also use photographs, many of which were taken by our foreign students during their adventures in Japan. The kanji taught here are, clearly, based on everyday use. (Please note that prices mentioned in these authentic materials may have changed.)

Also, for each kanji we include either etymologies or memory aids, which will help students to understand and memorize the kanji systematically. The list of kanji compounds will also help learners understand how new words are created by combining the familiar kanji, and to realize the power that mastering kanji offers them.

Each lesson helps you master a new group of kanji, and consists of several sections.
- **Introductory Quiz** introduces some familiar, everyday situations where the kanji is likely to be used.
- **Vocabulary** contains the readings and meanings of the kanji that you've encountered in the Quiz.
- **New Characters** teaches you the kanji systematically, by introducing the meaning, the basic **on-kun** readings, the etymologies or memory aids, and compound words.
- **Practice** will help you improve your kanji reading and writing skills.
- **Advanced Placement Exam Practice Questions** will test your competence in reading and writing semi-authentic natural Japanese. These questions reflect the format of the College Board's Japanese Language and Culture examination.

We wish to thank Yuichi Ikeda for the illustrations, and also Koichi Maekawa, Michael Handford, Su Di, Sandra Korinchak, and Cathy Layne. Junko Ishida and Akiyo Nishino revised the 2008 edition; Junko Ishida, Kaori Kaieda, Mikiko Shibuya, and Akiyo Nishino revised the 2015 edition.

We received funding from the Japan Foundation to publish the original edition of this book.

The following books were useful in compiling the kanji charts: *Reikai Gakushu Kanji Jiten*, published by Shogakukan, and *Kanjigen* published by Gakushu Kenkyusha.

We sincerely hope that this book will help all learners—yes, even you who have been stymied by kanji before!—begin to enjoy learning kanji.

The Kanji Text Research Group, The University
  of Tokyo 漢字教材研究グループ
Japanese Language Class 日本語教室
Department of Civil Engineering 社会基盤学専攻
The University of Tokyo 東京大学大学院

Authors: 著者:
Junko Ishida   石田 順子
Kaori Kaieda   海江田 香
Kazuko Nagatomi   長富 和子
Akiyo Nishino   西野 章代
Junko Sagara   相良 淳子
Mikiko Shibuya   渋谷 幹子
Masako Watanabe   渡辺 雅子
Yoshiko Yamazaki   山崎 佳子

CONTENTS

INTRODUCTION

This book contains 21 lessons introducing 250 kanji. Each lesson focuses on an everyday situation in Japan.

There is a short explanation of kanji and kana before the lessons begin. You will also find the Appendices, the **On-Kun** Index and the Vocabulary Index useful to refer to as you learn.

From Lesson 1 through Lesson 10, the Japanese is written with a space between words except in the Advanced Placement Exam Practice Questions at the end of every chapter. A modified Hepburn system of romanization has been used.

Each lesson is composed of the following sections.

1. **Introductory Quiz** — This section describes situations that you may encounter in daily life, and is followed by a quiz. By referring first to the words in **Vocabulary**, you'll learn the readings and the meanings of the words that are introduced in the lesson. And by solving the quiz, you will understand the situation that's presented. Try the quiz again *after* the lesson, and you'll find out how much you have learned.

2. **Vocabulary** — This section contains the readings and meanings of the words used in the **Introductory Quiz.** Refer to it when studying the illustrations or taking the quiz. The numeral above each kanji indicates the lesson where the kanji is introduced.

3. **New Characters** — This section introduces the kanji of the lesson using **Kanji Charts** with their meanings, basic **on-kun** readings, stroke orders, etymologies or memory-aid hints, and compounds with their English translations.

   The compounds essentially consist of newly or previously introduced kanji. (Kanji that are not included in the 250 taught in volume 1 are marked with ×.) More important compounds are shown in the upper part of the list. However, you are encouraged to study those in the lower part of the list as well. When kana is optionally added to kanji (**okurigana**), the most common usage is adopted and formal usages are shown in parentheses.

4. **Practice** — This section provides practice for reading and writing the kanji found mainly in the upper part of the kanji charts. You should use the practice as a final check for the kanji learned in each lesson. Answers to this section are not provided.

5. **Advanced Placement Exam Practice Questions** — This section provides an exercise similar in format to the College Board's Advanced Placement examination for Japanese Language and Culture. You can try the exercise after each lesson, or after completing all the lessons.

UNDERSTANDING KANJI

The oldest Chinese characters, the precursors of kanji, originated more than 3,000 years ago. Originally they were simple illustrations of objects and phenomena in everyday life, and developed as a writing tool mainly characterized by pictography and ideography. Thus each of the Chinese characters carries its own meaning within itself.

Chinese characters, or kanji, can be classified according to origin and structure into four main categories:

1. Pictographic characters are derived from the shapes of concrete objects.

    🌳 → 木 → 木 = tree

    ☀ → ⊖ → 日 = sun

2. Sign characters are composed of points and lines that express abstract ideas.

    • → 上 → 上 = above, on, up

    • → 下 → 下 = below, down, under

3. Ideographic characters are composed of combinations of other characters.

    木 (tree) ＋ 木 (tree) → 林 = forest

    日 (sun) ＋ 月 (moon) → 明 = bright

4. Phonetic-ideographic characters are composed of combinations of ideographic and phonetic elements. Upper parts or righthand parts often indicate the reading of the kanji. About 90% of all kanji fall into this category.

    先 (セン previous) → 洗 (セン wash)
    安 (アン peaceful) → 案 (アン proposal)

The Japanese had no writing symbols until kanji were introduced from China in the fifth century. Soon after this, kanji were simplified into phonetic symbols known as **hiragana** and **katakana**. Thus the Japanese language came to be written in combinations of **kanji** and **kana** (see page 11).

This kanji-kana writing system is more effective than writing with kana only. As the written Japanese language doesn't leave spaces between words, kanji among kana make it easier for readers to distinguish units of meaning and to understand the context. Readers can easily grasp the rough meaning of written text by following kanji only.

Kanji can usually be read two ways. These readings are referred to as **on-yomi** and **kun-yomi**. **On-yomi** is the Japanese reading taken from the original Chinese pronunciation. **Kun-yomi** is the pronunciation of an original Japanese word applied to a kanji according to its meaning. Hiragana added after **kun-yomi** readings are called **okurigana**. **Okurigana** primarily indicates the inflectional ending of a kanji, though the last part of the stem is occasionally included in the **okurigana**.

Most kanji are composed of two or more elements, and parts of one kanji are often found in different combinations in other kanji. Certain commonly shared parts are called radicals, or **bushu** in Japanese. Radicals are used to classify kanji in dictionaries; thus each kanji is allocated only one radical. Each radical also carries a core meaning. For example, the radical 言 means "word" or "speak." Therefore the kanji 語 (language), 話 (speak, story), 読 (read), 記 (note down), and 論 (discuss) all have something to do with the meaning of 言.

There are 214 radicals altogether. These are some frequently seen radicals:

1. 扌 hand	5. 言 word, speak	9. 金 metal, gold	13. 阝 village	17. 尸 corpse
2. 土 earth	6. 木 tree	10. 辶 road, proceed	14. 阝 wall, hill	18. 疒 sickness
3. 氵 water	7. 艹 plant	11. 儿 legs	15. 日 sun, day	19. 宀 roof, house
4. 亻 man, people	8. 糸 thread	12. 口 mouth	16. 門 gate	20. 十 add, many

(Note that the radical listed above as 13 is always used at the right of a character, and the one listed as 14 is always used at the left of a character.)

Kanji strokes are written in a fixed direction and order. There are several fundamental rules for writing the strokes.

1. Horizontal strokes: from left to right

三 (three)　土 (soil)　工 (engineering)

2. Vertical or slanting strokes: from top to bottom

十 (ten)　木 (tree)　人 (man)　八 (eight)

3. Hook strokes: from top left to right or left bottom

日 (day)　手 (hand)　分 (minute)　氏 (surname)

4. The center stroke first, followed by the left and right strokes

小 (small)　山 (mountain)

5. The outside strokes first, followed by the middle strokes

月 (moon)　中 (inside)

6. The horizontal stroke first, followed by the vertical stroke (usually followed by another horizontal stroke)

十 (ten)　土 (soil)

7. The left-hand slanting stroke first, followed by the right-hand side

八 (eight)　六 (six)

As your knowledge of kanji increases, kanji dictionaries become more helpful. There are three ways to refer to a kanji.

1. Look for the kanji by radical in the **bushu** (radical) index.
2. Look for the kanji by stroke number in the **kakusū** (stroke number) index.
3. Look for the kanji by pronunciation in the **on-kun** reading index.

UNDERSTANDING KANA

Japanese Writing Systems

There are four different kinds of characters used for writing Japanese: kanji, hiragana, katakana, and rōmaji (Roman alphabet). Kanji incorporates meanings as well as sounds. Hiragana, katakana, and rōmaji are phonetic characters that express only sounds. However, unlike English, one kana character can be pronounced only one way: 「あ」 or 「ア」 is only pronounced [a].

Japanese sentences are usually written with a combination of kanji, hiragana, and katakana. Katakana is mainly used for foreign words that are adapted to fit Japanese pronunciation. Kanji appears in nouns, verbs, adjectives, and adverbs. Hiragana is primarily used to show the inflectional endings of kanji (**okurigana**). Particles, conjunctions, and interjections are mostly written in hiragana. Although hiragana can substitute for kanji, a combination of kanji and hiragana is much faster to read. For example, compare these four ways of writing the same information:

Kanji and hiragana: 私は毎朝早く起きます。 出かける前にテレビを見ます。
Hiragana only: わたしはまいあさはやくおきます。 でかけるまえにテレビをみます。
Rōmaji: **Watashi-wa maiasa hayaku okimasu. Dekakeru mae-ni terebi-o mimasu.**
English: I get up early every morning. I watch TV before I leave home.

hiragana ── あ **a**
rōmaji ──
katakana ── ア

Japanese Syllabary Chart

Each square in the chart below represents one pronounced syllable.

	a	i	u	e	o
	あ a ／ ア	い i ／ イ	う u ／ ウ	え e ／ エ	お o ／ オ
k	か ka ／ カ	き ki ／ キ	く ku ／ ク	け ke ／ ケ	こ ko ／ コ
s	さ sa ／ サ	し shi ／ シ	す su ／ ス	せ se ／ セ	そ so ／ ソ
t	た ta ／ タ	ち chi ／ チ	つ tsu ／ ツ	て te ／ テ	と to ／ ト
n	な na ／ ナ	に ni ／ ニ	ぬ nu ／ ヌ	ね ne ／ ネ	の no ／ ノ
h	は ha ／ ハ	ひ hi ／ ヒ	ふ fu ／ フ	へ he ／ ヘ	ほ ho ／ ホ
m	ま ma ／ マ	み mi ／ ミ	む mu ／ ム	め me ／ メ	も mo ／ モ
y	や ya ／ ヤ		ゆ yu ／ ユ		よ yo ／ ヨ
r	ら ra ／ ラ	り ri ／ リ	る ru ／ ル	れ re ／ レ	ろ ro ／ ロ
w	わ wa ／ ワ				を o ／ ヲ

	ya	yu	yo
k	きゃ kya ／ キャ	きゅ kyu ／ キュ	きょ kyo ／ キョ
s	しゃ sha ／ シャ	しゅ shu ／ シュ	しょ sho ／ ショ
t	ちゃ cha ／ チャ	ちゅ chu ／ チュ	ちょ cho ／ チョ
n	にゃ nya ／ ニャ	にゅ nyu ／ ニュ	にょ nyo ／ ニョ
h	ひゃ hya ／ ヒャ	ひゅ hyu ／ ヒュ	ひょ hyo ／ ヒョ
m	みゃ mya ／ ミャ	みゅ myu ／ ミュ	みょ myo ／ ミョ
r	りゃ rya ／ リャ	りゅ ryu ／ リュ	りょ ryo ／ リョ

ん n ／ ン

g	が ga ガ	ぎ gi ギ	ぐ gu グ	げ ge ゲ	ご go ゴ
z	ざ za ザ	じ ji ジ	ず zu ズ	ぜ ze ゼ	ぞ zo ゾ
d	だ da ダ	ぢ ji ヂ	づ zu ヅ	で de デ	ど do ド
b	ば ba バ	び bi ビ	ぶ bu ブ	べ be ベ	ぼ bo ボ
p	ぱ pa パ	ぴ pi ピ	ぷ pu プ	ぺ pe ペ	ぽ po ポ

ぎゃ gya ギャ	ぎゅ gyu ギュ	ぎょ gyo ギョ
じゃ ja ジャ	じゅ ju ジュ	じょ jo ジョ

びゃ bya ビャ	びゅ byu ビュ	びょ byo ビョ
ぴゃ pya ピャ	ぴゅ pyu ピュ	ぴょ pyo ピョ

Additional Katakana

Created with small ア イ ウ エ オ ュ

	a	i	u	e	o	yu
y				イェ ye		
w		ウィ wi		ウェ we	ウォ wo	
kw	クァ kwa	クィ kwi		クェ kwe	クォ kwo	
gw	グァ gwa	グィ gwi		グェ gwe	グォ gwo	
sh				シェ she		
j				ジェ je		
t		ティ ti	トゥ tu			テュ tyu
d		ディ di	ドゥ du			デュ dyu
ts	ツァ tsa	ツィ tsi		ツェ tse	ツォ tso	
f	ファ fa	フィ fi		フェ fe	フォ fo	フュ fyu
v	ヴァ va	ヴィ vi	ヴ vu	ヴェ ve	ヴォ vo	ヴュ vyu

Derivation of Kana

Hiragana and katakana are Japanese phonetic syllabaries developed from kanji in the eighth century. Hiragana, which are cursive letters, derive from the shapes of entire kanji characters. Katakana, which are combinations of straight lines, derive from various parts of kanji characters. In some cases both hiragana and katakana are derived from the same kanji, such as **to**, **fu**, **he**, **ho**, **me**, and **wa**, shown below. Kana derived from some of the kanji introduced in this textbook are also shown.

A SAMPLE KANJI CHART

A sample from the kanji charts is explained below.

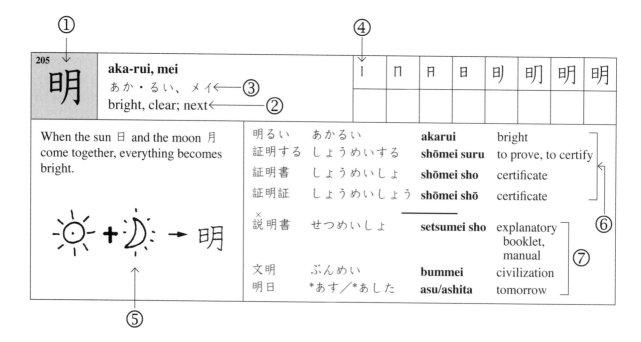

① The kanji and its serial number in this textbook.
② Meanings.
③ Readings: **kun**-readings in hiragana, and **on**-readings in katakana.
  Hiragana following a dot [・るい in the sample above] are **okurigana**.
  Readings in parentheses ( ) express euphonic change, i.e., modified readings. [For example, ヒャク、(ビャク)、(ピャク) seen in kanji 11, 百.]
④ Stroke order.
⑤ Etymology or memory-aid. (The authors have created new derivations for some kanji when the etymology is unclear or confusing.)
⑥ Important compound words, and their readings and meanings.
⑦ Additional compound words, and their readings and meanings.

Note that:

- Kanji marked × are not included in the 250 kanji taught in this volume of *Essential Japanese Kanji Characters*.
- Kana in parentheses ( ) in kanji compounds is optional when writing. [For example, 終（わ）る can be written 終わる or 終る]. Two sets of ( ) appear for most nouns derived from compound verbs. The kana in both ( ) or in the former ( ) only may be omitted, but the kana in the latter ( ) alone cannot be omitted. [For example, 取（り）消（し）can be written 取り消し、取消し、or 取消、but not 取り消.]
- * indicates exceptional readings.
- Small numbers placed above certain kanji in the Vocabulary sections refer to Lesson numbers in this book.

Let's Eat!

なにか たべましょう

In Japan, eating out is a popular alternative to cooking at home. There is a variety of restaurants, including **soba-ya** (**soba** shops), **shokudō** (inexpensive eateries), and **famirī resutoran** (family restaurants). Most **shokudō** serve simple Japanese, Western, or Chinese meals. Plastic models of some of the dishes are usually displayed with prices in an outside showcase as shown in the picture below.

In this lesson you will learn how to write numerals in kanji, since that's how they are written in restaurant menus, newspapers, books written vertically, and various other documents.

1 ▶ Introductory Quiz

Look at the illustration below and refer to the words in **Vocabulary**. Then try the following quiz.

In a **shokudō**, you will often find the names and prices of dishes written on paper and hung on the wall. Write the correct answers in the spaces provided below.

でんわ（五四三七）〇一七二

コーヒー　三百円

カレーライス　六百三十円

ラーメン　五百円

そば　四百五十円

うどん　四百六十円

Example: わたしは そばを たべました。
_____450_____ 円でした。

1. プレムさんは うどんを たべました。
_____ 円でした。

2. リーさんは カレーライスを たべました。
コーヒーも のみました。
_____ 円でした。

3. ラーメンは _____ 円です。

4. しょくどうの でんわばんごうは
_____ です。

5. あなたは この しょくどうで なにを たべますか。_____ を たべます。

6. いくらですか。_____ 円です。

2 ► Vocabulary

Study the readings and meanings of these words to help you understand the **Introductory Quiz**.

1. そば		**soba**	buckwheat noodles
2. 四百五十円	よん ひゃく ご じゅう えん	**yonhyaku gojū en**	450 yen
3. うどん		**udon**	Japanese noodles
4. 四百六十円	よん ひゃく ろく じゅう えん	**yonhyaku rokujū en**	460 yen
5. カレーライス		**karē raisu**	curry and rice
6. 六百三十円	ろっ ぴゃく さん じゅう えん	**roppyaku sanjū en**	630 yen
7. コーヒー		**kōhī**	coffee
8. 三百円	さん びゃく えん	**sambyaku en**	300 yen
9. ラーメン		**rāmen**	ramen
10. 五百円	ご ひゃく えん	**gohyaku en**	500 yen
11. でんわばんごう		**denwa bangō**	phone number
12. 五四三七 - 〇一七一	ご よん さん なな – れい いち なな いち	**go yon san nana - rei ichi nana ichi**	5437-0171

3 ► New Characters

Twelve characters are introduced in this lesson. Use the explanations to help you understand and remember the characters. Study the compound words to increase your vocabulary.

一 二 三 四 五 六 七 八 九 十 百 円

1 一	**hito-tsu, ichi, (i')** ひと・つ、イチ、（イッ） one	一							

一 derives from a pictograph of one finger.

一つ	ひとつ	**hitotsu**	one
一	いち	**ichi**	one

一人	*ひとり	**hitori**	one person
一円	いちえん	**ichi en**	one yen
一日	いちにち	**ichi nichi**	a day; all day
一本	いっぽん	**ippon**	one slender object
一日	*ついたち	**tsuitachi**	the first (date)

16

2 二	**futa-tsu, ni** ふた・つ、ニ two	一	二				

二 derives from a pictograph of two fingers.

二つ	ふたつ	**futatsu**	two
二	に	**ni**	two
二人	*ふたり	**futari**	two people
二月	にがつ	**ni gatsu**	February
二日	*ふつか	**futsuka**	the second (date); (for) two days

---

3 三	**mit-tsu, san** みっ・つ、サン three	一	二	三			

三 derives from a pictograph of three fingers.

三つ	みっつ	**mittsu**	three
三	さん	**san**	three
三日	みっか	**mikka**	the third (date); (for) three days
三月	さんがつ	**san gatsu**	March
三人	さんにん	**sannin**	three people

---

4 四	**yot-tsu, yon, yo, shi** よっ・つ、よん、よ、シ four	丨	冂	冂	四	四	

四 derives from a pictograph of four fingers.

四つ	よっつ	**yottsu**	four
四	よん	**yon**	four
四	し	**shi**	four
四日	よっか	**yokka**	the fourth (date); (for) four days
四百	よんひゃく	**yonhyaku**	four hundred
四円	よえん	**yo en**	four yen
四時	よじ	**yo ji**	four o'clock
四月	しがつ	**shi gatsu**	April

5 五	**itsu-tsu, go** いつ・つ、ゴ five	一	丁	五	五			

五 is 二 plus 三, meaning five.

五つ	いつつ	**itsutsu**	five
五	ご	**go**	five

五日	いつか	**itsuka**	the fifth (date); (for) five days
五月	ごがつ	**go gatsu**	May
五十	ごじゅう	**gojū**	fifty

6 六	**mut-tsu, roku, (ro')** むっ・つ、ロク、(ロッ) six	`	亠	宀	六			

六 derives from a pictograph of a hand showing the number six in the Chinese way of counting on one's fingers.

六つ	むっつ	**muttsu**	six
六	ろく	**roku**	six

六月	ろくがつ	**roku gatsu**	June
六十	ろくじゅう	**rokujū**	sixty
六分	ろっぷん	**roppun**	six minutes
六日	*むいか	**muika**	the sixth (date); (for) six days

7 七	**nana-tsu, nana, shichi** なな・つ、なな、シチ seven	一	七					

七 depicts two fingers on five fingers, meaning seven.

七つ	ななつ	**nanatsu**	seven
七	なな	**nana**	seven
七	しち	**shichi**	seven

七百	ななひゃく	**nanahyaku**	seven hundred
七月	しちがつ	**shichi gatsu**	July
七時	しちじ	**shichi ji**	seven o'clock
七日	*なのか	**nanoka**	the seventh (date); (for) seven days

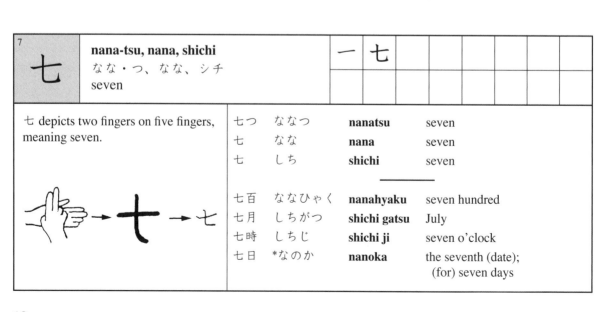

8 八	**yat-tsu, hachi, (ha')** やっ・つ、ハチ、（ハッ） eight	ノ 八				

八 derives from a pictograph of two hands, each showing four fingers, meaning eight. When 八 is used as part of other kanji, it often means "divide" because of its shape.

八つ	やっつ	**yattsu**	eight
八	はち	**hachi**	eight
			———
八月	はちがつ	**hachi gatsu**	August
八百	はっぴゃく	**happyaku**	eight hundred
八日	*ようか	**yōka**	the eighth (date); (for) eight days

9 九	**kokono-tsu, kyū, ku** ここの・つ、キュウ、ク nine	ノ 九				

九 depicts an arm with tightened muscles and is used to mean nine, the number that tightens up and completes the series of single digits.

九つ	ここのつ	**kokonotsu**	nine
九	きゅう	**kyū**	nine
九	く	**ku**	nine
			———
九日	ここのか	**kokonoka**	the ninth (date); (for) nine days
九十	きゅうじゅう	**kyūjū**	ninety
九州	きゅうしゅう	**Kyūshū**	Kyushu (island, district)
九月	くがつ	**ku gatsu**	September
九時	くじ	**ku ji**	nine o'clock

10 十	**tō, jū, ji', (ju')** とお、ジュウ、ジッ、（ジュッ） ten	一 十				

十 derives from a pictograph of two crossing hands with ten fingers. When used as part of other kanji, 十 often means "add" (e.g., 184 協, 204 博, 219 計, 239 汁).

十	とお	**tō**	ten
十	じゅう	**jū**	ten
十一	じゅういち	**jūichi**	eleven
三十	さんじゅう	**sanjū**	thirty
			———
十日	とおか	**tōka**	the tenth (date); (for) ten days
十一円	じゅういちえん	**jūichi en**	eleven yen
十分	じっぷん/じゅっぷん	**jippun/juppun**	ten minutes
二十日	*はつか	**hatsuka**	the twentieth (date); (for) twenty days

19

11 百	**hyaku, (byaku), (pyaku)** ヒャク、(ビャク)、(ピャク) hundred	一 ㄱ ㄈ 百 百 百

百 combines 一 one and 白 rice grain, and represents one bag of rice. This suggests a large number, at least one hundred. 白 by itself means white, the color of rice.

百	ひゃく	**hyaku**	one hundred
四百	よんひゃく	**yonhyaku**	four hundred
三百	さんびゃく	**sambyaku**	three hundred
六百	ろっぴゃく	**roppyaku**	six hundred
八百	はっぴゃく	**happyaku**	eight hundred
九百円	きゅうひゃくえん	**kyūhyaku en**	nine hundred yen
何百	なんびゃく	**nanbyaku**	how many hundreds; hundreds of ~

12 円	**en** エン circle, yen	丨 冂 円 円

円 derives from 圓, which combines □ encircle, 口 mouth or man (cf. 107), and 貝 money (cf. 200 費). Originally indicating encircled things, 円 then came to mean circle, round, and, as an associated meaning, yen, because yen coins are round.

円	えん	**en**	yen; circle
十円	じゅうえん	**jū en**	ten yen
五十円	ごじゅうえん	**gojū en**	fifty yen
百円	ひゃくえん	**hyaku en**	one hundred yen
七百円	ななひゃくえん	**nanahyaku en**	seven hundred yen
円高	えんだか	**endaka**	high value of the yen
円安	えんやす	**en'yasu**	low value of the yen

4 ▶ Practice

I. Write the readings of the following kanji in hiragana.

1. 一   2. 二   3. 三   4. 四
5. 五   6. 六   7. 七   8. 八
9. 九   10. 十   11. 四十   12. 九十
13. 二十九円   14. 七十四円   15. 九十七円   16. 百
17. 二百   18. 三百   19. 四百   20. 五百
21. 六百   22. 七百   23. 八百   24. 九百
25. 五つ   26. 三つ   27. 六つ   28. 二つ
29. 八つ   30. 四つ   31. 九つ   32. 一つ
33. 七つ   34. 三百十一円

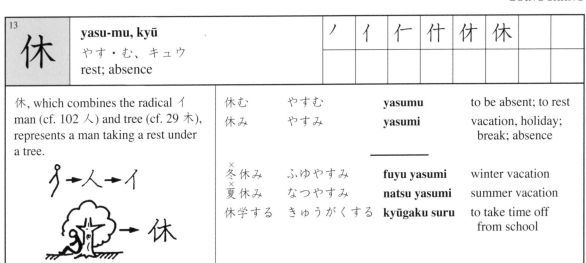

13 休 yasu-mu, kyū
やす・む、キュウ
rest; absence

ノ イ イ 仁 什 休 休

休, which combines the radical イ man (cf. 102 人) and tree (cf. 29 木), represents a man taking a rest under a tree.

彳 → 人 → イ

🌳 → 休

休む	やすむ	**yasumu**	to be absent; to rest
休み	やすみ	**yasumi**	vacation, holiday; break; absence
冬休み	ふゆやすみ	**fuyu yasumi**	winter vacation
夏休み	なつやすみ	**natsu yasumi**	summer vacation
休学する	きゅうがくする	**kyūgaku suru**	to take time off from school

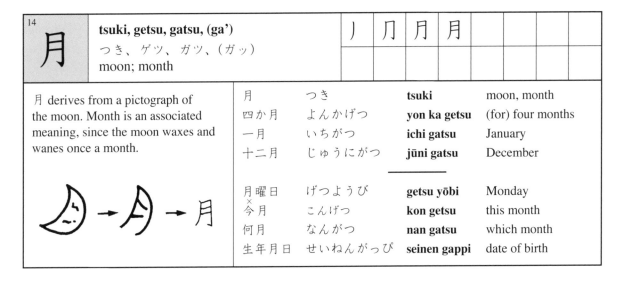

14 月 tsuki, getsu, gatsu, (ga')
つき、ゲツ、ガツ、（ガッ）
moon; month

丿 几 月 月

月 derives from a pictograph of the moon. Month is an associated meaning, since the moon waxes and wanes once a month.

🌙 → 月 → 月

月	つき	**tsuki**	moon, month
四か月	よんかげつ	**yon ka getsu**	(for) four months
一月	いちがつ	**ichi gatsu**	January
十二月	じゅうにがつ	**jūni gatsu**	December
月曜日	げつようび	**getsu yōbi**	Monday
今月	こんげつ	**kon getsu**	this month
何月	なんがつ	**nan gatsu**	which month
生年月日	せいねんがっぴ	**seinen gappi**	date of birth

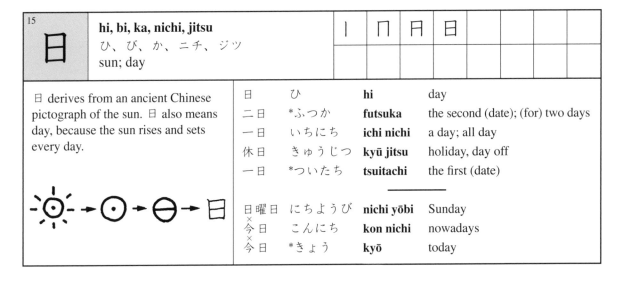

15 日 hi, bi, ka, nichi, jitsu
ひ、び、か、ニチ、ジツ
sun; day

| 冂 月 日

日 derives from an ancient Chinese pictograph of the sun. 日 also means day, because the sun rises and sets every day.

☀ → ⊙ → ⊖ → 日

日	ひ	**hi**	day
二日	*ふつか	**futsuka**	the second (date); (for) two days
一日	いちにち	**ichi nichi**	a day; all day
休日	きゅうじつ	**kyū jitsu**	holiday, day off
一日	*ついたち	**tsuitachi**	the first (date)
日曜日	にちようび	**nichi yōbi**	Sunday
今日	こんにち	**kon nichi**	nowadays
今日	*きょう	**kyō**	today

16 週	shū シュウ week	ノ	刀	月	月	用	用	周	周
		冑	周	週	週				

週 combines 周, paddy with rice from a basket scattered all around, and the radical ⻌, meaning proceed or road. Thus 週 suggests the time, perhaps a week, required to go all around a paddy to look after it.

週	しゅう	**shū**	week
毎週	まいしゅう	**mai shū**	every week
今週	こんしゅう	**kon shū**	this week
先週	せんしゅう	**sen shū**	last week
来週	らいしゅう	**rai shū**	next week
週末	しゅうまつ	**shū matsu**	weekend

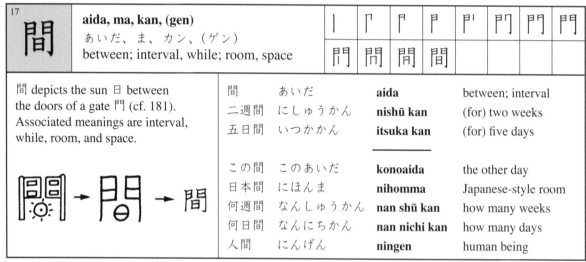

17 間	aida, ma, kan, (gen) あいだ、ま、カン、（ゲン） between; interval, while; room, space	l	冂	冋	冋	冋	門	門	門
		門	閂	間	間				

間 depicts the sun 日 between the doors of a gate 門 (cf. 181). Associated meanings are interval, while, room, and space.

間	あいだ	**aida**	between; interval
二週間	にしゅうかん	**nishū kan**	(for) two weeks
五日間	いつかかん	**itsuka kan**	(for) five days
この間	このあいだ	**konoaida**	the other day
日本間	にほんま	**nihomma**	Japanese-style room
何週間	なんしゅうかん	**nan shū kan**	how many weeks
何日間	なんにちかん	**nan nichi kan**	how many days
人間	にんげん	**ningen**	human being

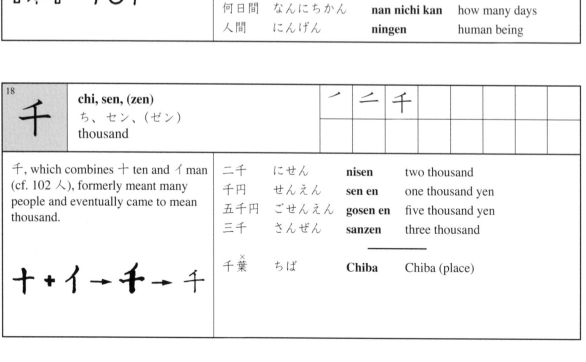

18 千	chi, sen, (zen) ち、セン、（ゼン） thousand	㇒	二	千					

千, which combines 十 ten and イ man (cf. 102 人), formerly meant many people and eventually came to mean thousand.

二千	にせん	**nisen**	two thousand
千円	せんえん	**sen en**	one thousand yen
五千円	ごせんえん	**gosen en**	five thousand yen
三千	さんぜん	**sanzen**	three thousand
千葉	ちば	**Chiba**	Chiba (place)

十 + イ → 千 → 千

19 万	**man, ban** マン、バン ten thousand	一	フ	万					

万 derives from an ancient Indian religious symbol 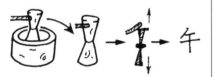, which changed into 卍 later in China, meaning ten thousand gods.	二万円	にまんえん	**niman en**	twenty thousand yen
	百万円	ひゃくまんえん	**hyakuman en**	one million yen
	万国	ばんこく	**bankoku**	all nations

20 午	**go** ゴ noon	ノ	┕	┕	午				

午 depicts a pestle used for pounding rice. The up-and-down motion of the pestle suggests the turning of morning to afternoon, namely, noon.

正午　しょうご　**shōgo**　noon

21 前	**mae, zen** まえ、ゼン front, before, earlier	丶	⸜	丷	亠	广	前	前	前	前
		前								

前 combines 歬 foot (cf. 149 止 stop) on a boat, suggesting a boat that cannot move, and 刂 sword. The sword is used to cut the boat's rope, allowing it to go forward. Thus 前 means front. Associated meanings are before and earlier.

前	まえ	**mae**	the front
午前	ごぜん	**gozen**	(in the) morning
前日	ぜんじつ	**zenjitsu**	the previous day, the day before
五分前	ごふんまえ	**gofun mae**	five minutes before/ago
三日前	みっかまえ	**mikka mae**	three days before/ago

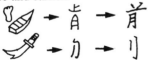

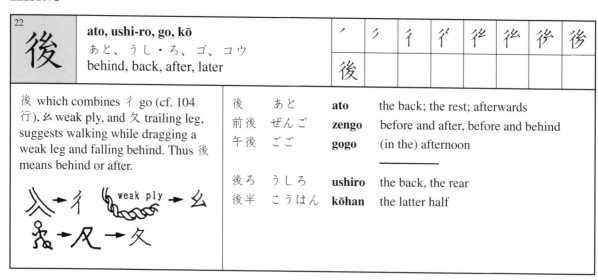

22 後	ato, ushi-ro, go, kō あと、うし・ろ、ゴ、コウ behind, back, after, later	ノ	ク	彳	彳	彳	丝	丝	後
		後							

後 which combines 彳 go (cf. 104 行), 幺 weak ply, and 夂 trailing leg, suggests walking while dragging a weak leg and falling behind. Thus 後 means behind or after.

後	あと	**ato**	the back; the rest; afterwards
前後	ぜんご	**zengo**	before and after, before and behind
午後	ごご	**gogo**	(in the) afternoon
後ろ	うしろ	**ushiro**	the back, the rear
後半	こうはん	**kōhan**	the latter half

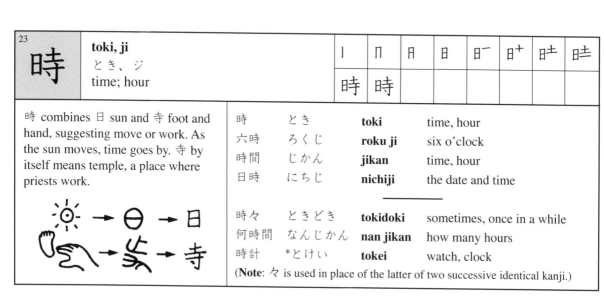

23 時	toki, ji とき、ジ time; hour	丨	冂	月	日	日-	日+	旪	旪
		時	時						

時 combines 日 sun and 寺 foot and hand, suggesting move or work. As the sun moves, time goes by. 寺 by itself means temple, a place where priests work.

時	とき	**toki**	time, hour
六時	ろくじ	**roku ji**	six o'clock
時間	じかん	**jikan**	time, hour
日時	にちじ	**nichiji**	the date and time
時々	ときどき	**tokidoki**	sometimes, once in a while
何時間	なんじかん	**nan jikan**	how many hours
時計	*とけい	**tokei**	watch, clock

(**Note**: 々 is used in place of the latter of two successive identical kanji.)

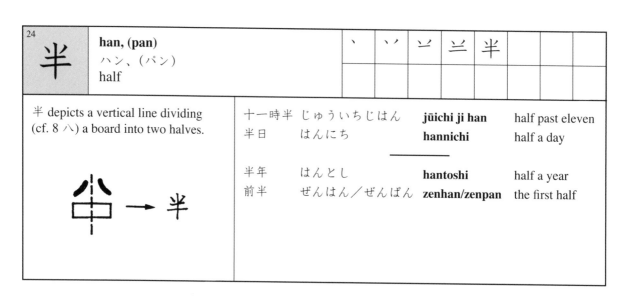

24 半	han, (pan) ハン、（パン） half	丶	丷	丷	半	半			

半 depicts a vertical line dividing (cf. 8 八) a board into two halves.

十一時半	じゅういちじはん	**jūichi ji han**	half past eleven
半日	はんにち	**hannichi**	half a day
半年	はんとし	**hantoshi**	half a year
前半	ぜんはん／ぜんぱん	**zenhan/zenpan**	the first half

25 分	**wa-karu, wa-keru, bun, fun, (pun)** わ・かる、わ・ける、ブン、フン、（プン） divide, portion; minute; understand	ノ	八	分	分				

分, which combines 八 divide (cf. 8) and 刀 knife, means divide or portion. One hour is divided into sixty minutes. Dividing a question into solvable pieces suggests understanding.

分（か）る	わかる	**wakaru**	to understand
分ける	わける	**wakeru**	to divide, to separate
半分	はんぶん	**hambun**	half
九分	きゅうふん	**kyū fun**	nine minutes
四分	よんぷん	**yon pun**	four minutes
三日分	みっかぶん	**mikka bun**	three days' worth

4 ▶ Practice

I. How to read time

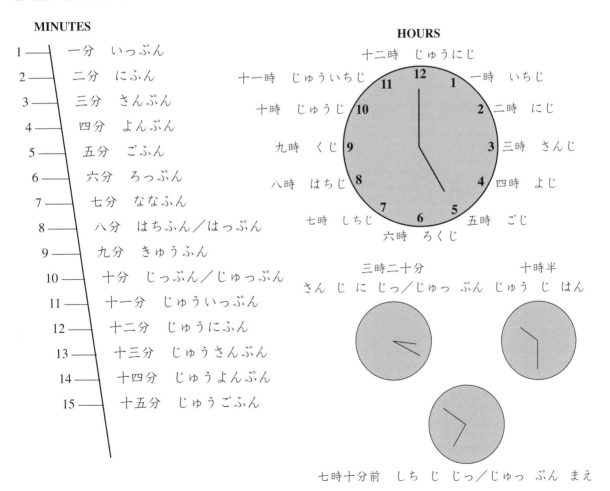

MINUTES

1 — 一分　いっぷん
2 — 二分　にふん
3 — 三分　さんぷん
4 — 四分　よんぷん
5 — 五分　ごふん
6 — 六分　ろっぷん
7 — 七分　ななふん
8 — 八分　はちふん／はっぷん
9 — 九分　きゅうふん
10 — 十分　じっぷん／じゅっぷん
11 — 十一分　じゅういっぷん
12 — 十二分　じゅうにふん
13 — 十三分　じゅうさんぷん
14 — 十四分　じゅうよんぷん
15 — 十五分　じゅうごふん

HOURS

十二時　じゅうにじ
十一時　じゅういちじ
十時　じゅうじ
九時　くじ
八時　はちじ
七時　しちじ
六時　ろくじ
一時　いちじ
二時　にじ
三時　さんじ
四時　よじ
五時　ごじ

三時二十分　さん　じ　に　じっ／じゅっ　ぷん
十時半　じゅう　じ　はん
七時十分前　しち　じ　じっ／じゅっ　ぷん　まえ

II. Write the readings of the following kanji in hiragana.

1. 十 二 月	2. 二 十 九 日	3. 一 月 一 日	4. 二 日
5. 三 日	6. 四 日 間	7. 五 日 間	8. 六 日 間
9. 午 後	10. 十 一 時 半	11. 午 前	12. 六 時 十 分
13. 三 万 円	14. 五 千 円	15. 七 日	16. 二 月
17. 三 月	18. 四 月	19. 五 月	20. 六 月
21. 七 月	22. 八 月	23. 九 月	24. 十 月
25. 十 一 月	26. 一 か 月	27. 四 か 月	28. 六 か 月
29. 九 か 月	30. 八 日	31. 九 日	32. 十 日
33. 十 九 日	34. 二 十 日	35. 千	36. 三 千
37. 四 千	38. 八 千	39. 九 千	40. 四 万
41. 九 万	42. 四 時	43. 一 分	44. 四 分
45. 六 分	46. 七 分	47. 八 分	48. 九 分

49. なつ 休 み は　なん 日 間 です か 。 十 四 日 間 、 二 週 間 で す 。

50. け さ　なん 時 に　お き ま し た か 。 九 時 で す 。

51. バ ス に　なん 時 間　の り ま す か 。 六 時 間 半　の り ま す 。

III. Fill in the blanks with appropriate kanji.

1. やす
□ む
to rest

2. きゅう じつ
□ □
day off

3. ひ
ははの □
Mother's Day

4. にち
十三 □
the 13th (date)

5. か
七 □
the 7th (date)

6. げつ
四か □
for 4 months

7. がつ
十 □
October

8. せん
□ 円
1,000 yen

9. ぜん
三 □ 円
3,000 yen

10. まん
百 □ 円
1,000,000 yen

11. しゅう かん
一 □ □
for 1 week

12. まえ　あと
□ と □
before and after

13. ご ぜん
□ □
in the morning

14. ご ご
□ □
in the afternoon

15. とき
□
time

16. じ　ふん
八 □ 五 □
8:05

17. ぷん
三 □
3 minutes

18. はん ぶん
□ □
half

5 ▶ Advanced Placement Exam Practice Questions

Answer the following questions about the schedule of the winter camp.

スキーキャンプ　スケジュール

	二月二十四日	二月二十五日	二月二十六日	
8:00		あさごはん	あさごはん	8:00
9:00		トレーニング	トレーニング	9:00
10:00	バス出発 (9:50) START			10:00
11:00				11:00
12:00	ひるごはん ARRIVE バス到着 (13:00)	ひるごはん	ひるごはん	12:00
13:00				13:00
14:00	オリエンテーション	トレーニング	バス出発 (13:20) START	14:00
15:00	トレーニング			15:00
16:00			ARRIVE バス到着 (16:40)	16:00
17:00		シャワー		17:00
18:00	シャワー	よるごはん		18:00
19:00	よるごはん			19:00
20:00				20:00

1. キャンプはいつからですか。
   A. にがつにじゅうよんにち
   B. にがつにじゅうようか
   C. にがつにじゅうよっか
   D. にがつにじゅうににち

2. 二十四日のバスはなんじにでますか。
   A. 午前九時十分前
   B. 午前十時十分前
   C. 午後九時十分前
   D. 午後十時十分前

3. トレーニングはいつありますか。
   A. まいにち、午前も午後もある。
   B. 午前はまいにちあるが、午後はない日がある。
   C. 午後はまいにちあるが、午前はない日がある。
   D. 午前も午後もあるのは、１日だけである。

4. 二十六日のトレーニング時間はどのくらいありますか。
   A. 三時半
   B. 三時半間
   C. 三時間半
   D. 三時三十分間

5. 二十六日のバスはなんじにつきますか。
   A. よじよんじゅうぷん　　B. よじよんじゅっぷん
   C. よんじよんじゅうぷん　D. よんじよんじゅっぷん

31

What Day Is Today?

きょうは なん曜日ですか

In addition to the Western system for counting years, a traditional system based on the reign of the emperors is used in Japan. There are 15 national holidays per year in Japan. One long series of holidays that occurs from the end of April to the beginning of May is known as Golden Week. Golden Week ends with Children's Day on May 5, during which parents with boys fly carp banners above their homes. This expresses their wish that their children grow up to be strong and healthy like carp. (**Hina Matsuri**, the Japanese Doll Festival held on March 3, is the day to hope for the well-being of girls.)

In this lesson, you will learn kanji used in calendars and other time-related words.

1 ▶ Introductory Quiz

Look at the calendar below and refer to the words in **Vocabulary**. Then try the following quiz.

Saturday and Sunday are holidays for most government offices, post offices, banks, and many companies. When a national holiday falls on a Sunday, the following Monday automatically becomes a holiday. Fill in the spaces provided with hiragana and Arabic numerals.

○ 祝日 （祭日）
③ 5月3日　けんぽう　きねん日　Constitution Day
④ 5月4日　みどりの　日　Greenery Day
⑤ 5月5日　こどもの　日　Children's Day

1. これは ＿＿＿＿＿＿＿＿＿＿ 十九年 （2007） の カレンダーです。

2. 五月の　祝日（祭日）は　みっかと ＿＿＿＿＿＿＿＿＿＿ と ＿＿＿＿＿＿＿＿＿＿ です。

3. それは ＿＿＿＿＿＿＿＿ 曜日と ＿＿＿＿＿＿＿＿ 曜日と ＿＿＿＿＿＿ 曜日です。

4. 五月には、もく曜日が ＿＿＿＿＿＿＿＿＿＿* かい あります。　(*times)

5. にち曜日が ＿＿＿＿＿＿＿＿＿＿ かい あります。

6. 五月十四日は ＿＿＿＿＿＿＿＿＿ 曜日です。

7. 五月二十九日は ＿＿＿＿＿＿＿＿＿ 曜日です。

8. 五月の　休日は ＿＿＿＿＿＿＿ かい あります。

9. 平日は ＿＿＿＿＿＿＿＿＿＿ 曜日から ＿＿＿＿＿＿＿＿＿＿ 曜日まででです。

2 ▶ Vocabulary

Study the readings and meanings of these words to help you understand the **Introductory Quiz**.

1.	平成	へい せい	**Heisei**	Heisei (era)
2.	十九年	じゅう きゅう ねん	**jūkyū nen**	the 19th year
3.	祝日	しゅく じつ	**shukujitsu**	national holiday
4.	祭日	さい じつ	**saijitsu**	national holiday (used interchangeably with しゅく じつ)
5.	日曜日	にち よう び	**nichi yōbi**	Sunday
6.	月曜日	げつ よう び	**getsu yōbi**	Monday
7.	火曜日	か よう び	**ka yōbi**	Tuesday
8.	水曜日	すい よう び	**sui yōbi**	Wednesday
9.	木曜日	もく よう び	**moku yōbi**	Thursday
10.	金曜日	きん よう び	**kin yōbi**	Friday
11.	土曜日	ど よう び	**do yōbi**	Saturday
12.	休日	きゅう じつ	**kyūjitsu**	holiday, day off
13.	平日	へい じつ	**heijitsu**	ordinary day, weekday

3 ▶ New Characters

Eleven characters are introduced in this lesson. Use the explanations to help you understand and remember the characters. Study the compound words to increase your vocabulary.

曜 火 水 木 金 土 平 成 年 祝 祭

26 曜	yō ヨウ day of the week	丨	冂	月	日	日ㄱ	日ㄱ	日ㅋ	日ㅋ
		日ㅋㅋ	日ㅋㅋ	日ㅋ	曜ㅋ	曜ㅋ	曜	曜	曜

曜 combines 日 sun, ㅋㅋ wings, and 隹 fat bird. The sun flying on a bird's wings suggests a day of the week.

日曜日	にちようび	**nichi yōbi**	Sunday
月曜日	げつようび	**getsu yōbi**	Monday
何曜日	なんようび	**nan yōbi**	what day of the week

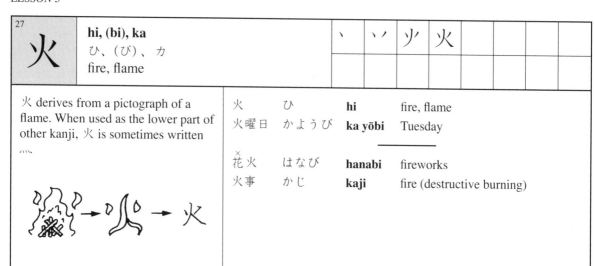

27	hi, (bi), ka	丶	` `	` `	火			
火	ひ、（び）、カ							
	fire, flame							

火 derives from a pictograph of a flame. When used as the lower part of other kanji, 火 is sometimes written 灬.

火	ひ	**hi**	fire, flame
火曜日	かようび	**ka yōbi**	Tuesday
		———	
×花火	はなび	**hanabi**	fireworks
火事	かじ	**kaji**	fire (destructive burning)

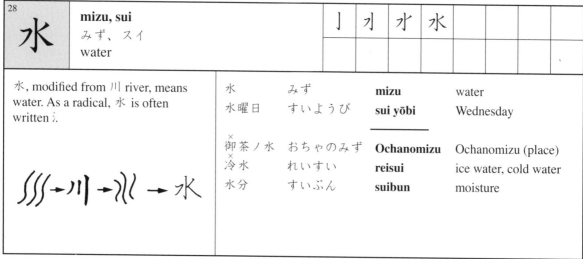

28	mizu, sui	亅	刀	水	水			
水	みず、スイ							`
	water							

水, modified from 川 river, means water. As a radical, 水 is often written 氵.

水	みず	**mizu**	water
水曜日	すいようび	**sui yōbi**	Wednesday
		———	
×御茶ノ水	おちゃのみず	**Ochanomizu**	Ochanomizu (place)
×冷水	れいすい	**reisui**	ice water, cold water
水分	すいぶん	**suibun**	moisture

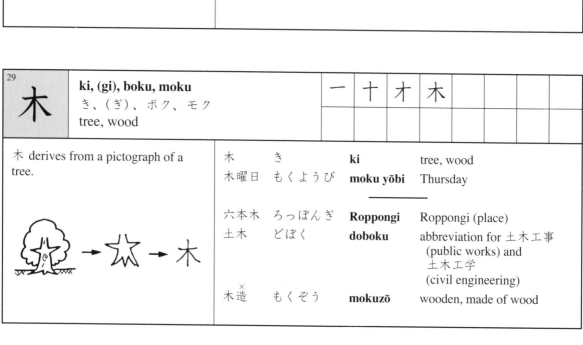

29	ki, (gi), boku, moku	一	十	才	木			
木	き、（ぎ）、ボク、モク							
	tree, wood							

木 derives from a pictograph of a tree.

木	き	**ki**	tree, wood
木曜日	もくようび	**moku yōbi**	Thursday
		———	
六本木	ろっぽんぎ	**Roppongi**	Roppongi (place)
土木	どぼく	**doboku**	abbreviation for 土木工事 (public works) and 土木工学 (civil engineering)
木×造	もくぞう	**mokuzō**	wooden, made of wood

30 金	**kane, kin** かね、キン gold, metal, money	ノ	八	全	全	仐	全	金	金

金, which depicts two nuggets in the earth 土 (cf. 31) piled up in a mound 스, indicates precious ore such as gold. Associated meanings are metal and money.

金	かね	**kane**	money/metal
金	きん	**kin**	gold
金曜日	きんようび	**kin yōbi**	Friday
─────			
金メダル	きんメダル	**kin medaru**	gold medal
現金	げんきん	**genkin**	cash
礼金	れいきん	**reikin**	gift money to landlord

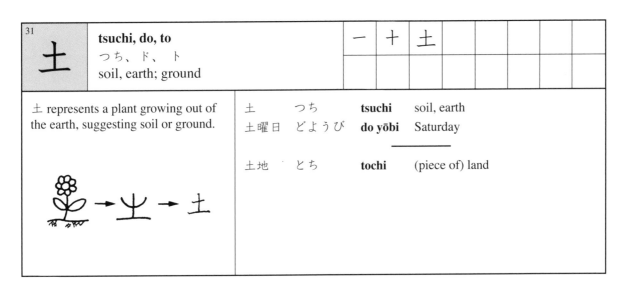

---

31 土	**tsuchi, do, to** つち、ド、ト soil, earth; ground	一	十	土					

土 represents a plant growing out of the earth, suggesting soil or ground.

土	つち	**tsuchi**	soil, earth
土曜日	どようび	**do yōbi**	Saturday
─────			
土地	とち	**tochi**	(piece of) land

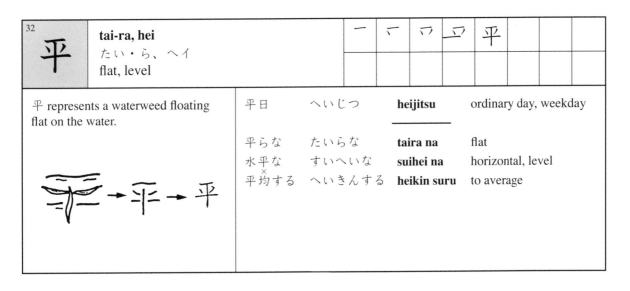

---

32 平	**tai-ra, hei** たい・ら、ヘイ flat, level	一	一	丆	立	平			

平 represents a waterweed floating flat on the water.

平日	へいじつ	**heijitsu**	ordinary day, weekday
平らな	たいらな	**taira na**	flat
水平な	すいへいな	**suihei na**	horizontal, level
平均する	へいきんする	**heikin suru**	to average

33 成	**na-ru, sei** な・る、セイ achieve; become, form	ノ 厂 万 成 成 成

成, which combines 戈 arms or weapon and 力 power or force (cf. 67 男), means achieve. Associated meanings are form and become. 	平成	へいせい	**Heisei**	Heisei (era)
	成田	なりた	**Narita**	Narita (place, airport)
	成績表	せいせきひょう	**seiseki hyō**	school report card
	成人の日	せいじんのひ	**Seijin no hi**	Coming of Age Day
	成功する	せいこうする	**seikō suru**	to succeed, to be successful

34 年	**toshi, nen** とし、ネン year; age	ノ ᅡ 二 ᅡ 二 年

年 depicts a man working in a rice paddy (cf. 102 人) and grain. This suggests the period between harvests, which is usually a year. 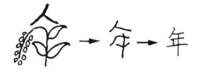	年	とし	**toshi**	year; age
	三年	さんねん	**san nen**	three years, the third year
	今年	ことし	**kotoshi**	this year
	去年	きょねん	**kyonen**	last year
	年度	ねんど	**nendo**	fiscal/academic year
	年金	ねんきん	**nenkin**	pension
	忘年会	ぼうねんかい	**bōnenkai**	year-end party

35 祝	**iwa-u, shuku** いわ・う、シュク celebrate, congratulate	` ᅳ ネ ネ ネ 祀 祀 祀 祝

祝 combines ネ and 兄. The radical ネ derives from 示 altar, and 兄 represents a kneeling priest. Thus 祝 means celebration. 兄 by itself means elder brother. 	祝う	いわう	**iwau**	to celebrate, to congratulate
	(お)祝い	(お)いわい	**(o)iwai**	congratulation, celebratory gift
	祝日	しゅくじつ	**shukujitsu**	national holiday, festival day
	内祝(い)	うちいわい	**uchi iwai**	family celebration
	祝電	しゅくでん	**shukuden**	congratulatory telegram

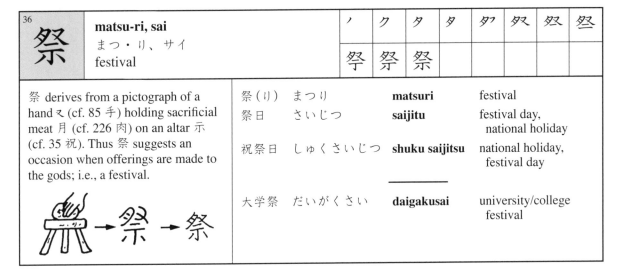

36 祭	matsu-ri, sai まつ・り、サイ festival	ノ	ク	タ	夕	夕フ	夗	夗	祭
		祭	祭	祭					

祭 derives from a pictograph of a hand ⺕ (cf. 85 手) holding sacrificial meat 月 (cf. 226 肉) on an altar 示 (cf. 35 祝). Thus 祭 suggests an occasion when offerings are made to the gods; i.e., a festival.

祭(り)	まつり	**matsuri**	festival
祭日	さいじつ	**saijitu**	festival day, national holiday
祝祭日	しゅくさいじつ	**shuku saijitsu**	national holiday, festival day
————			
大学祭	だいがくさい	**daigakusai**	university/college festival

4 ▶ Practice

I. Write the readings of the following kanji in hiragana.

1. 平成五年
2. 祝日
3. 祭日
4. 日曜日
5. 月曜日
6. 火曜日
7. 水曜日
8. 木曜日
9. 金曜日
10. 土曜日
11. 休日
12. 平日
13. 祝う
14. 祭り
15. 火は あかいです。
16. この 水は おいしいですね。
17. 五月は 木が きれいです。
18. お金は かばんの なかに あります。
19. 1964年は、とうきょう オリンピックの 年でした。2020年の オリンピックも とうきょうです。

II. Fill in the blanks with appropriate kanji.

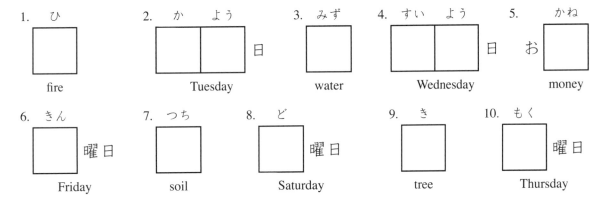

1. ひ □ — fire
2. か よう □□日 — Tuesday
3. みず □ — water
4. すい よう □□日 — Wednesday
5. かね お □ — money
6. きん □曜日 — Friday
7. つち □ — soil
8. ど □曜日 — Saturday
9. き □ — tree
10. もく □曜日 — Thursday

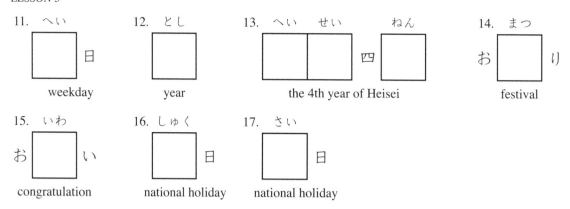

11. へい
☐日
weekday

12. とし
☐
year

13. へい　せい　　　　　ねん
☐☐四☐
the 4th year of Heisei

14. まつ
お☐り
festival

15. いわ
お☐い
congratulation

16. しゅく
☐日
national holiday

17. さい
☐日
national holiday

5 ▸ Advanced Placement Exam Practice Questions

Read the passage below and answer the questions.

日本（にほん）には祝日が十五日あります。いちばん祝日がおおい月は五月です。三日、四日、五日の三日間あります。祝日がない月は六月と八月です。

平成十九年に、四月と五月の祝日のなまえがかわりました。四月二十九日の「みどりの日」は「昭和（しょうわ）の日」に、五月四日の「こくみんの休日」は「みどりの日」になりました。

祝日が日曜日のときは、つぎの平日が休みです。これを「ふりかえ休日」といいます。

たとえば、二千七年（平成十九年）は四月二十九日が日曜日なので、三十日の月曜日がふりかえ休日になります。五月一日の火曜日と二日の水曜日を休みにすると、四月二十九日から五月六日までの、ながい休みになります。つづけて休む会社（かいしゃ）もあります。

このながい休みを、ゴールデンウィークといいます。たくさんの人（ひと）がたのしみにしています。

1. What day of the week is May 1, 2007?
   A. Monday
   B. Tuesday
   C. Wednesday
   D. Thursday

2. During what months are there no public holidays in Japan?
   A. June and August
   B. July and September
   C. August and October
   D. November and January

3. What day is May 4, 2007?
   A. Showa-no-hi
   B. Midori-no-hi
   C. Kokumin-no-kyūjitsu
   D. Furikae-kyūjitsu

4. What day is April 30, 2007?
   A. Showa-no-hi
   B. Midori-no-hi
   C. Kokumin-no-kyūjitsu
   D. Furikae-kyūjitsu

5. Which of the following statements about Golden Week（ゴールデンウィーク）is not true?
   A. Many Japanese are looking forward to these consecutive holidays.
   B. All days from April 29 to May 5 are holidays.
   C. Some companies close for the whole week during Golden Week.
   D. Midori-no-hi has changed to Showa-no-hi.

It's Nice to Meet You

はじめまして、どうぞ よろしく

The academic year in Japan begins in April. An entrance ceremony is held for incoming university freshmen, and the president and deans give welcoming addresses. When classes begin, new students are often asked to introduce themselves. This lesson will help you introduce yourself in Japanese.

The photo top left shows a street address sign, often attached to buildings or utility poles.

1 ▶ Introductory Quiz

Look at the illustration below and refer to the words in **Vocabulary**. Then try the quiz overleaf.

文京区 本郷（こう）七丁目 3

はじめまして、わたしは リーです。
マレーシアの 留学生です。四月から
東京大学の 工学部で べんきょう
します。専攻は 土木工学です。
わたしの 先生は 三木先生です。
日本語も べんきょうします。
都市工学科に ともだちが います。
あしたは 入学式です。

Mr. Lee, a student from Malaysia, is planning to study civil engineering in the Faculty of Engineering at the University of Tokyo; he will study Japanese, too. The entrance ceremony will be held tomorrow. Read the following sentences and choose the correct answers.

1. わたしは リーです。 (a. とうきょう　b. きょうと) 大学の がくせいです。
2. (a. こうがくぶ　b. ぶんがくぶ) の (a. とし　b. どぼく) 工学科で べんきょう します。
3. わたしの せんこうは (a. 日本語　b. 土木工学) です。
4. (a. 学生　b. 先生) のなまえは 三木せんせいです。
5. 大学の にゅうがくしきは (a. 四月　b. 八月) です。
6. 東京大学は (a. 左京区　b. 文京区)、本郷 (a. 七丁目　b. 七十日) に あります。

2 ▶ Vocabulary

Study the readings and meanings of these words to help you understand the **Introductory Quiz**.

1. 東京大学	とう きょう だい がく	**Tōkyō daigaku**	University of Tokyo
2. 京都大学	きょう と だい がく	**Kyōto daigaku**	Kyoto University
3. 学生	がく せい	**gakusei**	student
4. 留学生	りゅう がく せい	**ryūgakusei**	foreign student
5. 工学部	こう がく ぶ	**Kōgaku bu**	Faculty of Engineering
6. 文学部	ぶん がく ぶ	**Bungaku bu**	Faculty of Literature
7. 都市工学科	と し こう がっ か	**Toshi kōgakka**	Department of Urban Engineering
8. 土木工学科	ど ぼく こう がっ か	**Doboku kōgakka**	Department of Civil Engineering
9. 専攻	せん こう	**senkō**	major field of study
10. 日本語	に ほん ご	**Nihongo**	Japanese language
11. 先生	せん せい	**sensei**	professor, teacher
12. 三木	み き	**Miki**	Miki (name)
13. 入学式	にゅう がく しき	**nyūgaku shiki**	entrance ceremony
14. 左京区	さ きょう く	**Sakyō ku**	Sakyo Ward
15. 文京区	ぶん きょう く	**Bunkyō ku**	Bunkyo Ward
16. 本郷	ほん ごう	**Hongō**	Hongo (place)
17. 七丁目	なな ちょう め	**nana chōme**	the 7th block (in an address)

3 ▶ New Characters

Twenty-two characters are introduced in this lesson. Use the explanations to help you understand and remember the characters. Study the compound words to increase your vocabulary.

大 学 東 京 留 生 工 部 科 専 攻 先 本 語 都 市 入 式 文 区 丁 目

| 37 大 | **ō-kii, dai, tai**
おお・きい、ダイ、タイ
big, large, great | 一 | ナ | 大 | | | | | |

大 depicts a man with arms and legs spread wide, suggesting big and large.					
	大きい	おおきい	**ōkii**	big, large, great, tall	————
	大阪	おおさか	**Ōsaka**	Osaka	
	大都市	だいとし	**daitoshi**	big city	
	大仏	だいぶつ	**daibutsu**	great statue of Buddha	
	大会	たいかい	**taikai**	large meeting, convention; tournament	

| 38 学 | **mana-bu, gaku, (ga')**
まな・ぶ、ガク、（ガッ）
study, learn; school | 丶 | 丷 | 丷 | 丷 | 丷 | 学 | 学 | 学 |

学, simplified from 學, combines 子 child (cf. 116) and 丷, which represents a building with lights on. Thus 学 indicates a building where children are, namely, a school. An associated meaning is study.				
大学	だいがく	**daigaku**	university, college	
学年	がくねん	**gakunen**	school/academic year; grade at school	
				————
学ぶ	まなぶ	**manabu**	to study, to learn	
学校	がっこう	**gakkō**	school	

| 39 東 | **higashi, tō**
ひがし、トウ
east | 一 | 厂 | 厅 | 币 | 百 | 東 | 東 | 東 |

東, which combines 木 tree and 日 sun, depicts the sun rising from behind a tree in the east.				
東	ひがし	**higashi**	east	
東大	とうだい	**Tōdai**	abbreviation for 東京大学 (University of Tokyo)	
				————
JR東日本	JRひがしにほん	**JR Higashinihon**	East Japan Railway Company	
関東	かんとう	**Kantō**	Kanto (district)	

40 京	**kyō** キョウ capital	`	一	亠	亢	古	亨	京	京

京 represents a big building on a hill, a sight often seen in a capital city. It also represents stone lanterns that guarded ancient Chinese capitals.

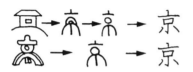

東京	とうきょう	**Tōkyō**	Tokyo
左京区	さきょうく	**Sakyō ku**	Sakyo Ward (in Kyoto)

---

41 留	**to-meru, ryū** と・める、リュウ stay, keep; fasten	´	ㇰ	㇉	𠂊	卯	𠃌	𠂉	留
		留	留						

卯 was originally written 丣, depicting closed doors. 田 means rice paddy (cf. 88), which can be thought of as limited space. Closed doors combined with limited space suggest staying or keeping something in a certain place.

留学する	りゅうがくする	**ryūgaku suru**	to study abroad
書留	かきとめ	**kakitome**	registered mail
国費留学	こくひ 　りゅうがく	**kokuhi** 　**ryūgaku**	study abroad on a government scholarship
×私費留学	しひりゅうがく	**shihi ryūgaku**	study abroad at one's own expense

---

42 生	**i-kiru, u-mareru, sei, (jō)** い・きる、う・まれる、セイ、(ジョウ) live, be born, life	ノ	丿	牛	牛	生			

生 depicts a flower in its prime, ready to give birth to a new life. Thus 生 means life, living, being born, or giving birth.

生まれる	うまれる	**umareru**	to be born
学生	がくせい	**gakusei**	student
留学生	りゅうがくせい	**ryūgakusei**	foreign student
生年月日	せいねんがっぴ	**seinen gappi**	date of birth
生きる	いきる	**ikiru**	to live
大学生	だいがくせい	**daigakusei**	university/college student
×学生課	がくせいか	**gakusei ka**	Student Affairs Section
一年生	いちねんせい	**ichinensei**	first-year student, freshman
×誕生日	たんじょうび	**tanjōbi**	birthday

43	**kō** コウ craft, industry	一	丁	工					
工									

工, representing a carpenter's ruler, means craft or industry. As part of other kanji, it often means straight.

工学	こうがく	**kōgaku**	engineering
土木工学	どぼくこうがく	**doboku kōgaku**	civil engineering
工場	こうじょう	**kōjō**	factory
工業	こうぎょう	**kōgyō**	(manufacturing) industry
人工	じんこう	**jinkō**	artificial

44	**bu** ブ part, section	'	亠	立	立	立	音	音	音
部		音	部	部					

部 combines 音, which derives from 剖 and means cutting something into parts, and 阝, indicating village (cf. 51 都, 150 郵). Thus 部 formerly meant part of a village, and now has come to mean part or section in general.

工学部	こうがくぶ	**Kōgaku bu**	Faculty of Engineering
部分	ぶぶん	**bubun**	part, portion
全部	ぜんぶ	**zembu**	all, whole
テニス部	テニスぶ	**tenisu bu**	tennis club
部屋	*へや	**heya**	room

45	**ka** カ department, course; academic subject	ノ	ニ	千	禾	禾	禾	禾	禾
科		科							

科 combines the radical 禾 grain and 斗, which derives from the shape of a dipper used to measure volume in ancient China. Formerly meaning measuring and sorting out, 科 now means subject of study or department.

学科	がっか	**gakka**	university/ college department
土木工学科	どぼく こうがっか	**Doboku kōgakka**	Department of Civil Engineering
科学	かがく	**kagaku**	science

46 専	**sen** セン specialize; exclusive	一	丆	冂	戸	叀	虫	車	専
		専							

専 combines 叀, depicting a tool used to weave one rope from many strands, and 寸 work (cf. 23 時). Thus 専 means working in one specific area or specializing.

専門	せんもん	**semmon**	major field of study, specialty
専門学校	せんもん がっこう	**semmon gakkō**	vocational/ professional school

---

47 攻	**kō** コウ attack	一	丁	エ	工'	丏'	攻	攻	

攻 combines エ straight (cf. 43) and 攵, representing a hand brandishing a whip. Thus 攻 means attacking in a straightforward way. 攵 is often used to indicate that the whole kanji is a verb.

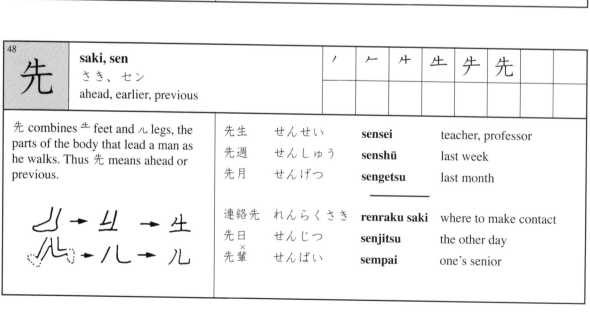

専攻する	せんこうする	**senkō suru**	to specialize/major in
攻撃する	こうげきする	**kōgeki suru**	to attack

---

48 先	**saki, sen** さき、セン ahead, earlier, previous	ノ	丨	牛	生	牛	先		

先 combines 生 feet and 儿 legs, the parts of the body that lead a man as he walks. Thus 先 means ahead or previous.

先生	せんせい	**sensei**	teacher, professor
先週	せんしゅう	**senshū**	last week
先月	せんげつ	**sengetsu**	last month
連絡先	れんらくさき	**renraku saki**	where to make contact
先日	せんじつ	**senjitsu**	the other day
先輩	せんぱい	**sempai**	one's senior

| 49 本 | **moto, hon, (bon), (pon)**
もと、ホン、（ボン）、（ポン）
origin, main; book; counter for long slender objects | 一 | 十 | 才 | 木 | 本 | | |

Adding a line to the base of 木 tree, 本 means basic, origin, or main. (If the line is added near the top as in 末, it means end or trifle.)

本	ほん	**hon**	book
日本	にほん／ にっぽん	**Nihon/ Nippon**	Japan
本部	ほんぶ	**hombu**	head office, headquarters
三本	さんぼん	**san bon**	three slender objects
山本さん	やまもとさん	**Yamamoto san**	Mr./Ms./Miss/Mrs. Yamamoto
本日	ほんじつ	**honjitsu**	today

| 50 語 | **go**
ゴ
talk, word, language | 、 | 二 | 三 | 言 | 言 | 言 | 言 | 言 |

訂 討 訶 語 語 語 語

語 combines 言 speak (cf. 78 話), 五 interact (cf. 5), and 口 mouth (cf. 107). 五 is associated with interact because of its crossing lines. Thus 語 means talk, word, or language.

日本語	にほんご	**Nihongo**	Japanese language
フランス語	フランスご	**Furansugo**	French language
×言語	げんご	**gengo**	language
×単語	たんご	**tango**	word, vocabulary
語学	ごがく	**gogaku**	language study, linguistics
×英語	えいご	**Eigo**	English language

| 51 都 | **to**
ト
capital, metropolis | 一 | 十 | 土 | 尹 | 耂 | 者 | 者 | 者 |

者ʾ 者ʳ 都

都 combines the radical ß village and 者, which depicts various foods gathered and cooked on a stove. 都 thus suggests a gathering of many villages, meaning capital city.

東京都	とうきょうと	**Tōkyōto**	Metropolis of Tokyo
京都	きょうと	**Kyōto**	Kyoto
×首都	しゅと	**shuto**	capital

| 52 市 | ichi, shi
いち、シ
city; market | ヽ | 亠 | 广 | 亣 | 市 | | |

市 combines 亠, simplified from 止 stop (cf. 149), and 巾, depicting a balance. Thus 市 means market, where people stop and bargain until a balanced agreement is reached. An associated meaning is city.

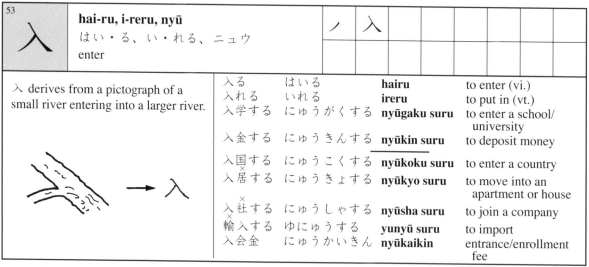

都市	とし	**toshi**	city
都市工学科	とし こうがっか	**Toshi kōgakka**	Department of Urban Engineering
京都市	きょうとし	**Kyōto shi**	the City of Kyoto
市場	いちば／ しじょう	**ichiba/ shijō**	market, marketplace
市役所	しやくしょ	**shiyakusho**	city/municipal office
市民	しみん	**shimin**	citizen
市長	しちょう	**shichō**	mayor

| 53 入 | hai-ru, i-reru, nyū
はい・る、い・れる、ニュウ
enter | ノ | 入 | | | | | |

入 derives from a pictograph of a small river entering into a larger river.

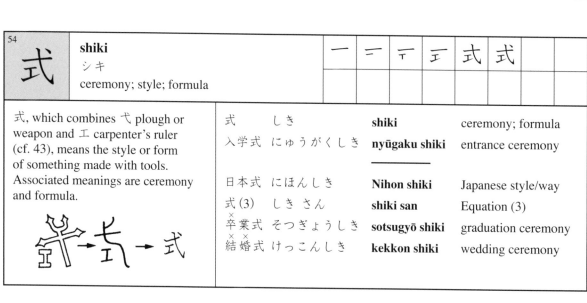

入る	はいる	**hairu**	to enter (vi.)
入れる	いれる	**ireru**	to put in (vt.)
入学する	にゅうがくする	**nyūgaku suru**	to enter a school/ university
入金する	にゅうきんする	**nyūkin suru**	to deposit money
入国する	にゅうこくする	**nyūkoku suru**	to enter a country
入居する	にゅうきょする	**nyūkyo suru**	to move into an apartment or house
入社する	にゅうしゃする	**nyūsha suru**	to join a company
輸入する	ゆにゅうする	**yunyū suru**	to import
入会金	にゅうかいきん	**nyūkaikin**	entrance/enrollment fee

| 54 式 | shiki
シキ
ceremony; style; formula | 一 | 二 | 〒 | 工 | 式 | 式 | |

式, which combines 弋 plough or weapon and 工 carpenter's ruler (cf. 43), means the style or form of something made with tools. Associated meanings are ceremony and formula.

式	しき	**shiki**	ceremony; formula
入学式	にゅうがくしき	**nyūgaku shiki**	entrance ceremony
日本式	にほんしき	**Nihon shiki**	Japanese style/way
式(3)	しき さん	**shiki san**	Equation (3)
卒業式	そつぎょうしき	**sotsugyō shiki**	graduation ceremony
結婚式	けっこんしき	**kekkon shiki**	wedding ceremony

55 文	**bun, mon** ブン、モン literature; sentence; culture	丶	一	ナ	文			

文 was often used as a design on ancient clay pottery. Originally associated with design, it has now come to mean written passage, sentence, literature, and also culture.

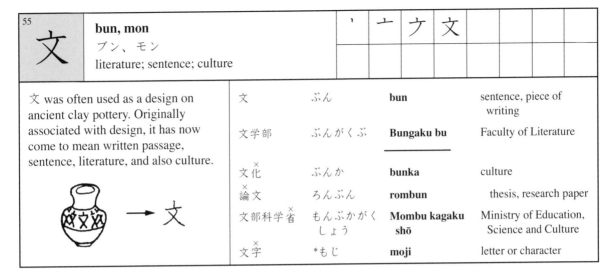

文	ぶん	**bun**	sentence, piece of writing
文学部	ぶんがくぶ	**Bungaku bu**	Faculty of Literature
文化	ぶんか	**bunka**	culture
論文	ろんぶん	**rombun**	thesis, research paper
文部科学省	もんぶかがく しょう	**Mombu kagaku shō**	Ministry of Education, Science and Culture
文字	*もじ	**moji**	letter or character

56 区	**ku** ク ward; district	一	フ	ヌ	区			

区 derives from 區, which depicts many mouths or people (cf. 107 口) inside a boundary ⊏. 区 thus indicates a district or ward.

文京区	ぶんきょうく	**Bunkyō ku**	Bunkyo Ward
区間	くかん	**kukan**	interval (between two points long a railway or a road)
区役所	くやくしょ	**kuyakusho**	ward office
東京都区内	とうきょうと くない	**Tōkyōto kunai**	within the twenty-three wards of Tokyo

57 丁	**chō** チョウ counter for blocks of houses	一	丁					

丁 represents a sign showing a town or street name, and is used as a counter for blocks of houses, blocks of tōfu, and other food dishes.

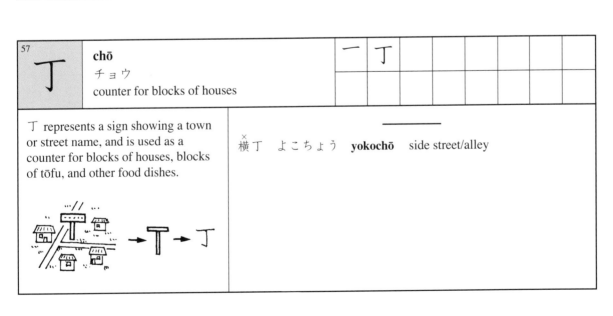

横丁	よこちょう	**yokochō**	side street/alley

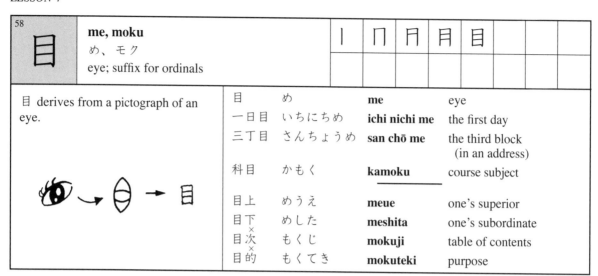

58 目	me, moku め、モク eye; suffix for ordinals		一	冂	冃	月	目		

目 derives from a pictograph of an eye.	目	め	**me**	eye
	一日目	いちにちめ	**ichi nichi me**	the first day
	三丁目	さんちょうめ	**san chō me**	the third block (in an address)
	科目	かもく	**kamoku**	course subject
	目上	めうえ	**meue**	one's superior
	目下	めした	**meshita**	one's subordinate
	目次	もくじ	**mokuji**	table of contents
	目的	もくてき	**mokuteki**	purpose

4 ▶ Practice

I. Write the readings of the following kanji in hiragana.

1. 東 京 大 学　　2. 留 学 生　　3. 工 学 部　　4. 都 市 工 学 科
5. 三 木 先 生　　6. 専 攻　　　7. 日 本 語　　8. 土 木 工 学 科
9. 入 学 式　　　10. 文 京 区　　11. 七 丁 目　　12. 東
13. 部 分　　　　14. 先 月　　　15. 入 る　　　16. 科 目
17. ピ ー タ ー さ ん の 　目 は 　大 き い で す ね 。
18. 科 学 や 　文 学 を 　べ ん き ょ う し ま す 。
19. 先 週 、 京 都 へ 　い き ま し た 。
20. わ た し は 　日 本 で 　生 ま れ ま し た 。
21. こ こ に 　あ な た の 　生 年 月 日 を 　か い て く だ さ い 。
22. フ ラ ン ス 語 で 　*み じ か い 　文 を 　か き ま し た 。 (*short)

II. Fill in the blanks with appropriate kanji.

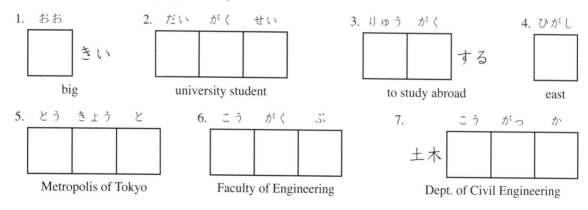

1. おお
□ きい
big

2. だい　がく　せい
□□□
university student

3. りゅう　がく
□□ する
to study abroad

4. ひがし
□
east

5. とう　きょう　と
□□□
Metropolis of Tokyo

6. こう　がく　ぶ
□□□
Faculty of Engineering

7. こう　がっ　か
土木 □□□
Dept. of Civil Engineering

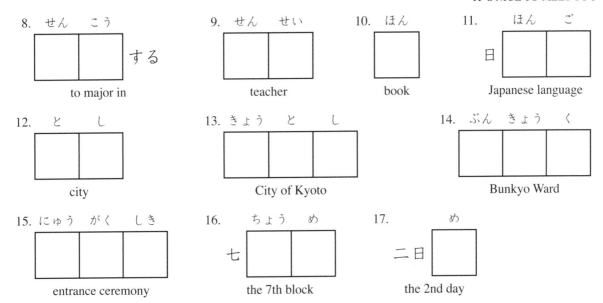

8. せん こう
□□する
to major in

9. せん せい
□□
teacher

10. ほん
□
book

11. ほん ご
日□□
Japanese language

12. と し
□□
city

13. きょう と し
□□□
City of Kyoto

14. ぶん きょう く
□□□
Bunkyo Ward

15. にゅう がく しき
□□□
entrance ceremony

16. ちょう め
七□□
the 7th block

17. め
二日□
the 2nd day

5 ▶ Advanced Placement Exam Practice Questions

The setting is Bunkyo Ward's civic center hall. During Golden Week, people are having an international party for the foreigners living in this ward. Four young people are introducing themselves in a circle. Read their statements and answer the following questions.

Mr. A:

イランからきた留学生です。東京大学の工学部でべんきょうしています。専攻は都市工学です。はたちです。国（くに）の日本語学校（がっこう）で二年間日本語をべんきょうしました。一か月前にきたばかりで、なにも分かりませんが、よろしくおねがいします。

Ms. B:

わたしは一年前に中国（ちゅうごく）からきました。平日は九時から十二時半まで日本語学校でべんきょうしています。午後はスーパーでアルバイトをしています。日本の大学に入って、[1]経済（けいざい）をべんきょうしたいです。ともだちになってください。休日は時間があるので、いろいろなところへいきたいです。あ、年は十八です。どうぞよろしく。

Mr. C:

ぼくは十七歳（さい）です。オーストラリア人（じん）です。きょ年の十月に日本の高校（こうこう）へ留学生としてきました。はじめて漢字（かんじ）をべんきょうしましたが、日本語はむずかしいですね。べんきょうはたいへんですが、日本のまんがやアニメが大すきなので、まい日テレビをみています。まんがやアニメがすきな人はいませんか。

[1]経済（けいざい）: economics

Ms. D:

わたしはアメリカからきました。いま日本の高校[こうこう]で英[えい]語をおしえています。八年前、大学生のときも日本の大学で一年間べんきょうしたことがあるんです。Aさんの大学の文学部です。だからわたしの年は、みなさんわかりますね。「おすし」や「てんぷら」が大すきなので日本の生活[せいかつ]はたのしいです。

1. Who is the oldest?
   A. Mr. A
   B. Ms. B
   C. Mr. C
   D. Ms. D

2. Who says that the Japanese language is difficult?
   A. Mr. A
   B. Ms. B
   C. Mr. C
   D. Ms. D

3. Who has come to Japan before?
   A. Mr. A
   B. Ms. B
   C. Mr. C
   D. Ms. D

4. Who has stayed in Japan the shortest amount of time?
   A. Mr. A
   B. Ms. B
   C. Mr. C
   D. Ms. D

5. Who hopes to enter a Japanese university?
   A. Mr. A
   B. Ms. B
   C. Mr. C
   D. Ms. D

Buying a Commuter Pass

定期券を かいます

If you commute to work or school by train every day, you'll find it convenient to buy a commuter pass. Good for one, three, or six months, the pass can be used as often as you like between the stations indicated on it. It normally costs about two thirds the price of using ordinary tickets, and only about one third if you are a student. These passes can be purchased at major stations. The IC card commuter pass, shown left, was introduced more recently, and many people use it. You simply touch it to the automatic ticket scanner, making it very easy to use.

In this lesson, you will learn how to fill in the application form to buy a commuter pass. This knowledge will then help you fill in other kinds of forms as well.

1 ▸ Introductory Quiz

Look at the illustration below and refer to the words in **Vocabulary**. Then try the following quiz.

The commuter pass above shows all of the following information.

① It is valid between Yotsuya station and Shinjuku station.
② It is valid for 6 months, from March 14 to September 13, in the 20th year of Heisei (2008).
③ It costs ¥13,740.
④ It belongs to Mr. Sudō.
⑤ Mr. Sudō is a 20-year-old student.

I. Look at the commuter pass below, and then answer the following questions.

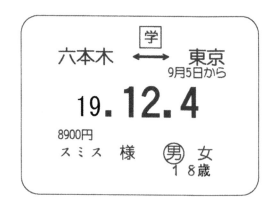

1. この 定期券は _____ 駅から _____ 駅までです。

2. この 定期券は 平成19年____月____日から 平成19年____月____日までです。

3. この 定期券は _____円です。

4. この 定期券は _____さんのです。

5. この 人は （ a. 学生です。　　b. 学生ではありません。）

II. To buy a commuter pass you need to fill in an application form like the one shown below. Look at the completed application, then try to fill in the blank copy of the application form as best you can.

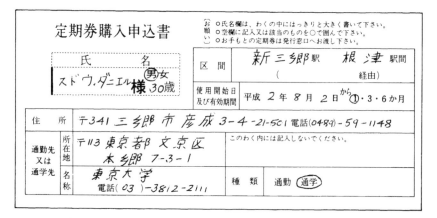

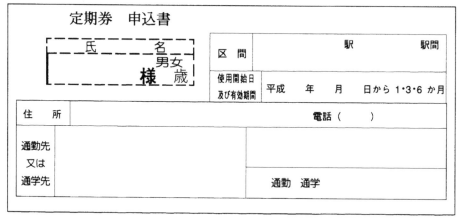

2 **Vocabulary**

Study the readings and meanings of these words to help you understand the **Introductory Quiz**.

1.	定期券	てい き けん	**teiki ken**	commuter pass
2.	駅	え き	**eki**	station
3.	〜様	〜さ ま	**~sama**	Mr. ~, Ms. ~, Miss ~, Mrs. ~
4.	通学	つう がく	**tsūgaku**	commuting to school
5.	六本木	ろっ ぽん ぎ	**Roppongi**	Roppongi (station)
6.	申込書	もうし こみ しょ	**mōshikomi sho**	application form
7.	氏名	し めい	**shimei**	full name
8.	男	おとこ	**otoko**	man
9.	女	おんな	**onna**	woman
10.	〜歳	〜 さい	**~sai**	~ years old
11.	区間	く かん	**kukan**	interval (between two railway points)
12.	使用	し よう	**shiyō**	use
13.	開始日	かい し び	**kaishi bi**	starting date
14.	有効	ゆう こう	**yūkō**	validity
15.	期間	き かん	**kikan**	period
16.	〜か月	〜 か げつ	**~ka getsu**	~ month(s)
17.	住所	じゅう しょ	**jūsho**	address
18.	電話	でん わ	**denwa**	telephone
19.	通勤	つう きん	**tsūkin**	commuting to work
20.	通勤先	つう きん さき	**tsūkin saki**	one's place of work
21.	通学先	つう がく さき	**tsūgaku saki**	one's school
22.	所在地	しょ ざい ち	**shozaichi**	location
23.	名称	めい しょう	**meishō**	name
24.	種類	しゅ るい	**shurui**	types

3 **New Characters**

Twenty-one characters are introduced in this lesson. Use the explanations to help you understand and remember the characters. Study the compound words to increase your vocabulary.

定 期 券 申 込 書 氏 名 男 女 歳 駅 使 用 開
始 住 所 電 話 通

59 定	**tei** テイ fix, decide; regular, definite	ヽ	゛	宀	宀	宇	宇	定	定

定 combines the radical 宀 house, 一 one, and 疋 a variation of 止 stop (cf. 149). Stopping in one part of a house implies a fixed place. Associated meanings include decide, regular and definite.

定休日	ていきゅうび	**teikyū bi**	regular holiday, shop/company holiday
定年	ていねん	**teinen**	retirement age
定価	ていか	**teika**	list price
定員	ていいん	**teiin**	seating/passenger capacity; fixed number of personnel
未定	みてい	**mitei**	undecided, unscheduled

---

60 期	**ki** キ period of time, term	一	十	廿	廿	甘	甚	其	其
		斯	期	期	期				

期 combines 月 month and 其, a stiff basket made of tightly woven bamboo. From this association, 期 has come to mean fixed period of time or term.

定期	ていき	**teiki**	regular; abbreviation for 定期券 (commuter pass)
学期	がっき	**gakki**	school term/semester
期間	きかん	**kikan**	term, period
期限	きげん	**kigen**	deadline, time limit
短期大学	たんきだいがく	**tanki daigaku**	junior college
同期生	どうきせい	**dōki sei**	graduates in the same year

---

61 券	**ken** ケン ticket	ヽ	゛	丷	쓰	半	关	券	券

券 combines 丷 bamboo sheet marked with an ×, and 刀 sword or knife. Ancient Chinese would scratch a thin bamboo scroll with a knife and give one half to another person as a certificate. From this, 券 has come to mean ticket.

券	けん	**ken**	ticket
定期券	ていきけん	**teiki ken**	commuter pass
乗車券	じょうしゃけん	**jōsha ken**	train/bus ticket
指定券	していけん	**shitei ken**	seat reservation ticket
旅券	りょけん	**ryoken**	passport

62 申 mō-su, shin
もう・す、シン
say, report

Stroke order: 丨 冂 日 日 申

申 derives from 电, which is part of the kanji for lightning 電 (cf. 77). One speaks to a superior with the same awe or fear one has in the presence of lightning. Thus 申 means say in a humble form.

申す	もうす	**mōsu**	to say (humble form)
申請する	しんせいする	**shinsei suru**	to apply/petition for
申告する	しんこくする	**shinkoku suru**	to report, to notify

63 込 ko-mu
こ・む
be crowded; counted in

Stroke order: 丿 入 込 込 込

込, which combines 入 enter (cf. 53) and 辶 proceed (cf. 16 週), is a kanji created in Japan. From its original meaning of enter or gather, 込 has come to mean counted or be crowded.

込む	こむ	**komu**	to be crowded
申(し)込む	もうしこむ	**mōshi komu**	to apply for (enrollment, etc.); to propose (marriage)
払(い)込む	はらいこむ	**harai komu**	to pay into
振(り)込む	ふりこむ	**furi komu**	to transfer money by bank

64 書 ka-ku, sho
か・く、ショ
write; book

Stroke order: 乛 ユ ヨ ヨ 聿 聿 書 書 書 書

書 depicts a hand holding a brush and writing on a piece of paper.

書く	かく	**kaku**	to write
申込書	もうしこみしょ	**mōshikomi sho**	application form
書状	しょじょう	**shojō**	letter
読書	どくしょ	**dokusho**	reading books
参考書	さんこうしょ	**sankōsho**	reference book
辞書	じしょ	**jisho**	dictionary
書類	しょるい	**shorui**	documents, written materials

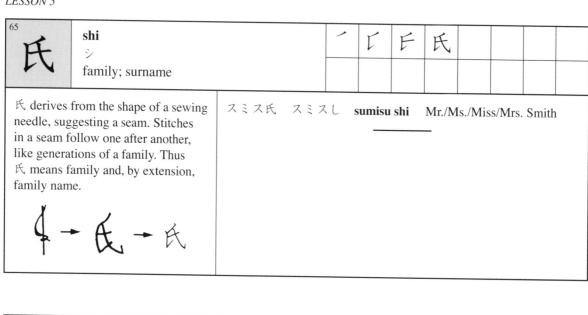

65 氏 shi
シ
family; surname

〔 ⸀ 仟 氏

氏 derives from the shape of a sewing needle, suggesting a seam. Stitches in a seam follow one after another, like generations of a family. Thus 氏 means family and, by extension, family name.

スミス氏　スミスし　**sumisu shi**　Mr./Ms./Miss/Mrs. Smith

66 名 na, mei
な、メイ
name; reputation

ノ ク タ 夕 名 名

名 combines 夕, which depicts the moon above a mountain and means evening, and 口 mouth (cf. 107), which implies speak. When it's difficult to recognize people on dark evenings, their names must be spoken aloud.

名前	なまえ	**namae**	name
氏名	しめい	**shimei**	full name
名人	めいじん	**meijin**	expert, master
20名	にじゅうめい	**nijū mei**	twenty people
名古屋	なごや	**Nagoya**	Nagoya
有名な	ゆうめいな	**yūmei na**	famous, well-known
名刺	めいし	**meishi**	business card, name card

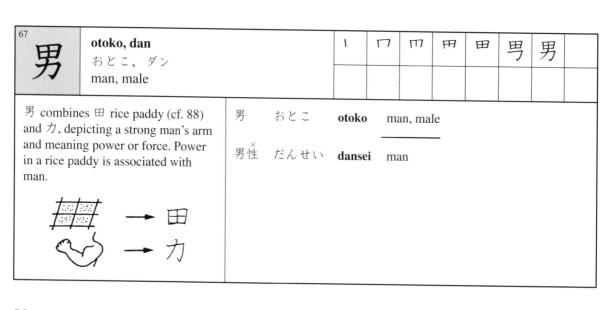

67 男 otoko, dan
おとこ、ダン
man, male

丨 冂 冂 甲 田 男 男

男 combines 田 rice paddy (cf. 88) and 力, depicting a strong man's arm and meaning power or force. Power in a rice paddy is associated with man.

男	おとこ	**otoko**	man, male
男性	だんせい	**dansei**	man

68 女 — onna, jo / おんな、ジョ / woman

く	夕	女					

女 derives from a pictograph of a woman holding a baby in her arms.

女	おんな	**onna**	woman, female
男女	だんじょ	**danjo**	men and women
女性	じょせい	**josei**	woman

69 歳 — toshi, sai, (zai) / とし、サイ、(ザイ) / age, year, years old

ノ	上	止	止	产	卢	虍	岸
岸	崇	歳	歳	歳			

The right and left foot 止 suggest the passage of time. A pike 戈 and a tree 木 suggest the harvest. Thus 歳 means the passage of time until the harvest, one year.

歳	とし	**toshi**	age
25歳	にじゅうごさい	**nijūgo sai**	25 years old
何歳	なんさい	**nan sai**	how old
万歳	ばんざい	**banzai**	hurrah
歳月	さいげつ	**saigetsu**	time
歳入	さいにゅう	**sainyū**	annual revenue

70 駅 — eki / エキ / station

l	厂	厂	厍	馬	馬	馬	馬
馬	馬	馬ㄱ	馬ㄱ	馬っ	駅		

駅 combines 馬 horse and 尺, a unit of length deriving from the shape of stretched fingers. In the past, stations were placed at regular intervals for travelers and horses to stop and rest.

駅	えき	**eki**	station
駅前	えきまえ	**ekimae**	in front of a station
駅名	えきめい	**ekimei**	station name
駅長	えきちょう	**ekichō**	stationmaster
駅員	えきいん	**ekiin**	station employee/staff
駅弁	えきべん	**ekiben**	box lunch sold at a station
駅ビル	えきビル	**ekibiru**	station building

71 使	tsuka-u, shi つか・う、シ use, messenger	ノ	イ	仁	仨	仴	佢	伊	使

使 combines イ man and 吏, a hand holding a brush and papers, representing a government officer. Thus 使 suggests a superior employing or using his officers, and has come to mean use in general.

使う	つかう	**tsukau**	to use
大使	たいし	**taishi**	ambassador

使い方	つかいかた	**tsukaikata**	how to use, directions for use
大使館	たいしかん	**taishikan**	embassy

72 用	mochi-iru, yō もち・いる、ヨウ use, usage; business	ノ	刀	月	月	用			

用 depicts a fence used to keep sheep in one place, and has come to mean use in general.

用	よう	**yō**	something to do, business
使用する	しようする	**shiyō suru**	to use
学生用	がくせいよう	**gakusei yō**	for students
専用	せんよう	**sen'yō**	for private/exclusive use

用いる	もちいる	**mochiiru**	to use
用×紙	ようし	**yōshi**	blank form/paper
利用×者	りようしゃ	**riyōsha**	user
採×用する	さいようする	**saiyō suru**	to adopt; to employ

73 開	hira-ku, a-ku, a-keru, kai ひら・く、あ・く、あ・ける、カイ open	丨	冂	冃	阝	阝	門	門	門
		門	閂	開	開				

開 depicts two hands 廾 (cf. 85 手) removing the bolt 一 from a gate 門 (cf. 181) in order to open it.

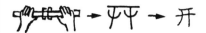

開く	ひらく	**hiraku**	to open
開く	あく	**aku**	to open (vi.)
開ける	あける	**akeru**	to open (vt.)

開店する	かいてんする	**kaiten suru**	to open a shop; for a shop to open
開発する	かいはつする	**kaihatsu suru**	to develop (vt.)

74 始	haji-maru, haji-meru, shi はじ・まる、はじ・める、シ begin, start	く	夕	女	女	女	始	始	始

始 combines 女 woman (cf. 68) and 台 foundation. A woman is the foundation of all our beginnings.

始まる	はじまる	**hajimaru**	to start/begin (vi.)
始める	はじめる	**hajimeru**	to start/begin (vt.)
開始する	かいしする	**kaishi suru**	to start/begin
開始日	かいしび	**kaishi bi**	starting date
始業式	しぎょうしき	**shigyō shiki**	opening ceremony for a new semester at school

75 住	su-mu, jū す・む、ジュウ live	ノ	イ	イ	亠	什	住	住	

住, which combines イ man and 主 candle with a still flame, means stay still or live in one place. As part of other kanji, 主 often means stay still.

住む	すむ	**sumu**	to live
住まい	すまい	**sumai**	residence, house
住民票	じゅうみんひょう	**jūminhyō**	resident registration certificate
住宅	じゅうたく	**jūtaku**	house, residence

76 所	tokoro, sho, (jo) ところ、ショ、（ジョ） place	一	三	ヨ	戸	戸	所	所	所

戸 derives from a pictograph of a door, and 斤 from that of an ax. The place to keep an ax is near the door.

所	ところ	**tokoro**	place
住所	じゅうしょ	**jūsho**	address
名所	めいしょ	**meisho**	famous place
現住所	げんじゅうしょ	**genjūsho**	present address
所在地	しょざいち	**shozaichi**	location, address
近所	きんじょ	**kinjo**	neighborhood

77 電

den
デン
electricity

一	厂	冖	币	市	乕	雨	雨
雫	雫	雪	雷	電			

電 is a variation of 雷 thunder, which combines 雨 rain and 田 rice paddy (cf. 88). 電 indicates lightning, and has come to mean electricity.

電気	でんき	**denki**	electricity
電子	でんし	**denshi**	electron
電力	でんりょく	**denryoku**	electric power
電池	でんち	**denchi**	battery
電報	でんぽう	**dempō**	telegram

78 話

hana-su, hanashi, wa
はな・す、はなし、ワ
speak, talk; story

丶	亠	亖	言	言	言	言	言
訁	訐	訐	話	話			

話, which combines 言 word or say and 舌 tongue, means speak or story.

話す	はなす	**hanasu**	to talk, to speak
話	はなし	**hanashi**	story, talk, speech
電話	でんわ	**denwa**	telephone
会話	かいわ	**kaiwa**	conversation
話題	わだい	**wadai**	topic, subject of conversation/speech
市外通話	しがいつうわ	**shigai tsūwa**	out-of-town/ long-distance call

79 通

tō-ru, (dō-ri), tsū
とお・る、（どお・り）、ツウ
go through, pass; commute

丆	マ	マ	刁	甬	甬	甬	甬
通	通						

通 combines 辶 go (cf. 16 週) and 甬, a man putting a stick through a fence. Thus 通 means go through or pass.

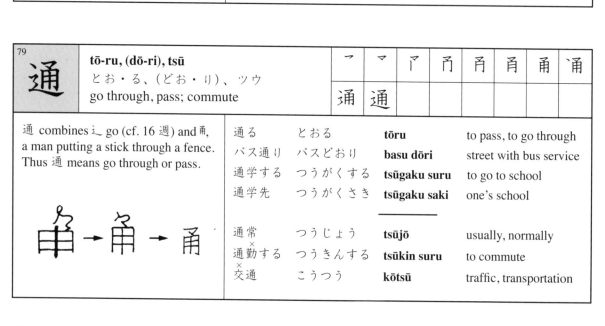

通る	とおる	**tōru**	to pass, to go through
バス通り	バスどおり	**basu dōri**	street with bus service
通学する	つうがくする	**tsūgaku suru**	to go to school
通学先	つうがくさき	**tsūgaku saki**	one's school
通常	つうじょう	**tsūjō**	usually, normally
通勤する	つうきんする	**tsūkin suru**	to commute
交通	こうつう	**kōtsū**	traffic, transportation

4 ▶ Practice

I. Write the readings of the following kanji in hiragana.

1. 定 期 券　　　2. 申 込 書　　　3. 通 学　　　4. 駅
5. 氏 名　　　　6. 男　　　　　7. 女　　　　　8. 〜 歳
9. 区 間　　　　10. 使 用　　　11. 開 始 日　　　12. 期 間
13. 住 所　　　14. 電 話　　　15. 定 休 日　　　16. 学 期
17. 通 る　　　18. 駅 名　　　19. 大 使　　　20. 所
21. 申 し 込 む　　　22. あ な た の　名 前　を　書 い て く だ さ い 。
23. 駅 前 か ら　タ ク シ ー に　の り ま し た 。
24. い い　て ん き で す 。　ま ど を　開 け ま し ょ う 。
25. ク ラ ス は　十 時 に　始 ま り ま す 。
26. わ た し は　東 京 に　住 ん で い ま す 。
27. き の う の　よ る　と も だ ち と　電 話 で　話 し ま し た 。

II. Fill in the blanks with appropriate kanji.

1. か

く
to write

2. もうしこみ　しょ
application form

3. てい　き　けん

commuter's pass

4. し
スミス □
Mr. Smith

5. だん　じょ

men and women

6. さい
30 □
30 years old

7. えき
□
station

8. つか

う
to use

9. し　よう

する
to use

10. す　　ところ
□ む □
place to live

11. めい　しょ
famous place

12. ひら

く
to open

13. はじ

める
to begin

14. かい　し

する
to begin

15. どお
バス □ り
street with bus service

16. つう
□ 学先
one's school

17. はな
□ す
to talk

5 ▶ **Advanced Placement Exam Practice Questions**

Now you are going to buy a commuter pass. Fill in the application form.

You are a student of the University of Tokyo and your address and the stations which you want to use are as follows:

- Address: みなと区六本木1丁目2-1
- Telephone: 03-4321-5678
- Stations: 六本木一丁目駅 から 東大前駅 まで

There are three choices for the time period. This is from September 3 to March 2, in the 19th year of Heisei (平成) (2007).

定期券 申込書

氏　　名		区　間	駅　　　　駅　間 （　　　　経　由　）
	男 女	使用開始日 及び 有 効 期 間	平成　年　月　日から **1・3・6** ヶ月
様	歳		

住　所	
	電話　（　　）

通勤先 又は 通学先	通勤　　　通学

REVIEW EXERCISE: LESSONS 1–5

I. Connect each kanji to its corresponding pictograph.

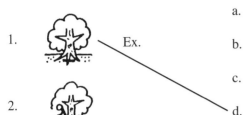

1.   Ex.

a. 日

b. 火

2.

c. 水

d. 本

3.

e. 休

f. 分

g. 金

4.

h. 先

i. 式

5.

j. 科

k. 門

l. 男

6.

m. 書

n. 曜

7.

o. 週

8.

p. 祭

9.

10.

11.

12.

13.

14.

15.

16.

II. Choose the correct kanji for the given readings.

(1) ご = { a. 牛 b. 午 }

(2) と = { a. 都 b. 部 }

(3) かい = { a. 間 b. 開 }

(4) はん = { a. 半 b. 羊 }

(5) つき = { a. 月 b. 目 }

(6) こう = { a. 土 b. 工 }

(7) まん = { a. 方 b. 万 }

(8) つう = { a. 週 b. 通 }

(9) わ = { a. 話 b. 語 }

Which Line Do You Take?

LESSON 6

何線に のりますか

In major cities in Japan, subways are the primary means of transportation. Left is a Tokyo subway map, which may seem complicated, but most people find the subway the most convenient way to get around. All lines are marked with a different color, and these colors are also displayed on signs in the stations. The Tokyo subway system consists of the Tokyo Metro Lines and the Toei Lines, and links up with the JR (Japan Railway) and private railway lines. Subway stations are marked with big signs above station entrances, as shown in the photo.

In this lesson you'll learn kanji to help you in using the subway system.

1 ▶ Introductory Quiz

Look at the illustration below and refer to the words in **Vocabulary**. Then try the following quiz.

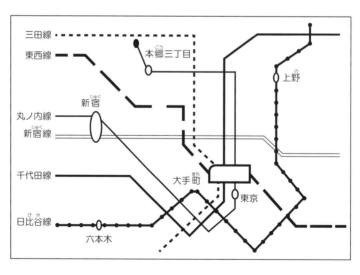

I. Look at the simplified Tokyo subway map and match the kanji for the station names with their readings.

1. ろっぽんぎ（　　）　2. おおてまち（　　）　3. うえの（　　）
4. とうきょう（　　）　5. しんじゅく（　　）　6. ほんごうさんちょうめ（　　）

　　a. 東京　　b. 新宿　　c. 大手町　　d. 上野　　e. 本郷 三丁目　　f. 六本木

II. Using the map at the bottom of the opposite page, identify the lines that pass through the following
stations. Then enter the correct letters in the spaces provided.

1. 大手町 (　　　)(　　　)(　　　)(　　　)　　　2. 六本木 (　　　)
3. 新宿　(　　　)(　　　)　　　　　　　　　　4. 東京　(　　　)

　a. ひびや線　　b. しんじゅく線　　c. みた線　　d. ちよだ線　　e. まるのうち線　　f. とうざい線

III. Subway lines in Tokyo are finely meshed; you can go in from one entrance to four stations in a few cases.
春日駅 and 後楽園駅 are connecting stations. Look at the signboard on the entrance and try the quiz:

とえいせんは　(a. **N11**　b. **M22**　c. **E07**　d. **I12**) です。

---

2 ▶ **Vocabulary**

Study the readings and meanings of these words to help you understand the **Introductory Quiz**.

1.	何線	なに せん	**nani sen**	what line, which line
2.	地下鉄	ち か てつ	**chikatetsu**	subway
3.	六本木	ろっ ぽん ぎ	**Roppongi**	Roppongi (station)
4.	大手町	おお て まち	**Ōtemachi**	Otemachi (station)
5.	上野	うえ の	**Ueno**	Ueno (station)
6.	新宿	しん じゅく	**Shinjuku**	Shinjuku (station)
7.	本郷三丁目	ほん ごう さん ちょう め	**Hongō san chōme**	Hongo-Sanchome (station)
8.	日比谷線	ひ び や せん	**Hibiya sen**	Hibiya Line
9.	新宿線	しん じゅく せん	**Shinjuku sen**	Shinjuku Line
10.	三田線	み た せん	**Mita sen**	Mita Line
11.	千代田線	ち よ だ せん	**Chiyoda sen**	Chiyoda Line
12.	丸ノ内線	まる の うち せん	**Marunouchi sen**	Marunouchi Line
13.	東西線	とう ざい せん	**Tōzai sen**	Tozai Line
14.	東京メトロ線	とう きょう メトロ せん	**Tōkyō metoro sen**	Tokyo Metro Line
15.	都営線	と えい せん	**Toei sen**	Toei Line (municipal)

---

3 ▶ **New Characters**

Fourteen characters are introduced in this lesson. Use the explanations to help you understand and remember
the characters. Study the compound words to increase your vocabulary.

何　線　地　下　鉄　手　上　新　田　代　丸　内　西　営

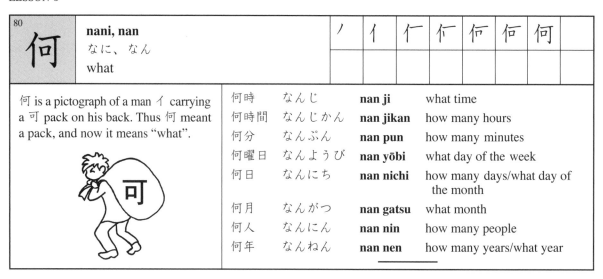

| 80 何 | **nani, nan**
なに、なん
what | ノ | イ | 仁 | 仃 | 仃 | 何 | 何 |

何 is a pictograph of a man イ carrying a 可 pack on his back. Thus 何 meant a pack, and now it means "what".

何時	なんじ	**nan ji**	what time
何時間	なんじかん	**nan jikan**	how many hours
何分	なんぷん	**nan pun**	how many minutes
何曜日	なんようび	**nan yōbi**	what day of the week
何日	なんにち	**nan nichi**	how many days/what day of the month
何月	なんがつ	**nan gatsu**	what month
何人	なんにん	**nan nin**	how many people
何年	なんねん	**nan nen**	how many years/what year

| 81 線 | **sen**
セン
line | く | 幺 | 幺 | 糸 | 糸 | 糸 | 糸' | 糸' |
| | | 紵 | 紵 | 絎 | 紵 | 綧 | 線 | 線 | |

線 combines 糸, twisted bundle of thread, 白 white (cf. 11 百), and 水 water. 泉 means spring, whose water is clean and white. Water from a spring flows in a line like thread.

線	せん	**sen**	line
丸ノ内線	まるのうちせん	**Marunouchi sen**	Marunouchi Line
JR線	JRせん	**JR sen**	Japanese Railway Line
内線	ないせん	**naisen**	extension (telephone)
国内線	こくないせん	**kokunai sen**	domestic route/flight
国際線	こくさいせん	**kokusai sen**	international route/flight
新幹線	しんかんせん	**Shinkan sen**	Shinkansen (bullet train)
無線タクシー	むせんタクシー	**musen takushī**	radio taxi

| 82 地 | **chi, ji**
チ、ジ
land, earth | 一 | 十 | 土 | 圫 | 地 | 地 | | |

地 combines ∮ modified from 土 ground (cf. 31) and 也 snake. Since snakes slither on the ground, 地 has come to mean land or earth.

土地	とち	**tochi**	(piece of) land
地名	ちめい	**chimei**	place name
地図	ちず	**chizu**	map
地球	ちきゅう	**chikyū**	the earth, the globe
地震	じしん	**jishin**	earthquake

83 下	**shita, kuda-ru, ka, ge** した、くだ・る、カ、ゲ below, under, down, lower; fall, descent	一	丁	下					

To indicate below, under, or down, the ancient Chinese drew a dot below a line. This was later modified to 下.	下	した	**shita**	below, under, down, lower
	下り	くだり	**kudari**	down, descent; abbreviation for 下り電車 (outbound train)
	地下	ちか	**chika**	underground
	下着	したぎ	**shitagi**	underwear
	下町	したまち	**shitamachi**	the traditional shopping, entertainment and residential districts (of Tokyo); downtown
	下水	げすい	**gesui**	sewerage
	千円以下	せんえん いか	**sen en ika**	one thousand yen or less

84 鉄	**tetsu** テツ iron	ノ	ハ	ム	스	牟	牟	金	金
		釘	針	鉄	鉄	鉄			

鉄, which combines 金 metal (cf. 30) and 失 lose, means iron, a metal that loses its value when it rusts.	鉄	てつ	**tetsu**	iron, steel
	地下鉄	ちかてつ	**chikatetsu**	subway
	鉄道	てつどう	**tetsudō**	railway
	私鉄	してつ	**shitetsu**	private railway line/company

85 手	**te, shu** て、シュ hand	ノ	二	三	手				

手 derives from a pictograph of a hand. All the elements shown below are used to refer to hand.	手	て	**te**	hand
	山手線	やまのてせん	**Yamanote sen**	Yamanote Line
	大手町	おおてまち	**Ōtemachi**	Otemachi (place)
	手紙	てがみ	**tegami**	letter
	手数料	てすうりょう	**tesūryō**	fee, charge, commission
	歌手	かしゅ	**kashu**	singer
	助手	じょしゅ	**joshu**	research associate, assistant
	選手	せんしゅ	**senshu**	athlete

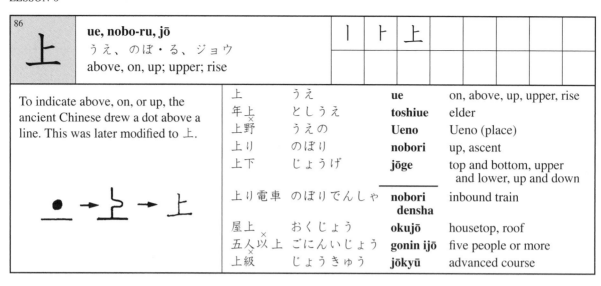

86 上	**ue, nobo-ru, jō** うえ、 のぼ・る、 ジョウ above, on, up; upper; rise	一	卜	上					

To indicate above, on, or up, the ancient Chinese drew a dot above a line. This was later modified to 上.

上	うえ	**ue**	on, above, up, upper, rise
年上	としうえ	**toshiue**	elder
上野	うえの	**Ueno**	Ueno (place)
上り	のぼり	**nobori**	up, ascent
上下	じょうげ	**jōge**	top and bottom, upper and lower, up and down
上り電車	のぼりでんしゃ	**nobori densha**	inbound train
屋上	おくじょう	**okujō**	housetop, roof
五人以上	ごにんいじょう	**gonin ijō**	five people or more
上級	じょうきゅう	**jōkyū**	advanced course

87 新	**atara-shii, shin** あたら・しい、 シン new	`	立	亠	宀	立	立	辛	辛
		亲	新	新	新	新			

新 combines 立 stand (cf. 167), 木 tree, and 斤 ax (cf. 76 所). From the idea of cutting a standing tree with an ax to produce fresh timber, 新 has come to mean new. Another version says that standing trees are cut to clear new land.

新しい	あたらしい	**atarashii**	new
新年	しんねん	**shinnen**	the New Year
新入生	しんにゅうせい	**shinnyūsei**	new student/pupil
新宿	しんじゅく	**Shinjuku**	Shinjuku (place)
新人	しんじん	**shinjin**	newcomer, new face
新住所	しんじゅうしょ	**shin jūsho**	new address
新学期	しんがっき	**shin gakki**	new term/semester
新聞	しんぶん	**shimbun**	newspaper

88 田	**ta, (da)** た、 （だ） rice field, paddy	丨	冂	冂	田	田			

田 derives from a pictograph of a rice field.

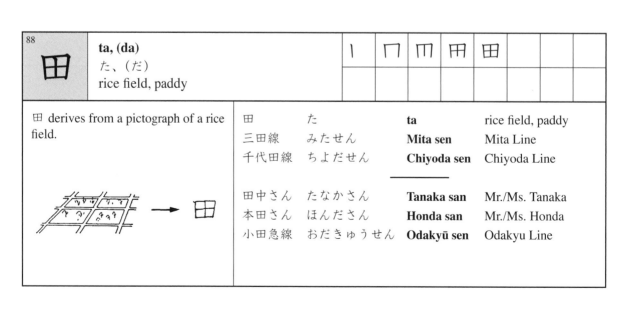

田	た	**ta**	rice field, paddy
三田線	みたせん	**Mita sen**	Mita Line
千代田線	ちよだせん	**Chiyoda sen**	Chiyoda Line
田中さん	たなかさん	**Tanaka san**	Mr./Ms. Tanaka
本田さん	ほんださん	**Honda san**	Mr./Ms. Honda
小田急線	おだきゅうせん	**Odakyū sen**	Odakyu Line

89

代

ka-waru, yo, dai
か・わる、よ、ダイ
substitute, replace; price; generation

ノ	イ	仁	代	代			

代, which combines イ man and 弋 weapon (cf. 54 式), came to mean substitute from the idea of an army getting stronger as weapons were substituted for man power. When buying things, money is substituted for a commodity; thus 代 also means price. An associated meaning is generation.

代(わ)りに	かわりに	**kawari ni**	instead
代々木	よよぎ	**Yoyogi**	Yoyogi (place)
バス代	バスだい	**basu dai**	bus fare
時代	じだい	**jidai**	period, epoch, era
代金	だいきん	**daikin**	price, charge
電気代	でんきだい	**denki dai**	electricity charges
現代	げんだい	**gendai**	present age, modern times
世代	せだい	**sedai**	generation
代理人	だいりにん	**dairinin**	deputy, agent, substitute

90

丸

maru, maru-i
まる、まる・い
circle; round

ノ	九	丸					

丸, which depicts a man rounding his back to enter a cave, means round. An associated meaning is circle.

丸	まる	**maru**	circle
丸い	まるい	**marui**	round, circular, spherical

91

内

uchi, nai
うち、ナイ
inside

丨	冂	内	内				

内 depicts a man 人 inside a house 冂, meaning inside.

都内	とない	**tonai**	inside Tokyo
年内	ねんない	**nennai**	within the year
内科	ないか	**naika**	internal medicine unit; internal medicine
内側	うちがわ	**uchigawa**	inside
学内便	がくないびん	**gakunai bin**	campus mail
家内	かない	**kanai**	my wife
市内	しない	**shinai**	inside a city

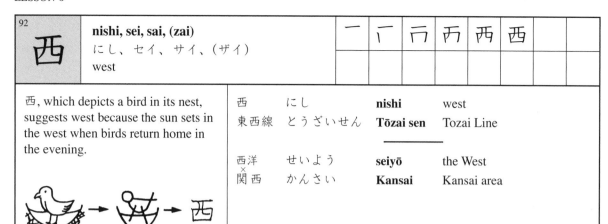

| 92 西 | nishi, sei, sai, (zai) にし、セイ、サイ、(ザイ) west | 一 | 亠 | 兀 | 丙 | 西 | 西 | | |

西, which depicts a bird in its nest, suggests west because the sun sets in the west when birds return home in the evening.

西	にし	**nishi**	west
東西線	とうざいせん	**Tōzai sen**	Tozai Line
		———	
西洋	せいよう	**seiyō**	the West
関西	かんさい	**Kansai**	Kansai area

| 93 営 | ei エイ perform, manage | ` | ` | ` | `` | `` | `` | `` | `` |
| | | 営 | 営 | 営 | 営 | | | | |

営 derives from 營. 宀 indicates house 宀 with lights 火 on, and 呂 represents rooms. From this, 営 has come to mean perform work or manage business in an office.

都営地下鉄	とえいちかてつ	**toei chikatetsu**	metropolitan subway
市営	しえい	**shiei**	municipally-managed
		———	
経営者	けいえいしゃ	**keieisha**	manager, executive

4 Practice

I. Write the readings of the following kanji in hiragana.

1. 地下鉄
2. 六本木
3. 大手町
4. 上野
5. 新宿
6. 日比谷線
7. 三田線
8. 千代田線
9. 丸ノ内線
10. 東西線
11. 何線
12. 都営線
13. 地名
14. 下り
15. 内線
16. 時代
17. 西
18. 新年
19. 上り

20. 東の そらに、丸い 月が でています。
21. 上田さんは わたしより 二つ 年上です。
22. 新宿には 新しい ビルが たくさん あります。

II. Fill in the blanks with appropriate kanji.

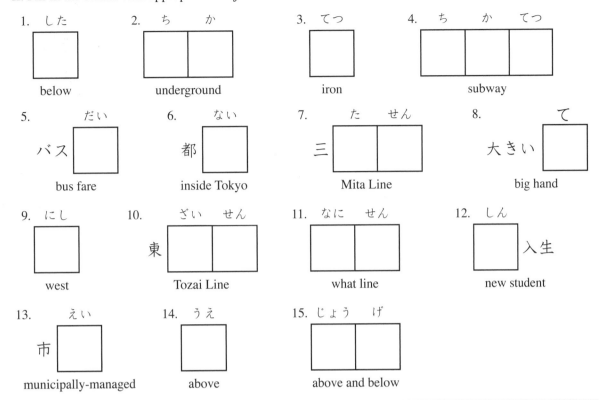

1. した
□
below

2. ち か
□□
underground

3. てつ
□
iron

4. ち か てつ
□□□
subway

5. だい
バス □
bus fare

6. ない
都 □
inside Tokyo

7. た せん
三 □□
Mita Line

8. て
大きい □
big hand

9. にし
□
west

10. ざい せん
東 □□
Tozai Line

11. なに せん
□□
what line

12. しん
□ 入生
new student

13. えい
市 □
municipally-managed

14. うえ
□
above

15. じょう げ
□□
above and below

---

5 ▶ Advanced Placement Exam Practice Questions

Miyuki will go shopping tomorrow in Roppongi with her friend Ichiro on her way home from her university, which is at Hongo. She is supposed to meet him at Roppongi Station (六本木) at 4:00 p.m. She can go to Hongo-sanchome Station (本郷三丁目), near the university, at about 3:15 p.m. She is checking the route on the Internet.

ROUTE 1

のりかえ1回 ／ 時間23分

■ 本郷三丁目
15:21 ～ 15:30　東京メトロ丸ノ内線
○ 銀座　　　　190円
15:34 ～ 15:43　東京メトロ日比谷線
■ 六本木

ROUTE 2

のりかえ2回 ／ 時間28分

■ 本郷三丁目
15:20 ～ 15:22　都営大江戸線
○ 春日
15:27 ～ 15:35　都営三田線　　260円
○ 日比谷
15:40 ～ 15:48　東京メトロ日比谷線
■ 六本木

Look at the route information above and on the previous page and answer the following questions.

1. Which route is the fastest?
   A. Route 1
   B. Route 2
   C. Route 3
   D. Route 4

2. Which route takes the most time?
   A. Route 1
   B. Route 2
   C. Route 3
   D. Route 4

3. Which route doesn't take the Toei lines?
   A. Route 1
   B. Route 2
   C. Route 3
   D. Route 4

4. Which route is the cheapest?
   A. Route 1
   B. Route 2
   C. Route 3
   D. Route 4

5. Which route changes trains from one Toei line to another Toei line?
   A. Route 1
   B. Route 2
   C. Route 3
   D. Route 4

Buying Tickets

きっぷを かいましょう

Except for long-distance tickets, ordinary subway and railroad tickets are valid only on the day of issue. Coupon tickets are also available for about a 10% discount. Since different kinds of tickets are required by the Tokyo-Metro, Toei, JR, and private lines, care should be taken to use the proper vending machines in stations serving many lines. Long-distance tickets are usually purchased at ticket windows.

1 ▶ Introductory Quiz

Look at the illustrations below and refer to the words in **Vocabulary**. Then try the following quiz.

I. Below is a simplified route map of the Yamanote (■■■) and Chuo (▭▭) Lines. The stations marked ◎ are connecting stations. The Chuo Line starts from Tokyo station, cuts through the center of the Yamanote Line, which is a loop. Study the fare chart at Shinjuku station, and then answer the questions overleaf.

自動きっぷうりば ご案内

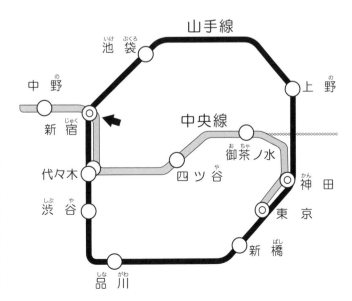

駅　　　名	料金（円）
代 々 木	130
渋　　　谷	150
池　　　袋	150
品　　　川	190
上　　　野	190
新　　　橋	190
東　　　京	190
中　　　野	150
四 ツ 谷	150
御茶ノ水	160
神　　　田	160

1. 新宿から つぎの 駅までは いくらですか。

    a. しんばし（　　　）円　　　b. よよぎ（　　　）円　　　c. おちゃのみず（　　　）円　　　d. なかの（　　　）円

2. 山手線と 中央線の 連絡駅は どれと どれですか。

    a. 新宿　　　　　　　　　b. 上野　　　　　　　　　c. 御茶ノ水　　　　　　　　　d. 東京

II. Shown below are various kinds of ordinary tickets and a coupon ticket for the JR lines, purchased at Shinjuku station. The coupon ticket is valid for a specified journey. The child's ticket looks the same as the adult's ticket, but it is marked with a kanji meaning "small." Also included is the IC card SUICA that lets the user go through automatic ticket gates with a touch on the scanner at either end of a journey, and calculate the appropriate fare.

    Match the appropriate ticket to each statement below, and write the correct letters (*a* through *e*) in the spaces provided.

a.

b.

c.

d.

e.

Example:
（　d　）は 新宿から 渋谷行きの きっぷです。

1. 新宿から 代々木行きは 大人は 130円（　　　）、こどもは 60円（　　　）です。

2. （　　　）は この 区間だけの 回数券です。

3. （　　　）は JRや 地下鉄など 全線に のれます。

74

2 ▸ Vocabulary

Study the readings and meanings of these words to help you understand the **Introductory Quiz**.

1. きっぷ		**kippu**	ticket
2. 代々木	よ よ ぎ	**Yoyogi**	Yoyogi (station) (*see Lesson 2, 23 時)
3. 自動	じ どう	**jidō**	automatic
4. うりば		**uriba**	(ticket) vending area
5. (ご)案内	(ご) あん ない	**(go)annai**	information
6. 駅名	えき めい	**ekimei**	station name
7. 料金	りょう きん	**ryōkin**	fare
8. 渋谷	しぶ や	**Shibuya**	Shibuya (station)
9. 池袋	いけ ぶくろ	**Ikebukuro**	Ikebukuro (station)
10. 品川	しな がわ	**Shinagawa**	Shinagawa (station)
11. 新橋	しん ばし	**Shimbashi**	Shinbashi (station)
12. 中野	なか の	**Nakano**	Nakano (station)
13. 四ツ谷	よつ や	**Yotsuya**	Yotsuya (station)
14. 御茶ノ水	お ちゃ の みず	**Ochanomizu**	Ochanomizu (station)
15. 神田	かん だ	**Kanda**	Kanda (station)
16. 山手線	やま の て せん	**Yamanote sen**	Yamanote Line
17. 中央線	ちゅう おう せん	**Chūō sen**	Chuo Line
18. 連絡	れん らく	**renraku**	connection
19. 〜行き	〜 い き／ゆ き	**~iki/yuki**	bound for ~
20. 大人	おとな	**otona**	adult
21. 小	しょう	**shō**	abbreviation for child
22. こども		**kodomo**	child
23. 回数券	かい すう けん	**kaisū ken**	coupon ticket
24. 全線	ぜん せん	**zensen**	all along the line

3 ▸ New Characters

Twelve characters are introduced in this lesson. Use the explanations to help you understand and remember the characters. Study the compound words to increase your vocabulary.

山 中 央 連 絡 自 動 小 人 全 行 回

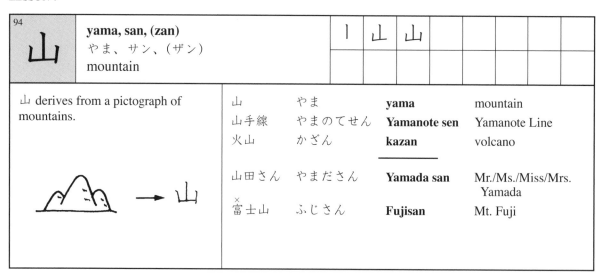

94	**yama, san, (zan)** やま、サン、（ザン） mountain	丨	凵	山				

山 derives from a pictograph of mountains.

山	やま	**yama**	mountain
山手線	やまのてせん	**Yamanote sen**	Yamanote Line
火山	かざん	**kazan**	volcano
山田さん	やまださん	**Yamada san**	Mr./Ms./Miss/Mrs. Yamada
×富士山	ふじさん	**Fujisan**	Mt. Fuji

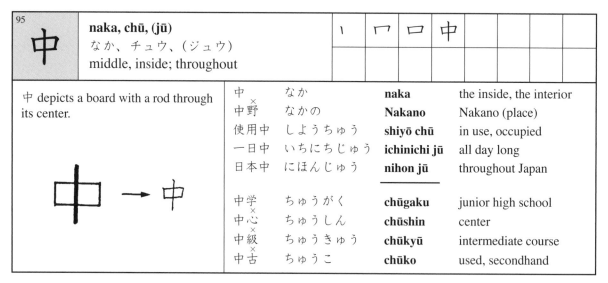

95	**naka, chū, (jū)** なか、チュウ、（ジュウ） middle, inside; throughout	丶	冂	口	中			

中 depicts a board with a rod through its center.

中	なか	**naka**	the inside, the interior
×中野	なかの	**Nakano**	Nakano (place)
使用中	しようちゅう	**shiyō chū**	in use, occupied
一日中	いちにちじゅう	**ichinichi jū**	all day long
日本中	にほんじゅう	**nihon jū**	throughout Japan
×中学	ちゅうがく	**chūgaku**	junior high school
×中心	ちゅうしん	**chūshin**	center
中級	ちゅうきゅう	**chūkyū**	intermediate course
×中古	ちゅうこ	**chūko**	used, secondhand

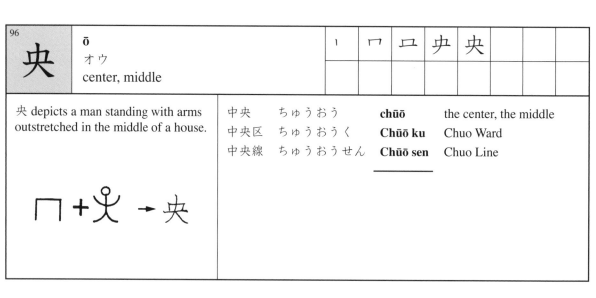

96	**ō** オウ center, middle	丶	冂	口	央	央		

央 depicts a man standing with arms outstretched in the middle of a house.

中央	ちゅうおう	**chūō**	the center, the middle
中央区	ちゅうおうく	**Chūō ku**	Chuo Ward
中央線	ちゅうおうせん	**Chūō sen**	Chuo Line

97 連

tsu-reru, ren
つ・れる、レン
connect, link; take along

一	厂	冂	百	百	亘	車	亘
連	連						

連 means connect or link, because vehicles 車 (cf. 106) on a road 辶 (cf. 16 週) follow one after another like links in a chain.

連れて行く	つれていく	**tsureteiku**	to take (someone) along / with
連休	れんきゅう	**renkyū**	consecutive holidays
関連	かんれん	**kanren**	relation, connection
国連	こくれん	**Kokuren**	abbreviation for 国際連合 (the United Nations)

98 絡

kara-mu, raku
から・む、ラク
get tangled; connect

∠	纟	幺	糸	糸	糸	糸	絞
絞	終	絡	絡				

絡 combines 糸 thread (cf. 81 線) and 各, which by itself means each (cf. 120) but here indicates a knotted thread. A thread with knots gets tangled easily. An associated meaning is connect.

連絡する	れんらくする	**renraku suru**	to connect with, to make contact
連絡先	れんらくさき	**renraku saki**	where to contact
連絡駅	れんらくえき	**renraku eki**	connecting station, junction
絡む	からむ	**karamu**	to get tangled
連絡口	れんらくぐち	**renraku guchi**	connection gate
連絡通路	れんらくつうろ	**renraku tsūro**	connecting passageway

99 自

ji, shi
ジ、シ
self

′	亻	冂	白	自	自		

自 derives from a pictograph of a nose. In Japan, pointing at one's nose indicates I or me.

自分	じぶん	**jibun**	oneself, one's own
自由な	じゆうな	**jiyū na**	free, unrestricted
自宅	じたく	**jitaku**	one's own home/house
自然	しぜん	**shizen**	nature

100 動	ugo-ku, dō うご・く、ドウ move	一	二	亍	盲	盲	盲	重	重
		重	動	動					

動 combines 重, man standing on a pile of heavy things on the ground, and 力 force (cf. 67 男). Even heavy things will move if great forces are exerted on them.

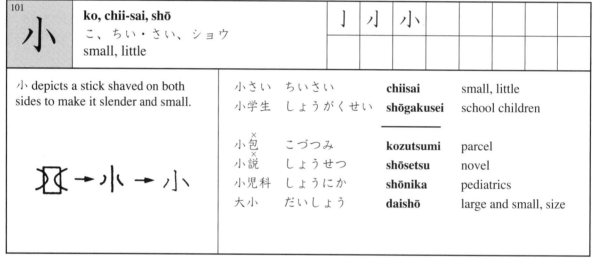

動く	うごく	**ugoku**	to move (vi.)
自動	じどう	**jidō**	automatic
手動	しゅどう	**shudō**	manually operated, hand-powered
×運動する	うんどうする	**undō suru**	to exercise, to campaign, to move

---

101 小	ko, chii-sai, shō こ、ちい・さい、ショウ small, little	亅	丿	小					

小 depicts a stick shaved on both sides to make it slender and small.

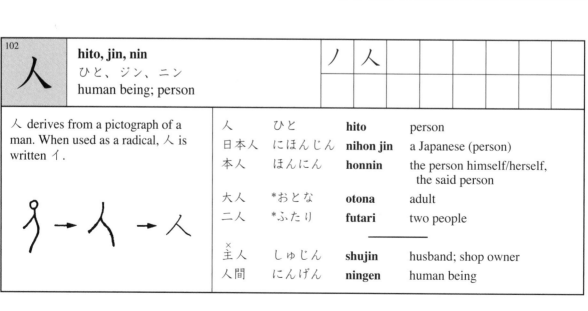

小さい	ちいさい	**chiisai**	small, little
小学生	しょうがくせい	**shōgakusei**	school children
×小包	こづつみ	**kozutsumi**	parcel
×小説	しょうせつ	**shōsetsu**	novel
小児科	しょうにか	**shōnika**	pediatrics
大小	だいしょう	**daishō**	large and small, size

---

102 人	hito, jin, nin ひと、ジン、ニン human being; person	丿	人						

人 derives from a pictograph of a man. When used as a radical, 人 is written イ.

人	ひと	**hito**	person
日本人	にほんじん	**nihon jin**	a Japanese (person)
本人	ほんにん	**honnin**	the person himself/herself, the said person
大人	*おとな	**otona**	adult
二人	*ふたり	**futari**	two people
×主人	しゅじん	**shujin**	husband; shop owner
人間	にんげん	**ningen**	human being

103 全 — zen / ゼン / all, whole; entirely

Stroke order: ノ 人 人 仐 仐 全

全 represents a mound 亼 of 土 earth containing everything or covering the whole area underneath.

全線	ぜんせん	**zensen**	all (train/bus) lines, all along the line
全学	ぜんがく	**zengaku**	the whole university
全部	ぜんぶ	**zembu**	all, whole
全国	ぜんこく	**zenkoku**	the whole country
全体	ぜんたい	**zentai**	the whole
全員	ぜんいん	**zen'in**	all members
完全な	かんぜんな	**kanzen na**	perfect, complete

104 行 — i-ku, yu-ku, kō, gyō / い・く、ゆ・く、コウ、ギョウ / go; line (of a text)

Stroke order: ノ ノ イ 彳 行 行

行 derives from the shape of a crossroad, meaning go. The radical 彳 refers to go or a road.

艹 → 彳 → 行

行く	いく/ゆく	**iku/yuku**	to go
行き先	いきさき/ゆきさき	**ikisaki/yukisaki**	destination of a journey, one's whereabouts
三行目	さんぎょうめ	**sangyō me**	the third line (on a page)
～行(き)	いき/ゆき	**～iki/yuki**	bound for ～
旅行する	りょこうする	**ryokō suru**	to travel, to make a trip

105 回 — mawa-ru, mawa-su, kai / まわ・る、まわ・す、カイ / go around; times

Stroke order: 丨 冂 冂 冋 回 回

回 derives from a pictograph of a whirlpool, which goes around in circles.

◎ → 回 → 回

回る	まわる	**mawaru**	to turn/go around, to make a tour (vi.)
回す	まわす	**mawasu**	to turn/move/pass (something) round (vt.)
回数券	かいすうけん	**kaisū ken**	coupon ticket
四回目	よんかいめ	**yonkai me**	the fourth time
前回	ぜんかい	**zenkai**	the last time
次回	じかい	**jikai**	the next time
回送	かいそう	**kaisō**	out-of-service car/train

4 Practice

I. Write the readings of the following kanji in hiragana.

1. 代々木　　　　2. 自動　　　　　3. 中野 (の)　　　4. 山手線
5. 中央線　　　　6. 連絡　　　　　7. ～行き　　　　8. 大人
9. 小　　　　　　10. 回数 (すう) 券　11. 全線　　　　　12. 使用中
13. 日本中　　　14. 中央　　　　　15. 自分　　　　　16. 小学生
17. 日本人　　　18. 一人　　　　　19. 二人　　　　　20. 三人
21. 回す　　　　22. バス の 中 で ともだち に あいました。
23. 五月 の 連休は どこ へ 行きますか。山 へ 行きます。
24. 日曜日は エレベーター が 動きません。
25. 小さい 駅には とまりません。
26. 三行目を よんでください。

II. Fill in the blanks with appropriate kanji.

1. やま

本さん
Mr./Ms. Yamamoto

2. ざん

火
volcano

3. なか
へやの

inside a room

4. じゅう
日本

throughout Japan

5. ちゅう おう

区
Chuo Ward

6. つ　　い

れて　く
to take (someone) with

7. れん らく

駅
connecting station

8. うご

く
to move

9. じ どう
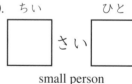
ドア
automatic door

10. ちい　　ひと

さい
small person

11. じん
メキシコ

a Mexican

12. にん
本

the said person

13. い

き先
destination

14. ぎょう
九

目
the 9th line

15. ぜん

部
all

16. まわ

る
to turn around

17. かい
四

目
the 4th time

5 ▶ Advanced Placement Exam Practice Questions

You are at Shinjuku station. Below is a simplified route map of the Yamanote (■■) and Chuo (▭) Lines. The stations marked ◎ are connecting stations. The number in the square ▭ is the fare from Shinjuku station.

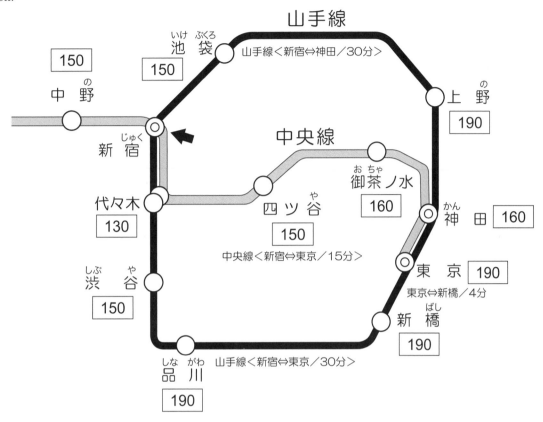

山手線

いけ ぶくろ
池 袋　　150
150

山手線＜新宿⇔神田／30分＞

上 野　　190
の

中 野　　150
の

新 宿
じゅく

中央線

御茶ノ水　160
お ちゃ

神 田　160
かん

代々木　130

四ツ谷　150
や

中央線＜新宿⇔東京／15分＞

東 京　190

東京⇔新橋／4分

渋 谷　150
しぶ や

新 橋　190
ばし

品 川　190
しな がわ　山手線＜新宿⇔東京／30分＞

1. You are going to Ueno station. How much is the ticket?
   A. ¥130
   B. ¥150
   C. ¥160
   D. ¥190

2. You are going to Tokyo station. Which route is the fastest?
   A. Yamanote Line via Ikebukuro station
   B. Yamanote Line via Shinagawa station
   C. Chuo Line via Yotsuya station
   D. Chuo Line via Nakano station

3. You are a graduate student. You go to Yotsuya a few times a week. Which is the cheapest?
   A. ordinary ticket
   B. coupon ticket
   C. IC card
   D. child's ticket

4. Now you are at Shimbashi station. When you go to Nakano station, which route is the fastest?
   A. Yamanote Line via Ikebukuro station
   B. Yamanote Line via Shinagawa station
   C. transfer to Chuo Line at Shinjuku station
   D. transfer to Chuo Line at Tokyo station

Taking the Train

電車に のりましょう

After buying a ticket, finding the right platform can be a challenge. Near the ticket gates in the station, there are guide boards that show all the stations along the line, and indicate the station where you are and the platform numbers for different destinations. If you take the Marunouchi Line from Tokyo station, for example, the platforms will be marked 1 新宿方面 and 2 池袋方面. Guide boards on the platforms show the terminal stations and other major stations along the way. Thus, to go from Tokyo to Yotsuya, you will need to recognize at least three signs— 東京, 四ツ谷, and 新宿 —and proceed to platform number 1.

1 ▶ Introductory Quiz

Look at the illustrations below and refer to the words in **Vocabulary**. Then try the following quiz.

Suppose this is Tokyo station. Look at the signs and choose the correct answers.

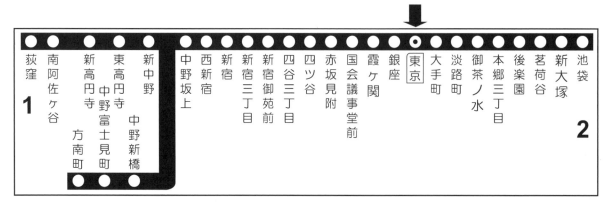

入口　　　　　出口

1. 駅の ホームには（a. 入口　　b. 出口）から はいります。
2. 新宿 行きは（a. 1　　b. 2）番線です。
3. 大手町 方面は（a. 1　　b. 2）番線です。
4. 四ツ谷 方面の 電車は（a. 1　　b. 2）番線 です。

2 ▶ Vocabulary

Study the readings and meanings of these words to help you understand the **Introductory Quiz**.

1. 電車	でん しゃ	**densha**	train
2. ホーム		**hōmu**	platform
3. 入口	いり ぐち	**iriguchi**	entrance
4. 出口	で ぐち	**deguchi**	exit
5. ～番線	～ばん せん	**～bansen**	track no. ～
6. ～方面	～ほう めん	**～hōmen**	bound for ～
7. 四ツ谷	よつ や	**Yotsuya**	Yotsuya (station)

3 ▶ New Characters

Six characters are introduced in this lesson. Use the explanations to help you understand and remember the characters. Study the compound words to increase your vocabulary.

車 口 出 方 面 番

106

車

kuruma, sha
くるま、シャ
wheel, car, vehicle

一 ／ 厂 ／ 一 ／ 一 ／ 百 ／ 亘 ／ 車

車 derives from a pictograph of a carriage with wheels, meaning wheel or car.

車	くるま	**kuruma**	car, wheel
電車	でんしゃ	**densha**	train
車内	しゃない	**shanai**	the inside of a car/train
自動車	じどうしゃ	**jidōsha**	automobile
自転車	じてんしゃ	**jitensha**	bicycle
下車する	げしゃする	**gesha suru**	to get off (a train/car)

107

口

kuchi, (guchi), kō
くち、（ぐち）、コウ
mouth

＼ ／ 冂 ／ 口

口 derives from a pictograph of a mouth. Associated meanings include opening, entrance, exit, and man.

口	くち	**kuchi**	mouth; opening
入口	いりぐち	**iriguchi**	entrance
東口	ひがしぐち	**higashi guchi**	east exit
中央口	ちゅうおうぐち	**chūō guchi**	central exit
人口	じんこう	**jinkō**	population
改札口	かいさつぐち	**kaisatsu guchi**	ticket gate, wicket
口座	こうざ	**kōza**	bank account
窓口	まどぐち	**madoguchi**	window (in a public office, bank, or station)

108 出	de-ru, da-su, shutsu, (shu') で・る、だ・す、シュツ、（シュッ） go out, come out; take out; send; leave	丨	屮	屮	出	出		

出 depicts a plant coming out of the ground a little more than the plant in the kanji 土 (cf. 31).

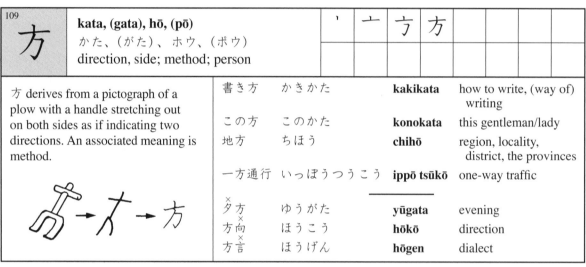

出る	でる	**deru**	to go/come out
出口	でぐち	**deguchi**	exit
出入口	でいりぐち	**deiriguchi**	doorway, entrance and exit
出す	だす	**dasu**	to take something out; to send (a letter); to submit
		————	
出前	でまえ	**demae**	ordering out for food
提出する	ていしゅつする	**teishutsu suru**	to submit
輸出する	ゆしゅつする	**yushutsu suru**	to export
出席する	しゅっせきする	**shusseki suru**	to attend, to be present
出国する	しゅっこくする	**shukkoku suru**	to leave the country

109 方	kata, (gata), hō, (pō) かた、（がた）、ホウ、（ポウ） direction, side; method; person	`	一	方	方			

方 derives from a pictograph of a plow with a handle stretching out on both sides as if indicating two directions. An associated meaning is method.

書き方	かきかた	**kakikata**	how to write, (way of) writing
この方	このかた	**konokata**	this gentleman/lady
地方	ちほう	**chihō**	region, locality, district, the provinces
一方通行	いっぽうつうこう	**ippō tsūkō**	one-way traffic
		————	
夕方	ゆうがた	**yūgata**	evening
方向	ほうこう	**hōkō**	direction
方言	ほうげん	**hōgen**	dialect

110 面	men メン face, surface	一	丆	厂	冇	而	而	面
		面						

面 represents a face enclosed in a square. Surface is an associated meaning.

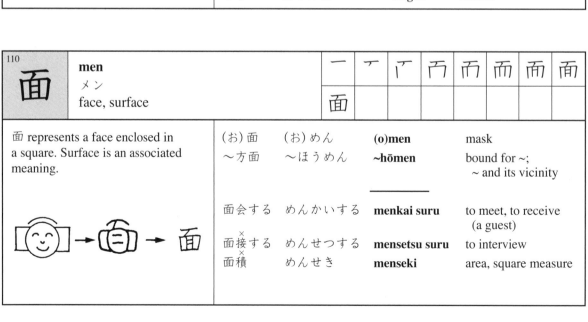

（お）面	（お）めん	**(o)men**	mask
〜方面	〜ほうめん	**〜hōmen**	bound for 〜; 〜 and its vicinity
		————	
面会する	めんかいする	**menkai suru**	to meet, to receive (a guest)
面接する	めんせつする	**mensetsu suru**	to interview
面積	めんせき	**menseki**	area, square measure

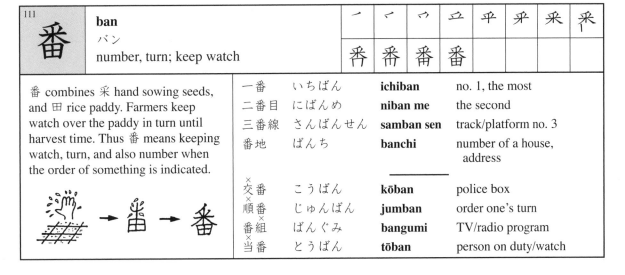

番 combines 釆 hand sowing seeds, and 田 rice paddy. Farmers keep watch over the paddy in turn until harvest time. Thus 番 means keeping watch, turn, and also number when the order of something is indicated.

一番	いちばん	**ichiban**	no. 1, the most
二番目	にばんめ	**niban me**	the second
三番線	さんばんせん	**samban sen**	track/platform no. 3
番地	ばんち	**banchi**	number of a house, address
×交番	こうばん	**kōban**	police box
×順番	じゅんばん	**jumban**	order one's turn
番組×	ばんぐみ	**bangumi**	TV/radio program
当番	とうばん	**tōban**	person on duty/watch

4 ▶ Practice

I. Write the readings of the following kanji in hiragana.

1. 電車
2. 入口
3. 出口
4. 〜番線
5. 〜方面
6. 車
7. 車内
8. 中央口
9. 人口
10. 出入口
11. 書き方
12. 地方
13. 一方通行
14. 番地
15. 口を 大きく 開けて 話してください。
16. 山と 山の 間から 日が 出てきました。
17. この 方は どなたですか。
18. お祭りで お面を かいました。

II. Fill in the blanks with appropriate kanji.

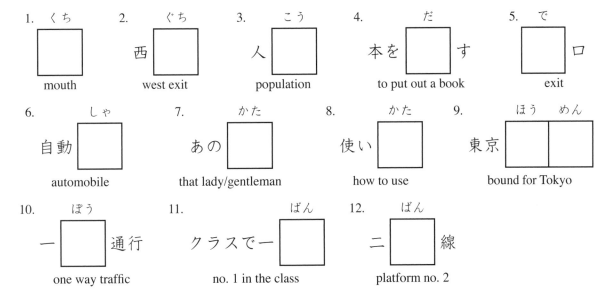

1. くち — mouth
2. ぐち 西〔 〕 — west exit
3. こう 人〔 〕 — population
4. だ 本を〔 〕す — to put out a book
5. で 〔 〕口 — exit
6. しゃ 自動〔 〕 — automobile
7. かた あの〔 〕 — that lady/gentleman
8. かた 使い〔 〕 — how to use
9. ほう めん 東京〔 〕〔 〕 — bound for Tokyo
10. ぽう 一〔 〕通行 — one way traffic
11. ばん クラスで一〔 〕 — no. 1 in the class
12. ばん 二〔 〕線 — platform no. 2

85

5 ▶ Advanced Placement Exam Practice Questions

Read the dialogue below involving two girls on their mobile phones and answer the questions.

リサ： もしもし、あいこちゃん？

あいこ： うん。どうしたの？

リサ： 待ち合わせにおくれてごめんね。今、まだ新宿にいるの。
上野まで、どうやって行けばいいの？

あいこ： 山手線にのればいいわ。

リサ： 渋谷方面と池袋方面の電車があるけど、どっちにのればいい？

あいこ： 池袋方面よ。上野まで、25分くらいかかるわ。

リサ： ありがとう。3時までには着くかな。

あいこ： 上野駅中央出口にいるから、着いたらまた電話して。
ホームも出口もたくさんあるから、迷ってしまうとおもう。
あ、それからなるべくいちばん前にのって。

リサ： どうして？

あいこ： 中央出口は前のほうにあるの。
3番線に着くよ。そして階段をおりて出口の方へ来て。

リサ： わかった。あ、電車がきた。着いたら電話する。

リサ： 今、着いた、階段おりている、あ、中央出口って書いてあるのが見えるわ。すぐ行く。

あいこ： ここよ。

リサ： 待たせてゴメン。

1. What time did Lisa first make a call?
   A. 11:00 A.M.
   B. 11:30 A.M.
   C. 3:30 P.M.
   D. 2:30 P.M.

2. Which train and which part of the train should Lisa get on?
   A. The front of the train towards Ikebukuro
   B. The back of the train towards Ikebukuro
   C. The front of the train towards Shibuya
   D. The back of the train towards Shibuya

3. Which of the following statements about Ueno station is correct?
   A. Although there are many platforms, it is not difficult to understand the way because there are not very many exits.
   B. You must be careful in finding the way because there are many exits and platforms.
   C. Because there are not many stairs and exits, you will not be lost.
   D. Because there are many exits and stairs it is hard to find the way.

4. What can be said about the relation between the central exit and the platform Lisa's train arrives at?
   A. The central exit and the platform are on the same floor.
   B. The central exit is on the floor below the platform.
   C. The central exit is on the floor above the platform.
   D. The central exit is in front of the platform.

Inside the Station

駅 の 中

$\mathbf{H}$ave you ever been frustrated because you cannot understand station signs? When you need to go to the bathroom, you'll look for the sign お手洗い. And once you reach it, you have to face another dilemma: which doorway to enter! Leaving the station, which exit do you use? 東口 or 西口? And when you want to buy coupon tickets, you must be able to recognize the appropriate ticket machine.

Fortunately, most of these problems are solved when you understand a few key kanji.

1 ▶ Introductory Quiz

Look at the illustration below and refer to the words in **Vocabulary**. Then try the following quiz.

I. The station below has ticket vending machines, an information desk, washrooms, information about taxis, and an emergency notice. Fill in the spaces provided with the correct letters (*a* through *f*).

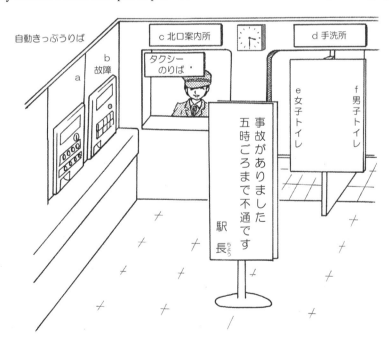

1. 駅の あんないじょは （　　　　　　　） です。
2. おとこの 人の トイレは （　　　　　　　） です。
3. おんなの 人の お手洗いは （　　　　　　　　） に あります。
4. きっぷは （　　　　　　　） で かいます。

87

II. Choose the correct answers by studying the illustration on the previous page.

1. 電車は すぐに きますか。　　(a. はい。　b. いいえ。)
2. どうしてですか。　　(a. じこが あった　b. 日曜日だ) からです。
3. 電車は 何時ごろに きますか。　　(a. 3時　b. 5時) ごろに きます。
4. きっぷうりばの　(a.　　b.　) の *きかいは 使えません。(*machine)
5. ここは　(a. きた口　b. みなみ口) です。

▶ 2 ▶ Vocabulary

Study the readings and meanings of these words to help you understand the **Introductory Quiz**.

1. 案内所	あん ない じょ／しょ	**annai jo/sho**	information desk
2. 男子	だん し	**danshi**	gentlemen
3. 女子	じょ し	**joshi**	ladies
4. (お) 手洗い	(お) て あらい	**(o)tearai**	washroom, toilet
5. 手洗所	て あらい じょ	**tearai jo**	washroom, toilet (formal)
6. 事故	じ こ	**jiko**	accident
7. 不通	ふ つう	**futsū**	interruption of train service
8. 故障	こ しょう	**koshō**	out of order
9. 北口	きた ぐち	**kita guchi**	north exit
10. 南口	みなみ ぐち	**minami guchi**	south exit

▶ 3 ▶ New Characters

Eight characters are introduced in this lesson. Use the explanations to help you understand and remember the characters. Study the compound words to increase your vocabulary.

北　南　案　洗　子　事　故　不

112 北	kita, hoku, (boku), (ho') きた、ホク、(ボク)、(ホッ) north	一	ナ	土	土'	北		

北 derives from a pictograph of two men sitting back to back and facing opposite directions. Men usually prefer facing the sun or south. Thus 北 has come to mean north, which is the opposite of south.	北	きた	**kita**	north
	北口	きたぐち	**kita guchi**	north exit
	東北地方	とうほくちほう	**Tōhoku chihō**	Tohoku district
	北部	ほくぶ	**hoku bu**	northern district/part
	南北	なんぼく	**namboku**	south and north
	北国	きたぐに	**kitaguni**	northern provinces/country
	北米	ほくべい	**Hokubei**	North America
	北海道	ほっかいどう	**Hokkaidō**	Hokkaido (island, district)

88

113 南 minami, nan / みなみ、ナン / south

	一	十	广	内	内	内	南	南
南								

南 depicts a plant inside a shed. Since plants turn to face the sun (south), 南 has come to mean south.

南	みなみ	**minami**	south
南口	みなみぐち	**minami guchi**	south exit
東南 アジア	とうなん アジア	**Tōnan Ajia**	Southeast Asia
東西南北	とうざいなんぼく	**tōzai namboku**	east, west, south and north
南アメリカ	みなみ アメリカ	**Minami Amerika**	South America
南国	なんごく	**nangoku**	southern provinces/ country
南東の風	なんとうのかぜ	**nantō no kaze**	southeasterly wind
南極	なんきょく	**nankyoku**	South Pole, Antarctic

114 案 an / アン / idea, plan, proposal

	'	'	宀	宀	安	安	安	宰
窣	案							

案 combines peaceful 安 (cf. 233) and 木 tree. Under the peaceful shade of a tree, one may come up with a good idea. Associated meanings are plan and proposal.

案	あん	**an**	idea, plan, proposal
案内する	あんないする	**annai suru**	to guide, to show
案内所	あんない じょ/しょ	**annai jo/sho**	information center
案内書	あんないしょ	**annai sho**	guidebook
入学案内	にゅうがく あんない	**nyūgaku annai**	guide to admission into school
原案	げんあん	**gen'an**	original plan/bill
案内図	あんないず	**annai zu**	guide/information map
名案	めいあん	**meian**	good idea/proposal

115 洗 ara-u, sen / あら・う、セン / wash

	`	`	氵	氵	汁	汁	汼	洗
洗								

洗 combines the radical 氵 water (cf. 28 水) and 先 feet (cf. 48). 洗 originally meant washing feet with water, and came to mean wash in general.

洗う	あらう	**arau**	to wash
（お）手洗い	（お）てあらい	**(o) tearai**	washroom, toilet
手洗所	てあらいじょ	**tearai jo**	washroom, toilet (formal)
洗面所	せんめんじょ	**semmen jo**	washroom, restroom
洗濯機	せんたくき	**sentaku ki**	washing machine
洗剤	せんざい	**senzai**	cleanser, detergent

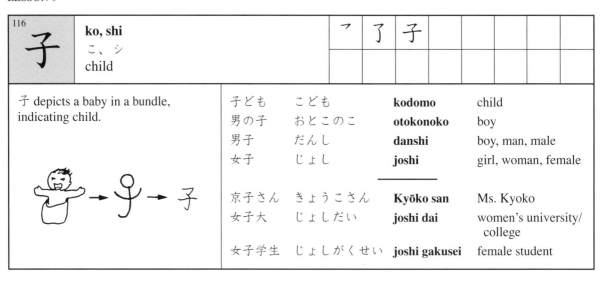

116 子	**ko, shi** こ、シ child	㇇	了	子					

子 depicts a baby in a bundle, indicating child.

子ども	こども	**kodomo**	child
男の子	おとこのこ	**otokonoko**	boy
男子	だんし	**danshi**	boy, man, male
女子	じょし	**joshi**	girl, woman, female
京子さん	きょうこさん	**Kyōko san**	Ms. Kyoko
女子大	じょしだい	**joshi dai**	women's university/ college
女子学生	じょしがくせい	**joshi gakusei**	female student

117 事	**koto, (goto), ji** こと、（ごと）、ジ thing, affair; job	一	一	一	写	写	写	写	事

事 depicts a hand holding a bamboo case containing fortunetelling sticks. A fortuneteller's job is to forecast various things.

事	こと	**koto**	things, matter
火事	かじ	**kaji**	fire (destructive burning)
用事	ようじ	**yōji**	business, errand, things to do
工事中	こうじちゅう	**kōji chū**	under construction
仕事	しごと	**shigoto**	work, job
大事な	だいじな	**daiji na**	important
事件	じけん	**jiken**	event, incident
返事する	へんじする	**henji suru**	to answer, to reply

118 故	**ko** コ deceased, old; accidental	一	十	十	古	古	古	古	故
		故							

故 combines 十 ten, 口 mouth, and 攵, indicating an action (cf. 47 攻). 古 implies the act of oral transmission through some ten generations, meaning old. 故 thus means deceased as well as old. An associated meaning is accidental, because old things break down easily.

事故	じこ	**jiko**	accident
故障する	こしょうする	**koshō suru**	(for a machine, etc.) to break down, to become out of order
故人	こじん	**kojin**	the deceased
故郷	こきょう	**kokyō**	hometown, native place

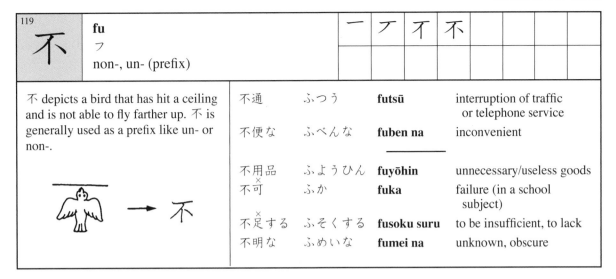

119 不	**fu** フ non-, un- (prefix)	一 フ 不 不

不 depicts a bird that has hit a ceiling and is not able to fly farther up. 不 is generally used as a prefix like un- or non-.

不通	ふつう	**futsū**	interruption of traffic or telephone service
不便な	ふべんな	**fuben na**	inconvenient
不用品	ふようひん	**fuyōhin**	unnecessary/useless goods
不可	ふか	**fuka**	failure (in a school subject)
不足する	ふそくする	**fusoku suru**	to be insufficient, to lack
不明な	ふめいな	**fumei na**	unknown, obscure

4 ▶ Practice

I. Write the readings of the following kanji in hiragana.

1. 案内所 2. 男子 3. 女子 4. お手洗い
5. 手洗所 6. 事故 7. 不通 8. 故障
9. 北口 10. 南口 11. 北部 12. 東南アジア
13. 東西南北 14. 入学案内 15. 洗面所 16. 男の子
17. 火事 18. わたしの 大学を 案内しました。
19. ごはんの 前に 手を 洗います。
20. 子どもは すぐ 大きくなります。

II. Fill in the blanks with appropriate kanji.

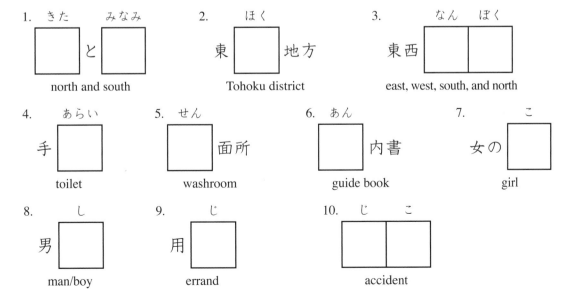

1. きた みなみ □ と □ north and south
2. ほく 東 □ 地方 Tohoku district
3. なん ぼく 東西 □ □ east, west, south, and north
4. あらい 手 □ toilet
5. せん □ 面所 washroom
6. あん □ 内書 guide book
7. こ 女の □ girl
8. し 男 □ man/boy
9. じ 用 □ errand
10. じ こ □ □ accident

5 ▶ Advanced Placement Exam Practice Questions

Heavy snow is falling in the Tokyo area. A reporter for a news program is broadcasting from Tokyo Station.

レポーター：こんにちは。わたしは、今、東京駅にいます。みてください。雪がたくさんふっていま
す。今日は¹関東地方が大雪のため、中央線の東京と新宿の間が不通です。山手線の東
京と新橋の間も不通です。また、私鉄、地下鉄も²のろのろ運転です。東京にこんなに雪
がふるのは、20年ぶりのことです。
タクシー乗り場にもたくさんの人がならんでいます。では、こちらの男性にインタビュ
ーしてみましょう。
こんにちは。すごい雪ですね。

男性：電車が動かなくて、こまったよ。タクシーに乗ろうと北口に行ったんだ。そうしたら、
事故があって道は車でいっぱい。ぜんぜん動いてなかったんだ。案内所できいて、いそ
いで南口にきたんだよ。でも、もう1時間もまっている。

レポーター：この雪じゃタクシーもあまりきませんね。

男性：東京は雪によわいね。

¹関東地方: Kanto region
²のろのろ運転: low speed service

1. What is the situation with the Chuo Line between Tokyo and Shinjuku station?
   A. interruption of train service
   B. operating a special train
   C. low speed service
   D. construction delay

2. What is the situation with the subway and the private railway?
   A. interruption of train service
   B. operating a special train
   C. low speed service
   D. construction delay

3. What is the situation with the north exit?
   A. Bus services were interrupted.
   B. blocked by heavy snow
   C. major traffic jam
   D. There was no cabstand.

4. What does the man think of Tokyo?
   A. It is very convenient.
   B. The person in the information office is kind.
   C. Sometime he gets lost, because it is very wide and complicated.
   D. It becomes gridlocked with traffic when it snows.

5. Which item does not match the text?
   A. Many people are waiting for the taxi at the south exit.
   B. The traffic system of Tokyo is weak in snow.
   C. People of Tokyo are used to snow.
   D. When it snows, a taxi will seldom come.

LESSON 10

On the Platform

駅の ホーム

If you've lived in Japan for some time, you have probably had the experience of taking the wrong train and wasting time and money. Most lines have local trains, semi-express trains, express trains, and special express trains. Maps posted inside the stations and trains show where each type of train stops.

1 ▶ Introductory Quiz

Look at the illustration below and refer to the words in **Vocabulary**. Then try the following quiz.

I.   The guide below shows all the stops between terminal stations on a particular line. The various types of trains are marked with ○▲■◎ and labeled in kanji. Naturally, the fewer stops a train makes, the faster it goes. Fill in the spaces with the correct letters (*a* through *g*).

○ 各駅停車（各停、普通）

○ ○

▲ 準急（快速）

▲　　▲　　　▲　　▲　　　　▲　　　　▲　　　▲　　　▲

■ 急行

■　　　　　■　　■　　　　　　　■　　　　　　　　　■

◎ 特急

◎　　　　　　　　　◎　　　　　　　　　　　　　　　◎

回送

1.　（　　　　）と（　　　　）と（　　　　）は どの 駅にも とまります。
2.　（　　　　）が 一番 はやいです。　　3.（　　　　）には だれも のりません。
4.　（　　　　）は 二番目に はやいです。　5.（　　　　）は 三番目に はやいです。

　　a. かくえきていしゃ　　b. とっきゅう　　　c. じゅんきゅう　　　d. きゅうこう
　　e. かくてい　　　　　　f. かいそう　　　　g. ふつう

93

II. Timetables for both weekdays and Sundays/holidays are found on the platforms. Shown below is part of a timetable for the Marunouchi Line. Read the timetable and fill in the spaces with the correct times.

発車時刻表

時	平日(新宿・荻窪	時	休日(新宿・荻窪
5	00 13 25 34 42 50 55	5	03 13 25 35 42 54
6	01 07 13 19 24 30 35 40 45 49 53 57	6	02 10 16 22 28 34 39 46 52 58
7	01 05 09 13 16 18 21 23 26 28 31 33 38	7	04 10 16 22 28 34 39 45 50 56
8	00 02 04 06 08 09 11 ⌐1 22 24	8	01 07 1⌐ ⌐4 40 45 50 56
	⌐8 58		⌐12 16 21 29 37 45 52 58
21	03 09 14 19 24 29 34 39 44 49 54 56	22	06 11 15 23 30 37 41 46 55
22	04 09 14 19 24 30 34 39 44 49 56	23	00 05 11 16 26 32 38 46 55
23	02 07 16 25 31 38 46 55 **0** 02 17	0	03

1. 水曜日の　始発は　（　　　　）時（　　　　）分です。

2. 日曜日の　終発は　（　　　　）時（　　　　）分です。

III. This is part of a timetable for the Shinkansen Nozomi のぞみ, Hikari ひかり, and Kodama こだま trains. Along the top row from left to right is a list of trains. Along the left-hand column from top to bottom is a list of stations. Departure and arrival track numbers are also indicated.

Choose the answers that correctly complete the statements on the next page.

列車名		のぞみ34号	のぞみ140号	こだま586号	のぞみ96号	のぞみ142号	ひかり422号	こだま548号	のぞみ256号	のぞみ36号	のぞみ144号
発車番線		26	24		26	24	26	25	23	26	23
新大阪	発	16:53	16:59		17:10	17:16	17:19	17:23	17:27	17:30	17:40
京都	着	17:07	17:14	—	17:24	17:31	17:34	17:37	17:42	17:45	17:55
〃	発	17:09	17:15	—	17:26	17:32	17:35	17:39	17:43	17:46	17:57
米原	発	レ	レ		レ	レ	レ	18:06	レ	レ	レ
岐阜羽島	発	レ	レ		レ	レ	レ	18:21	レ	レ	レ
小田原	発	レ	レ	20:17	レ	レ	レ	20:47	レ	レ	レ
新横浜	発	19:11	レ	20:37	19:31	レ	レ	21:04	レ	19:48	20:01
品川	発	19:23	19:26	20:50	レ	19:46	20:06	21:16	19:53	20:00	レ
東京	着	19:30	19:33	20:56	19:46	19:53	20:13	21:23	20:00	20:06	20:16
到着番線		17	14	18	17	14	16	17	18	15	17

1. のぞみ34号は (a. 東京へ 行きます。　b. 東京から きます。)
2. こだま586号は 東京 (a. 発　b. 着) 20時56分です。
3. ひかり422号の 発車番線は (a. 16　b. 26) 番線です。
4. この 時刻表は (a. 上り　b. 下り) の 新幹線の 時刻表です。

2 ▶ Vocabulary

Study the readings and meanings of these words to help you understand the **Introductory Quiz**.

1. 各駅停車	かく えき てい しゃ	**kakueki teisha**	local train
2. 各停	かく てい	**kakutei**	local train (abbreviation for 各駅停車)
3. 普通	ふ つう	**futsū**	local train, slow train
4. 特急	とっ きゅう	**tokkyū**	special express
5. 回送	かい そう	**kaisō**	out-of-service
6. 急行	きゅう こう	**kyūkō**	express train
7. 準急	じゅん きゅう	**junkyū**	semi-express train
8. 快速	かい そく	**kaisoku**	semi-express train
9. 時刻表	じ こく ひょう	**jikoku hyō**	timetable
10. 始発	し はつ	**shihatsu**	the first train
11. 終発	しゅう はつ	**shūhatsu**	the last train
12. 〜号	〜ごう	**〜gō**	train number 〜
13. 〜発	〜はつ	**〜hatsu**	departure from/at 〜
14. 〜着	〜ちゃく	**〜chaku**	arrival at 〜
15. 発車番線	はっ しゃ ばん せん	**hassha bansen**	train departure track
16. 到着番線	とう ちゃく ばん せん	**tōchaku bansen**	train arrival track
17. 上り	のぼ り	**nobori**	inbound train (to Tokyo)
18. 下り	くだ り	**kudari**	outbound train (from Tokyo)
19. 新幹線	しん かん せん	**Shinkan sen**	Shinkansen (bullet train)

3 ▶ New Characters

Twelve characters are introduced in this lesson. Use the explanations to help you understand and remember the characters. Study the compound words to increase your vocabulary.

各 停 普 準 急 速 快 特 表 終 着 発

120 各	kaku, (ka') カク、（カッ） each, every	ノ	ク	夂	冬	各	各		

各 combines 夂 trailing leg (cf. 22 後) and 口 here representing a square stone. When limping down a rocky road, one must stop and rest at every stone.

各地	かくち	**kakuchi**	each/every place, various places/districts
各自	かくじ	**kakuji**	each person; respective

各位	かくい	**kakui**	Sirs (in a letter)
各国	かっこく	**kakkoku**	each/every country, various countries

121 停	tei ティ stop, stay	ノ	イ	イ`	宀	宀	停	停	停
		停	停	停					

停 combines イ man, 高 immovable building, and 丁, which here represents an inserted nail and suggests remaining still. 停 thus implies people who stop or stay in one place.

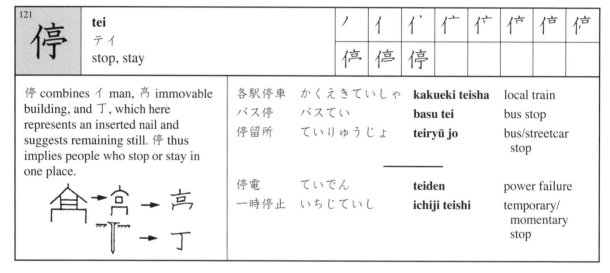

各駅停車	かくえきていしゃ	**kakueki teisha**	local train
バス停	バスてい	**basu tei**	bus stop
停留所	ていりゅうじょ	**teiryū jo**	bus/streetcar stop

停電	ていでん	**teiden**	power failure
一時停止	いちじていし	**ichiji teishi**	temporary/momentary stop

122 普	fu フ general, ordinary	丶	` `	丷	䒑	共	并	並	並
		並	普	普	普				

普 combines 並 and 日. 並 consists of two 立 stand (cf. 167), meaning side by side. Combined with 日, 普 implies that the sun's rays radiate out over a wide area. From this came the meaning of becoming widespread and eventually ordinary. By itself 並 also means ordinary.

普通	ふつう	**futsū**	ordinary, regular
普通電車	ふつうでんしゃ	**futsū densha**	local train

普通車	ふつうしゃ	**futsū sha**	ordinary-class car (train); ordinary-size car

123

jun
ジュン
level; semi-, sub-

`	`	シ	シ	沪	沪	汻	汼
汼	准	准	準	準			

準, which combines 氵 water, 隹 fat bird (cf. 26 曜), and 十 many, suggests calm water where many birds gather. The surface of calm water is level.

準備する	じゅんびする	**jumbi suru**	to prepare
×標準	ひょうじゅん	**hyōjun**	standard
水準	すいじゅん	**suijun**	level

124

急

iso-gu, kyū
いそ・ぐ、キュウ
hurry; urgent; sudden

ノ	ク	ク	勾	刍	刍	急	急
急							

急 combines 刍, a hand reaching out to grab the man ahead, and 心, which derives from a pictograph of a heart and means mind. Joining these together, 急 means hurry or urgent.

急ぐ	いそぐ	**isogu**	to hurry up
急行	きゅうこう	**kyūkō**	express train/bus
急用	きゅうよう	**kyūyō**	urgent business
準急	じゅんきゅう	**junkyū**	semi-express train

急停車する	きゅうていしゃ する	**kyūteisha suru**	to stop (car/train) suddenly
×救急車	きゅうきゅうしゃ	**kyūkyūsha**	ambulance
急行券	きゅうこうけん	**kyūkō ken**	express ticket

125

速

haya-i, soku
はや・い、ソク
fast, quick, prompt

一	一	一	日	束	束	束	束
速	速						

速 combines 束 bundle tied in the middle and 辶 go (cf. 79 通). Carrying things in a bundle is faster than carrying them one by one.

速い はやい	**hayai**	fast, rapid
時速 じそく	**jisoku**	speed per hour

×速達 そくたつ	**sokutatsu**	express mail
速×度 そくど	**sokudo**	speed, velocity

126 快

kai
カイ
pleasant, comfortable

| ' | ' | ＇| 忄 | 忄 | 快 | 快 | |

快 combines 忄, a variation of 心 mind, and 夬, which means open because the left side is open compared with 央 (cf. 96). Opening the mind makes one feel pleasant.

心 → 小 → 忄

快速	かいそく	**kaisoku**	high speed, semi-express train
快晴	かいせい	**kaisei**	clear and beautiful weather
全快する	ぜんかいする	**zenkai suru**	to recover completely from an illness

---

127 特

toku, (to')
トク、（トッ）
special

| ' | ﾉ | 牛 | 牛 | 牛 | 牛 | 牛 | 特 |
| 特 | 特 | | | | | | |

特 combines 牛, which is a variation of 牛 cow (cf. 227), a typical slow-moving animal, and 寺 move hands and feet (cf. 23 時). 特 thus indicates a cow moving quickly, which makes it special.

特に	とくに	**toku ni**	in particular, especially
特急	とっきゅう	**tokkyū**	special express train/bus
特別な	とくべつな	**tokubetsu na**	special
特長	とくちょう	**tokuchō**	strong point, merit
特徴	とくちょう	**tokuchō**	characteristic, peculiarity
特急券	とっきゅうけん	**tokkyū ken**	special express ticket

---

128 表

omote, hyō, (pyō)
おもて、ヒョウ、（ピョウ）
surface, front; list, table; expression

| 一 | 十 | 主 | 主 | 丰 | 丰 | 丰 | 表 |

表 combines 毛 hair or fur and 衣 clothes. A fur coat is an outer garment; thus 表 means surface. The surface of a thing can also express something about its content. An example of this is a list.

表	おもて	**omote**	the surface/front
表-4	ひょうよん	**hyō-yon**	Table 4
時間表	じかんひょう	**jikan hyō**	schedule (of classes, work), timetable
表面	ひょうめん	**hyōmen**	surface
表紙	ひょうし	**hyōshi**	front cover of a book
時刻表	じこくひょう	**jikoku hyō**	schedule (of trains), timetable
代表する	だいひょうする	**daihyō suru**	to represent

129 終 owa-ru, shū

お・わる、シュウ

end, come to an end

く	㇠	幺	糸	糸	糸	終	終
終	終	終					

糸 thread (cf. 81 線) suggests closing a bag by tying it. 冬 depicts foods being hung over ice to store for the winter, the season that ends the year. The two characters together make 終, meaning end.

終 (わ) る	おわる	**owaru**	to end, to be finished
終電	しゅうでん	**shūden**	last train
終日	しゅうじつ	**shūjitsu**	all day long
終点	しゅうてん	**shūten**	last stop, rail terminal
終了する	しゅうりょうする	**shūryō suru**	to be closed, to be completed

130 着 tsu-ku, ki-ru, (gi), chaku

つ・く、き・る、（ぎ）、チャク

arrive; wear, dress

丶	䒑	丷	㇒	半	羊	羊	羊
着	着	着	着				

着 combines 羊, which derives from 羊 sheep, and 目 eye. Sheep are easily seen when they arrive. Thus 着 means arrive. Associated meanings are attach and wear.

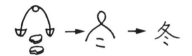

着く	つく	**tsuku**	to arrive
着る	きる	**kiru**	to put on clothes
上着	うわぎ	**uwagi**	coat, jacket
五時着	ごじちゃく	**go ji chaku**	five o'clock arrival
着物	きもの	**kimono**	Japanese clothes, kimono
下着	したぎ	**shitagi**	underwear
終着駅	しゅうちゃくえき	**shūchaku eki**	terminal station
発着時間	はっちゃくじかん	**hatchaku jikan**	departure and arrival times

131 発 hatsu, (ha'), (pa')

ハツ、（ハッ）、（パッ）

leave, depart; emit

㇒	㇆	癶	癶	癶	癶	発	発
発							

発 combines 癶, depicting outspread feet ready to start walking, and 几, indicating legs about to leave a starting line. Thus 発 has come to mean leave or depart.

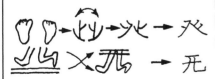

五時発	ごじはつ	**go ji hatsu**	five o'clock departure
始発	しはつ	**shihatsu**	the first train/bus
終発	しゅうはつ	**shūhatsu**	the last train/bus
発車する	はっしゃする	**hassha suru**	to depart (train/car)
出発する	しゅっぱつする	**shuppatsu suru**	to start/depart
発音する	はつおんする	**hatsuon suru**	to pronounce
発電所	はつでんしょ	**hatsuden sho**	power plant
発表する	はっぴょうする	**happyō suru**	to announce, to make a presentation

4 ▶ Practice

I. Write the readings of the following kanji in hiragana.

1. 各 駅 停 車　　　2. 普 通　　　3. 特 急　　　4. 回 送 ^(そう)^ ^(こく)^

5. 急 行　　　6. 準 急　　　7. 快 速　　　8. 時 刻 表

9. 始 発　　　10. 終 発　　　11. 〜 号 ^(かん)^　　　12. 〜 発

13. 〜 着　　　14. 発 車 番 線　　　15. 新 幹 線　　　16. 停 留 所

17. 急 用　　　18. 時 速　　　19. 特 に　　　20. 時 間 表

21. 出 発　　　22. きっぷ は 各 自 で かって く だ さ い 。

23. 電 車 が き ま す 。 急 い で く だ さ い 。

24. も う し ご と は 終 わ り ま し た 。

25. 十 時 に 東 京 駅 に 着 き ま し た 。

26. さ む い で す ね 。 上 着 を 着 て 出 か け ま し ょ う 。

II. Fill in the blanks with appropriate kanji.

1. ふ
 通電車
local train

2. じゅん きゅう

semi-express train

3. きゅう
 用
urgent business

4. てい
 車駅
station to stop at

5. かく　てい

local train

6. とく　　はや
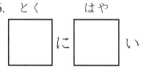 に　　い
especially fast

7. かい　そく
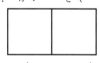
semi-express train

8. おもて

the surface

9. ひょう
 − 4
Table 4

10. お
 わる
to end

11. しゅう
 電
the last train

12. つ
 く
to arrive

13. ちゃく
五時
5:00 arrival

14. はつ
四時
4:00 departure

15. はっ
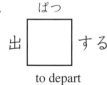 車する
to depart

16. ぱつ
出 ☐ する
to depart

5 ▶ Advanced Placement Exam Practice Questions

Read the passage and dialogue, and answer the questions.

　　東京に住んでいるジョンさんとポールさんは、はる休みに横浜へ行くことにしました。横浜はJR線でも東急線でも行くことができますが、まだのったことがないので東急線で行くことにきめました。いつもとちがう電車にのれば、旅行のようでたのしいとかんがえたからです。東急線は渋谷から横浜中華街までです。

　　いま二人は、渋谷駅ホームの時刻表をみながら、どの電車で行くか話しています。時間は10時45分です。横浜まで各駅停車ならだいたい40分、急行なら30分、特急なら25分かかります。

中華街方面下り時刻表

09	00特	01		....	43	47	50急	54
10	00特	01		....		46	50急	54
11	00特	01	05急	....			50急	54

特＝特急　　急＝急行

ジョン：ぼくは、横浜まで電車がどんな町をはしるのかゆっくりみたいからこの電車にしたいな。

ポール：ぼくは、はやく横浜へ行きたいから、速い電車がいい。40分も電車にのっているのはいやだよ。

ジョン：でも特急の発車までは15分もあるよ。ここでまつ？

ポール：そんなにまつなら、ほかの電車でもいいや。

ジョン：じゃ、この電車にしよう。すぐ発車するよ、それに各停じゃないからいいだろう。

1. What trains do John and Paul usually take?
   A. JR lines
   B. JR lines and Tokyu lines
   C. Tokyu lines
   D. Trains other than JR lines or Tokyu lines

2. Why did they choose the Tokyu Line to go to Yokohama?
   A. Because they are used to taking that line.
   B. Because Tokyu lines are faster than JR lines.
   C. Because Tokyu lines are cheaper than JR lines.
   D. Because they think it's more enjoyable to take the trains that they have never been on.

3. Choose the train that John wanted to get on.
   A. The local train which starts at 10:46
   B. The special express which starts at 11:00
   C. The express train which starts at 10:50
   D. The local train which starts at 10:54

4. Choose the train that Paul wanted to get on.
   A. The local train which starts at 10:46
   B. The special express which starts at 11:00
   C. The express train which starts at 10:50
   D. The local train which starts at 10:54

5. Choose the train which they eventually decided to take.
   A. The local train which starts at 10:46
   B. The special express which starts at 11:00
   C. The express train which starts at 10:50
   D. The local train which starts at 10:54

REVIEW EXERCISE: LESSONS 6–10

I. Find kanji having common radicals or elements, and write them or their corresponding letters in the blanks.

1. 後: ☐   2. 語: ☐   3. 定: ☐   4. 洗: ☐

5. 金: ☐   6. 学: ☐   7. 込: ☐ ☐

8. 終: ☐ ☐   9. 使: ☐ ☐ ☐ ☐

a. 行	b. 鉄	c. 営	d. 人	e. 準
f. 線	g. 停	h. 話	i. 連	j. 案
k. 絡	l. 何	m. 代	n. 速	

10. 時: ☐   11. 留: ☐   12. 内: ☐   13. 攻: ☐   14. 所: ☐

o. 新	p. 都	q. 故	r. 番	s. 特	t. 央

II. Find the antonyms to the kanji below, and write them or their corresponding letters in the blanks.

1. 大 ↔ ☐   2. 入 ↔ ☐

3. 上 ↔ ☐   4. 東 ↔ ☐

5. 南 ↔ ☐   6. 始 ↔ ☐

7. 発 ↔ ☐

a. 着   b. 西   c. 出

d. 央   e. 小   f. 子

g. 終   h. 人   i. 下

j. 北   k. 丑

At the Bank

銀行

All banks in Japan have automated teller machines (ATMs). Once you have opened an account and had a cash card with your Personal Identification Number made, you can withdraw or deposit money at any branch or affiliated bank. Becoming familiar with the kanji at ATMs will help you use any type of machine. Banks are usually open from 9:00 A.M. to 3:00 or 4:00 P.M. Monday through Friday, but ATMs operate 24 hours in some banks and convenience stores. ATMs are also conveniently located in department stores, large stations, and shopping streets.

1 ▶ Introductory Quiz

Look at the illustrations below and refer to the words in **Vocabulary**. Then try the following quiz.

a

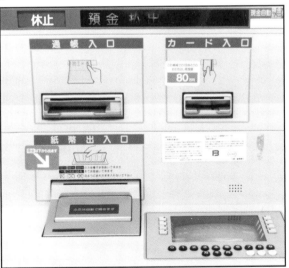

b

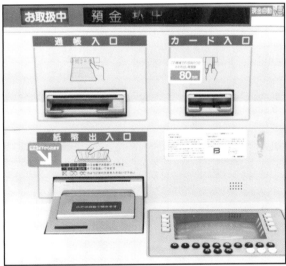

Here are some key words to know when using an ATM.

 押す   入れる   取る

Mr. Lee is at the bank with his cash card and bankbook. He wants to use the ATM but doesn't know the meaning of the kanji displayed on the machine. So he asks a bank employee for assistance.

I. Read the dialogue below and write (*a*) or (*b*) in the spaces provided.

リー　　　：「すみません。いま、どちらのきかいを使ったらいいですか。」

銀行の人：「＿＿＿＿＿＿　のきかいを使ってください。　＿＿＿＿＿＿　のきかいは使えません。」

II. Look at the kanji on the ATM screen below and write the correct letters (*A* – *F*) in the spaces provided.

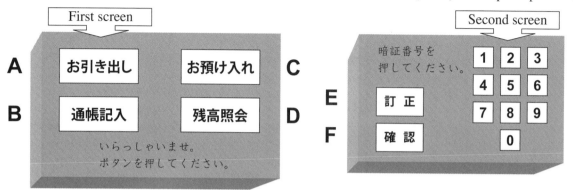

1. リー：　　「お金を預けたいんですが、どのボタンを押すんですか。」
　 銀行の人：「はじめに、＿＿のボタンを押してください。それから、通帳とお金を入れてくだ さい。」

2. リー：　　「25,000円、引き出したいんですが・・・。」
　 銀行の人：「はじめに ＿＿のボタンを押してください。それから、カードを入れて、暗証番号
　　　　　　を押します。つぎに、2・5・0・0・0のボタンを押して、正しかったら確認のボタンを
　　　　　　押してください。」

3. リー：　　「あっ、暗証番号をまちがえた！どうしたらいいですか。」
　 銀行の人：「＿＿のボタンを押してください。」

4. リー：　　「いま、お金がいくら残っているか、みたいんですが・・・。」
　 銀行の人：「＿＿のボタンを押して、カードを入れて、暗証番号を押してください。」

5. リー：　　「お金がいくらあるか通帳に記入したいんですが・・・。」
　 銀行の人：「＿＿のボタンを押して、通帳を入れてください。」

2 ▶ Vocabulary

Study the readings and meanings of these words to help you understand the **Introductory Quiz**.

1. 銀行	ぎん こう	**ginkō**	bank
2. 休止	きゅう し	**kyūshi**	out of use
3. （お）取扱中	（お）とり あつかい ちゅう	**(o)toriatsukai chū**	available for use
4. きかい		**kikai**	machine
5. 使う	つか う	**tsukau**	to use
6. 押す	お す	**osu**	to push
7. 入れる	い れる	**ireru**	to put in
8. 取る	と る	**toru**	to take out
9. ボタン		**botan**	button
10. （お）引き出し	（お）ひき だし	**(o)hikidashi**	withdrawal
11. （お）預け入れ	（お）あず け いれ	**(o)azukeire**	deposit
12. 通帳記入	つう ちょう き にゅう	**tsūchō kinyū**	entry in a bank book
13. 残高照会	ざん だか しょう かい	**zandaka shōkai**	checking the balance

14. 確認	かく にん	**kakunin**	confirmation
15. 訂正	てい せい	**teisei**	correction
16. 預ける 　　5	あず ける	**azukeru**	to deposit
17. 通帳 　　8	つう ちょう	**tsūchō**	bankbook
18. 暗証番号	あん しょう ばん ごう	**anshō bangō**	code number; Personal Identification Number
19. 正しい	ただ しい	**tadashii**	correct
20. まちがえる		**machigaeru**	to make a mistake
21. 残る 　　4	のこ る	**nokoru**	to remain
22. 記入する	き にゅう する	**kinyū suru**	to make an entry

3 ▶ New Characters

Eighteen characters are introduced in this lesson. Use the explanations to help you understand and remember the characters. Study the compound words to increase your vocabulary.

銀 引 預 押 号 暗 証 確 認 訂 正 残 高 記 帳 取 扱 止

132

銀　**gin**
ギン
silver

ノ	ハ	스	仝	牟	釒	釒	金
釗	鉓	鈤	鈤	銀	銀		

銀 combines 金 metal (cf. 30) and 艮 white root or white ground. White metal from the ground is silver. Another explanation is that 艮 is like 良 good (cf. 180 食) without `. Metal that is not as good as gold 金 is silver 銀.

白 + ✶ → 泉 → 艮

銀	ぎん	**gin**	silver
銀行	ぎんこう	**ginkō**	bank
銀座	ぎんざ	**Ginza**	Ginza (place)
銀メダル	ぎんメダル	**gin medaru**	silver medal
水銀	すいぎん	**suigin**	mercury

133

引　**hi-ku, (bi-ki), in**
ひ・く、（び・き）、イン
pull, draw; reduce

つ	コ	引	引				

引 derives from a pictograph of a bow and arrow. When shooting, the arrow is pulled back before it's let go.

ʒ + ↑ → ʒ| → 引

引く	ひく	**hiku**	to pull
引(き)出す	ひきだす	**hikidasu**	to pull ~ out; 　to withdraw money
引き出し	ひきだし	**hikidashi**	drawer; withdrawal 　(from bank account)
百円引(き)	ひゃくえん びき	**hyaku en biki**	one hundred yen discount
引力	いんりょく	**inryoku**	gravity

134 預	**azu-karu, azu-keru, yo** あず・かる、あず・ける、ヨ receive/entrust for safekeeping	⁻	マ	ヌ	予	予	予	矛	預
		預	預	預	預	預			

預 combines 予 in advance (cf. 243) and 頁 head or person. Preparing for something in advance allows people to feel safe. Thus 預 means entrust to or receive from someone for safekeeping.

預かる	あずかる	**azukaru**	to be entrusted with ~
預け入れ	あずけいれ	**azukeire**	depositing
預ける	あずける	**azukeru**	to leave ~ in someone's care; to deposit
預金する	よきんする	**yokin suru**	to deposit money
一時預 （か）り所	いちじ あずかりしょ	**ichiji azukari sho**	checkroom, temporary storage
定期預金	ていきよきん	**teiki yokin**	fixed deposit
普通預金	ふつうよきん	**futsū yokin**	ordinary deposit

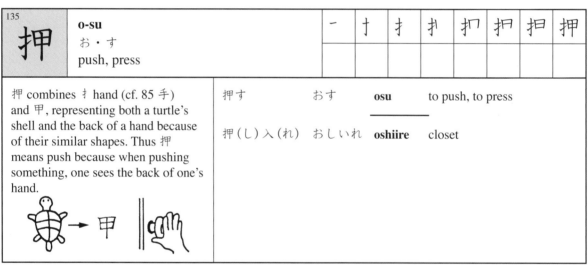

135 押	**o-su** お・す push, press	⁻	十	才	扌	扣	护	担	押

押 combines 扌 hand (cf. 85 手) and 甲, representing both a turtle's shell and the back of a hand because of their similar shapes. Thus 押 means push because when pushing something, one sees the back of one's hand.

押す	おす	**osu**	to push, to press
押（し）入（れ）	おしいれ	**oshiire**	closet

136 号	**gō** ゴウ number	⁻	口	口	므	号			

号 depicts a mouth shouting. In physical education class, students line up and shout out their numbers in order. Thus 号 means number when it shows the order of something.

番号	ばんごう	**bangō**	number (showing an order)
六号車	ろくごうしゃ	**rokugō sha**	car no. 6
年号	ねんごう	**nengō**	name of an era
信号	しんごう	**shingō**	signal
七月号	しちがつごう	**shichi gatsu gō**	July issue (magazine)

137 暗 — kura-i, an / くら・い、アン / dark, unseen

丨	冂	日	日	日'	日立	日立	日立
日立	暗	暗	暗	暗			

暗 combines 日 sun and 音, which is formed by adding a bar 一 to 口 of 言 say (cf. 78 話) and suggests confining someone's voice by covering his mouth. If the sun is covered, it becomes dark. By itself 音 means sound.

言 } → 音 → 音

暗い	くらい	**kurai**	dark	
		_____		
暗号	あんごう	**angō**	cipher, secret code	
暗室	あんしつ	**anshitsu**	photography darkroom	

138 証 — shō / ショウ / proof, certificate

丶	亠	ニ	訁	訁	言	言	訁
訂	訮	証	証				

証, which combines 言 say and 正 correct (cf. 142), suggests saying something correct. This has come to mean proof or certificate.

暗証番号	あんしょうばんごう	**anshō bangō**	Personal Identification Number
学生証	がくせいしょう	**gakusei shō**	student ID card
	_____		
保証する	ほしょうする	**hoshō suru**	to guarantee

139 確 — tashi-kameru, kaku / たし・かめる、カク / ascertain, make sure

一	丆	丆	石	石	石	石'	矿
矿	矿	矿	碏	確	確	確	

確 combines 石 stone, 宀 house, and 隹 bird (cf. 26 曜). If birds hide in a stone house, they can be sure of their safety.

確かめる	たしかめる	**tashikameru**	to make sure, to confirm
	_____		
確実な	かくじつな	**kakujitsu na**	sure, certain
正確な	せいかくな	**seikaku na**	accurate, exact

🗿 → 石 → 石

140 認	mito-meru, nin みと・める、ニン recognize, approve	ヽ	ニ	ニ	言	言	言	言	訂
		訒	訒	訒	認	認	認		

忍, which combines 刃 blade (cf. 61 券) and 心 mind (cf. 124 急), means bearing pain. With the addition of 言 words, 認 formerly meant bearing sharp words, and eventually came to mean recognize or approve.

認める	みとめる	**mitomeru**	to recognize, to approve
確認する	かくにんする	**kakunin suru**	to confirm, to make sure
———			
認定する	にんていする	**nintei suru**	to approve, to certify
公認する	こうにんする	**kōnin suru**	to approve/recognize officially

141 訂	tei テイ correct	ヽ	ニ	ニ	言	言	言	言	言
		訂							

訂 combines 言 words and 丁 nail hammered into a board at a right angle (cf. 121 停). Thus 訂 means righting or correcting what has been written or spoken.

丁 → 丁

———			
改訂する	かいていする	**kaitei suru**	to revise

142 正	tada-shii, shō, sei ただ・しい、ショウ、セイ correct, right; main	一	丁	下	正	正		

正, which combines 一 finish line and 止 stop walking (cf. 149), suggests stopping when one has correctly reached a goal (finish line). Now it means correct or right in general. Main is an associated meaning.

⻊ → ⻊ → 正

正しい	ただしい	**tadashii**	correct, right
正月	しょうがつ	**shōgatsu**	the New Year
正面	しょうめん	**shōmen**	the front
訂正する	ていせいする	**teisei suru**	to correct
———			
正式な	せいしきな	**seishiki na**	formal
正解	せいかい	**seikai**	correct answer

143 残

noko-ru, noko-su, zan
のこ・る、のこ・す、ザン
remain, left behind

一	丁	歹	歹	歹	歺	歺	残
残	残						

残, which combines 歹 bone and 㦮 two weapons (cf. 33 成), represents bones left after the meat has been taken off with weapons. Thus 残 means left behind or remain.

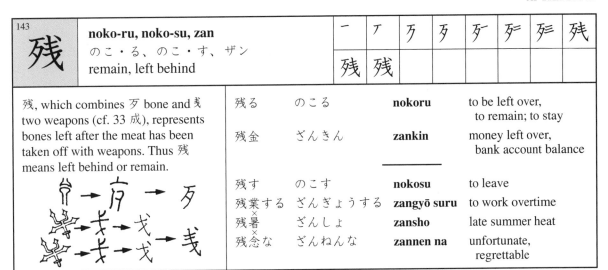

残る	のこる	**nokoru**	to be left over, to remain; to stay
残金	ざんきん	**zankin**	money left over, bank account balance
残す	のこす	**nokosu**	to leave
残業する	ざんぎょうする	**zangyō suru**	to work overtime
残暑	ざんしょ	**zansho**	late summer heat
残念な	ざんねんな	**zannen na**	unfortunate, regrettable

144 高

taka-i, (daka), kō
たか・い、(だか)、コウ
high; expensive

'	亠	亠	古	古	峝	高	高
高	高						

高 depicts a two-story house, which was considered high in ancient times. An associated meaning is high price, or expensive.

高い	たかい	**takai**	high; expensive
円高	えんだか	**endaka**	high value of the yen
残高	ざんだか	**zandaka**	bank account balance
高気圧	こうきあつ	**kō kiatsu**	high atmospheric pressure
高校	こうこう	**kōkō**	high school

145 記

ki
キ
take note, write

丶	亠	言	言	言	言	言	記
記	記						

己 suggests that something lying down has risen up and become noticeable. Together with 言 words, 記 implies words to note, and thus means take note or write.

記入する	きにゅうする	**kinyū suru**	to make an entry, to fill out/in
日記	にっき	**nikki**	diary
記号	きごう	**kigō**	mark, sign, symbol
暗記する	あんきする	**anki suru**	to learn by heart, to memorize
記事	きじ	**kiji**	news story, article
記念日	きねんび	**kinen bi**	memorial day, anniversary
新聞記者	しんぶんきしゃ	**shimbun kisha**	newspaper reporter

146	**chō**		｜	口	巾	巾′	巾″	巾‴	帪	帳
帳	チョウ notebook		帪	帳	帳					

帳 combines 巾 hanging cloth, and 長 long, which originally depicted an old man with long hair leaning on a cane. A long cloth was used as a notebook in ancient times.

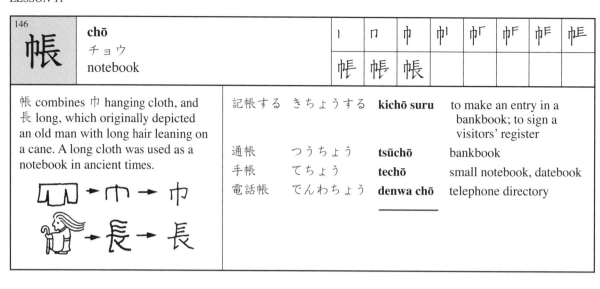

記帳する	きちょうする	**kichō suru**	to make an entry in a bankbook; to sign a visitors' register
通帳	つうちょう	**tsūchō**	bankbook
手帳	てちょう	**techō**	small notebook, datebook
電話帳	でんわちょう	**denwa chō**	telephone directory

147	**to-ru, (do-ri)**		一	厂	下	耳	王	耳	取	取
取	と・る、(ど・り) take, get, acquire									

取 combines 耳 ear and 又 hand. Ancient warriors used to take the ears off their conquered enemies. Now 取 means take or get in general.

取る	とる	**toru**	to take, to get
取 (り) 引 (き) する	とりひき する	**torihiki suru**	to trade, to make a deal
取 (り) 出す	とりだす	**toridasu**	to take out, to pick out
間取 (り)	まどり	**madori**	room arrangement of a house, floor plan
取 (り) 消 (し)	とりけし	**torikeshi**	cancellation

148	**atsuka-u**		一	十	扌	扌′	扔	扱		
扱	あつか・う treat, deal with, handle									

扱 combines 扌 hand (cf. 85 手) and 及 another hand reaching out for a man. Only when hands reach something, can one treat or handle it.

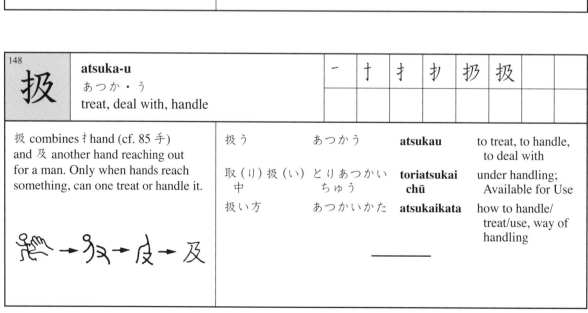

扱う	あつかう	**atsukau**	to treat, to handle, to deal with
取 (り) 扱 (い) 中	とりあつかい ちゅう	**toriatsukai chū**	under handling; Available for Use
扱い方	あつかいかた	**atsukaikata**	how to handle/ treat/use, way of handling

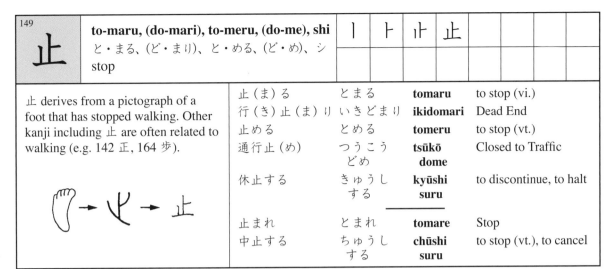

| 149 止 | to-maru, (do-mari), to-meru, (do-me), shi
と・まる、（ど・まり）、と・める、（ど・め）、シ
stop | 丨 | 卜 | 止 | 止 | | | | |

止 derives from a pictograph of a foot that has stopped walking. Other kanji including 止 are often related to walking (e.g. 142 正, 164 歩).

止（ま）る	とまる	**tomaru**	to stop (vi.)
行（き）止（ま）り	いきどまり	**ikidomari**	Dead End
止める	とめる	**tomeru**	to stop (vt.)
通行止（め）	つうこうどめ	**tsūkō dome**	Closed to Traffic
休止する	きゅうしする	**kyūshi suru**	to discontinue, to halt
止まれ	とまれ	**tomare**	Stop
中止する	ちゅうしする	**chūshi suru**	to stop (vt.), to cancel

4 ▶ Practice

I. Write the readings of the following kanji in hiragana.

1. 銀 行
2. 休 止
3. 高 い
4. 十 号 車
5. 引 き 出 し
6. 残 る
7. 預 金
8. 確 認
9. 預 ける
10. 暗 証 番 号
11. 訂 正
12. 記 号
13. 通 帳
14. 学 生 証
15. お 取 扱 中
16. 取 る
17. 暗 い
18. 引 く
19. 電 話 帳
20. 通 行 止 め
21. 円 高
22. 正 月
23. 残 高
24. 扱 い 方
25. ベ ル を 押 し て く だ さ い 。
26. 正 し い ほ う に 、 ○ を つ け な さ い 。
27. い つ も 、 日 記 を 書 い て い ま す 。
28. 通 帳 に 、 記 入 し て く だ さ い 。
29. い く ら お 金 が 残 っ て い る か 、 確 か め て み ま す 。
30. 手 を あ げ て 、 タ ク シ ー を 止 め ま す 。

II. Fill in the blanks with appropriate kanji.

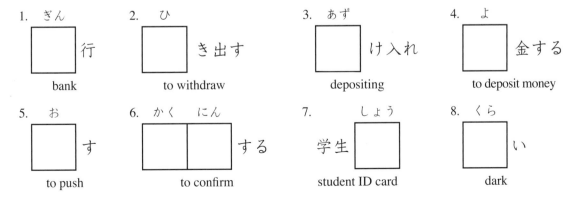

1. ぎん

□ 行

bank

2. ひ

□ き出す

to withdraw

3. あず

□ け入れ

depositing

4. よ

□ 金する

to deposit money

5. お

□ す

to push

6. かく にん

□ □ する

to confirm

7. しょう

学生 □

student ID card

8. くら

□ い

dark

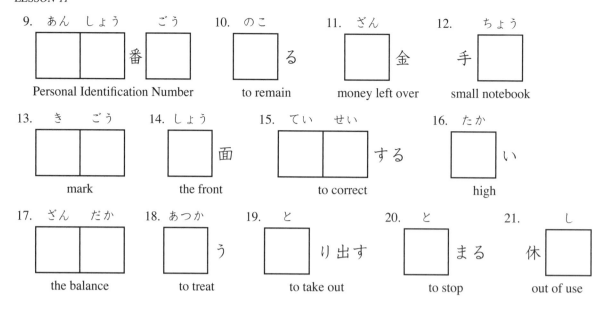

9. あん しょう ごう 番
Personal Identification Number

10. のこ る
to remain

11. ざん 金
money left over

12. ちょう 手
small notebook

13. き ごう
mark

14. しょう 面
the front

15. てい せい する
to correct

16. たか い
high

17. ざん だか
the balance

18. あつか う
to treat

19. と り出す
to take out

20. と まる
to stop

21. し 休
out of use

5 ▸ Advanced Placement Exam Practice Questions

Maria is a student from abroad. She tried to use an ATM for the first time at her new bank in Japan but she had some trouble. Now she is asking the bank clerk, Mr. Tanaka, how to use the ATM. Read their dialogue, then answer the questions.

マリア： 一万円、お金を出したいんですが。

田　中： はじめに「お引き出し」のボタンを押します。それからカードを入れて、暗証番号を押します。

マリア： あ、暗証番号をまちがえちゃった！どうしよう！

田　中： だいじょうぶですよ。「訂正」のボタンを押して、もう一回暗証番号を押してください。つぎに1・万・円のボタンを押して、正しければ「確認」のボタンを押してください。

マリア： あ、お金が出てきた。いま、お金がいくら残っているかもみたいんですが。

田　中： この「残高照会」のボタンを押せばみることができますよ。

マリア： お金を預けるときはどうしたらいいですか。

田　中： 「お預け入れ」のボタンを押して、通帳とお金を入れれば預けられます。通帳記入もいっしょにできますよ。

マリア： 通帳をわすれても、預けられますか。

田　中： はい、預けられます。

マリア： こんどは、預けにきます。ありがとう。

1. Which is the first button to be pushed?
   A. 残高照会
   B. お引き出し
   C. お預け入れ
   D. 暗証番号

2. If you make a mistake when entering the Personal Identification Number, which button should you push?
   A. だいじょうぶ
   B. 訂正
   C. 確認
   D. 暗証番号

3. Which of the buttons is to be pushed to check the balances?
   A. 残高照会
   B. 通帳記入
   C. お引き出し
   D. お預け入れ

4. What does Maria want to do, when she comes next time?
   A. Withdraw money alone
   B. Check her balances
   C. Deposit money
   D. Enter her Personal Identification Number without making a mistake

5. Choose the correct answer.
   A. Maria drew out 1000 yen.
   B. You cannot deposit money if you forget a bankbook.
   C. Depositing and making an entry in a bankbook cannot be performed simultaneously.
   D. When drawing out money, the second button to be pushed is a Personal Identification Number.

At the Post Office

郵便局

B uildings marked with 〒 are post offices. Inside are several windows, not only for the usual postal services, but also for savings accounts, money transfers, and other banking services. The window marked with はがき・切手 is where stamps, postcards, and aerogrammes can be bought. Stamps are also sold at any shop marked with 〒. For people who are unsure of the stamp value needed for their mail, lists of postal rates are available at post offices. City post boxes have two letter drops, with mailing instructions written below them.

1 ▶ Introductory Quiz

Look at the illustrations on this page and the facing page and refer to the words in **Vocabulary**. Then try the following quiz.

Refer to the lists of postal rates on page 115 and select the appropriate stamps for each of these 5 pieces of mail. One of the pieces needs two stamps, the express delivery rate plus the standard-sized letter rate. None of the letters exceeds 25g. Write the letter of the proper stamp in the spaces provided below.

国内むけ

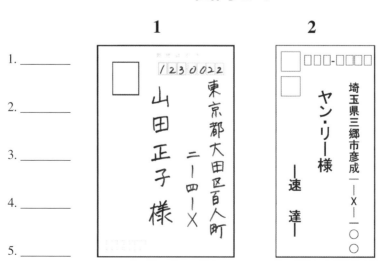

1. _____

2. _____

3. _____

4. _____

5. _____

外国むけ

3

Mr. I. Ronson

Lagos, NIGERIA

PAR AVION
BY AIR MAIL

4

Mr. M. Smith
Washington D. C.
DC 123456
U. S. A.

PAR AVION
BY AIR MAIL

5

Postal Rates
郵便料金表

【国際】通常郵便料金（航空）				
種類	重量	第1地帯	第2地帯	第3地帯
		アジア マーシャル グアム その他	北アメリカ 中央アメリカ オセアニア 中近東 ヨーロッパ	アフリカ 南アメリカ
書状	25g まで	90 円	110 円	130 円

郵便はがき	70 円

【国内】通常郵便料金	
通常はがき	50 円

定形	25g まで	80 円

【国内】速達料金		
通常 郵便	250g まで	270 円
	1kg まで	370 円
	4kg まで	630 円

日本の切手

a   **b**   **c**   **d**   **e**   **f**   **g**

2 ▶ Vocabulary

Study the readings and meanings of these words to help you understand the **Introductory Quiz**.

1. 郵便局	ゆう びん きょく		**yūbin kyoku**	post office
2. はがき			**hagaki**	postcard
3. 切手	きって		**kitte**	postage stamp
4. 外国	がい こく		**gaikoku**	overseas/foreign country
5. 航空(便)	こう くう (びん)		**kōkū (bin)**	airmail
6. 国際	こく さい		**kokusai**	international
7. 通常	つう じょう		**tsūjō**	ordinary
8. 郵便料金	ゆう びん りょう きん		**yūbin ryōkin**	postal rate
9. アジア			**Ajia**	Asia
10. その他	その た		**sono ta**	the others, et cetera
11. 北米	ほく べい		**Hokubei**	North America
12. アフリカ			**Afurika**	Africa
13. 書状／手紙	しょ じょう／て がみ		**shojō/tegami**	letter
14. 定形	てい けい		**teikei**	standard size (envelope)
15. 速達	そく たつ		**sokutatsu**	express mail
16. ～様	～さま		**～sama**	Mr. ~, Ms. ~, Miss ~, Mrs. ~

3 ▶ New Characters

Thirteen characters are introduced in this lesson. Use the explanations to help you understand and remember the characters. Study the compound words to increase your vocabulary.

郵 便 局 切 外 国 際 航 空 常 料 他 様

150 郵	**yū** ユウ mail		ノ	ニ	三	幵	乒	乓	垂	垂
			垂⁷	郵彡	郵					

垂 depicts a plant with leaves hanging vertically; vertical also refers to vertical cliffs far away. With the addition of ß village, 郵 formerly meant outposts for the relay of messages, and eventually came to mean mail.

郵便	ゆうびん	**yūbin**	mail service
郵便番号	ゆうびんばんごう	**yūbin bangō**	postal/ZIP code
郵送料	ゆうそうりょう	**yūsō ryō**	postage
郵便物	ゆうびんぶつ	**yūbin butsu**	mail

151 便 tayo-ri, ben, bin
たよ・り、ベン、ピン
convenience; mail

Stroke order: ノ 亻 仁 仁 仵 佢 佰 便 便

更 depicts various things 品 put together in one 一 place by hand 又. This makes them convenient for men 亻 to use. In the past, mail was the most convenient means of communication between people living far from each other.

便り	たより	**tayori**	letter, news
郵便	ゆうびん	**yūbin**	mail service
定期便	ていきびん	**teiki bin**	regular service flight/ mail
便利な	べんりな	**benri na**	convenient
学内便	がくないびん	**gakunai bin**	campus mail
船便	ふなびん	**funa bin**	surface/sea mail
宅急便	たっきゅうびん	**takkyū bin**	rapid door-to-door delivery

152 局 kyoku
キョク
bureau, office

Stroke order: ㄱ コ 尸 尹 局 局 局

局 combines 尹 enclose with two bent lines (as shown below), and 口 limited or divided space. Offices are enclosed spaces that are divided into sections.

郵便局	ゆうびんきょく	**yūbin kyoku**	post office
電話局	でんわきょく	**denwa kyoku**	telephone office
局番	きょくばん	**kyokuban**	district telephone number
テレビ局	テレビきょく	**terebi kyoku**	television station

153 切 ki-ru, (ki'), (gi'), setsu
き・る、（きっ）、（ぎっ）、セツ
cut

Stroke order: 一 七 切 切

切, which combines 七 branch being cut, and 刀 sword (cf. 25 分), means cut.

切る	きる	**kiru**	to cut
切手	きって	**kitte**	postage stamp
小切手	こぎって	**kogitte**	check
大切な	たいせつな	**taisetsu na**	important, valuable
締(め)切(り)	しめきり	**shimekiri**	deadline
切符	きっぷ	**kippu**	ticket
親切な	しんせつな	**shinsetsu na**	kind

117

154 外

soto, gai, ge
そと、ガイ、ゲ
outside, other

ノ	ク	タ	列	外					

外 combines 夕 evening (cf. 66 名) and 卜, which depicts a stick used by fortunetellers. In ancient China, fortunetellers worked outside in the evening.

外	そと	**soto**	outside
外出する	がいしゅつする	**gaishutsu suru**	to go out
時間外	じかんがい	**jikan gai**	before or after office/working hours; overtime
外科	げか	**geka**	surgical unit, surgery
外側	そとがわ	**sotogawa**	outside
外来	がいらい	**gairai**	coming from outside; for an outpatient
海外	かいがい	**kaigai**	overseas
内外	ないがい	**naigai**	inside and outside

155 国

kuni, koku, (goku), (ko')
くに、コク、（ゴク）、（コッ）
country, nation

丨	冂	冂	冃	国	国	国	国		

王 represents a man standing between heaven and earth with hands and legs spread wide, indicating a king. 丶 suggests treasure. A king and his treasures enclosed by borders 囗 represents country.

国	くに	**kuni**	country, nation
外国	がいこく	**gaikoku**	foreign country
外国人	がいこくじん	**gaikoku jin**	foreigner
中国	ちゅうごく	**Chūgoku**	China
四国	しこく	**Shikoku**	Shikoku (island, district)
国籍	こくせき	**kokuseki**	nationality
国内	こくない	**kokunai**	domestic, within the country
国会	こっかい	**kokkai**	the Diet

156 際

sai
サイ
inter-; occasion

⁊	彡	阝	阝	阝	阝	阝	阝		
阡	阡	阡	阡	際	際				

際 combines 阝, which as a left part of kanji means piled stones or hill, and 祭 festival (cf. 36). Festivals held on hills used to be important occasions during which people intermingled.

国際	こくさい	**kokusai**	international
国際線	こくさいせん	**kokusai sen**	international flight/route
国際電話	こくさいでんわ	**kokusai denwa**	international phone call
国際交流	こくさいこうりゅう	**kokusai kōryū**	international exchange
この際	このさい	**kono sai**	on this occasion

157 航 — kō / コウ — navigation, sailing

Stroke order: ′ 丿 亅 亅 舟 舟 舟′ 舟 舟 航

舟 derives from a pictograph of a boat, and 亢 represents a neck held up straight. Thus 航 means sailing straight forward.

日航	にっこう	**Nikkō**	abbreviation for 日本航空 (Japan Air Lines)
航海する	こうかいする	**kōkai suru**	to navigate, to sail, to voyage

158 空 — sora, kara, a-ku, kū / そら、から、あ・く、クウ — sky; empty, vacant

Stroke order: ′ ′′ 宀 宀 穴 空 空 空

穴 or 宂, which combines 宀 house and 八 divide (cf. 8), formerly meant pit or cave dwelling, and now means hole in general. エ indicates straight (cf. 43). The sky can be thought of as a large hole where one can go straight up and find nothing but emptiness.

空	そら	**sora**	sky
空手	からて	**karate**	karate
航空便	こうくうびん	**kōkū bin**	airmail
空車	くうしゃ	**kūsha**	vacant taxi
空オケ	からオケ	**karaoke**	karaoke (literally "empty orchestra") (commonly written カラオケ)
空きカン	あきカン	**aki kan**	empty can
成田空港	なりたくうこう	**Narita kūkō**	Narita Airport
空席	くうせき	**kūseki**	vacant/unoccupied seat

159 常 — jō / ジョウ — always, normal, usual

Stroke order: ′ ′′ ′′′ ′′′′ 尚 尚 常 常 常 常 常

常 combines 尚 long wisps of smoke coming out of a stove, and 巾 cloth (cf. 146 帳). Long cloth eventually came to mean long time, and now 常 means always or normal.

通常	つうじょう	**tsūjō**	usually, normally, in general
平常通り	へいじょうどおり	**heijō dōri**	as usual
正常な	せいじょうな	**seijō na**	normal
日常会話	にちじょうかいわ	**nichijō kaiwa**	daily conversation
非常の際	ひじょうのさい	**hijō no sai**	in case of emergency
非常階段	ひじょうかいだん	**hijō kaidan**	emergency stairs

119

160 料

ryō
リョウ
materials; fee, charge

丶	丷	丷	半	半	米	米	米
料	料						

料, which combines 米 rice and 斗 measure (cf. 45 科), originally meant measuring grain. It has come to mean materials or charge, since vendors always measure their materials and charge accordingly.

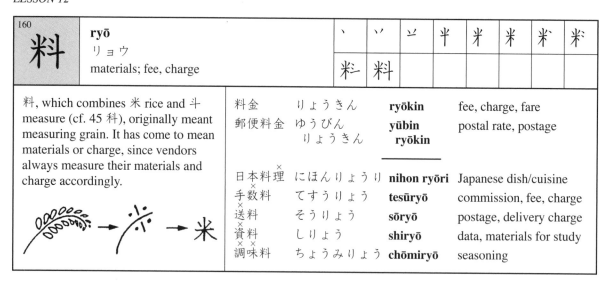

料金	りょうきん	**ryōkin**	fee, charge, fare
郵便料金	ゆうびん りょうきん	**yūbin ryōkin**	postal rate, postage

日本料理	にほんりょうり	**nihon ryōri**	Japanese dish/cuisine
手数料	てすうりょう	**tesūryō**	commission, fee, charge
送料	そうりょう	**sōryō**	postage, delivery charge
資料	しりょう	**shiryō**	data, materials for study
調味料	ちょうみりょう	**chōmiryō**	seasoning

161 他

ta
タ
other, another

ノ	イ	仒	仲	他			

他 combines 也 snake (cf. 82 地) and イ people. In ancient times, people were often as afraid of others as they were of snakes. Thus 他 came to mean other or another.

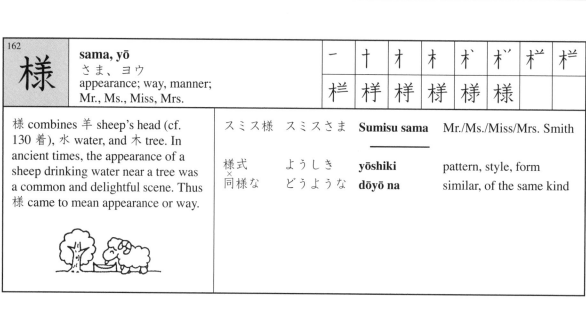

その他	そのた	**sonota**	the others, et cetera
他人	たにん	**tanin**	unrelated person, other people

162 様

sama, yō
さま、ヨウ
appearance; way, manner;
Mr., Ms., Miss, Mrs.

一	十	才	木	栏	栏	栏	栏
栏	栏	样	样	様	様		

様 combines 羊 sheep's head (cf. 130 着), 水 water, and 木 tree. In ancient times, the appearance of a sheep drinking water near a tree was a common and delightful scene. Thus 様 came to mean appearance or way.

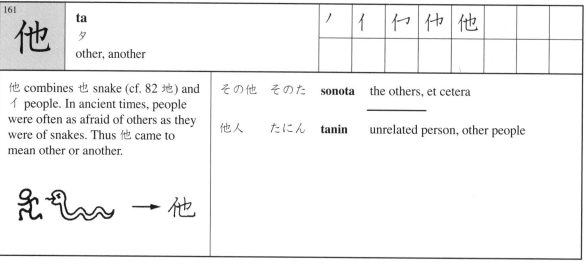

スミス様	スミスさま	**Sumisu sama**	Mr./Ms./Miss/Mrs. Smith
様式	ようしき	**yōshiki**	pattern, style, form
同様な	どうような	**dōyō na**	similar, of the same kind

4 Practice

I. Write the readings of the following kanji in hiragana.

1. 郵 便 局   2. 切 手   3. 航 空 便   4. 国 際
5. 通 常   6. 料 金   7. 書 状   8. 定 形
9. 速 達   10. そ の 他   11. 外 国   12. 〜 様
13. 郵 便 番 号   14. 電 話 局   15. 小 切 手   16. 時 間 外
17. 外 科   18. 国 際 線   19. 中 国   20. 空 車
21. 大 切 な ご 本 、 あ り が と う ご ざ い ま し た 。
22. 子 ど も が 、 外 で げ ん き に あ そ ん で い ま す 。
23. 国 か ら 便 り が あ り ま し た 。
24. ス ミ ス さ ん は 、 外 国 人 で す が 、 空 手 が じ ょ う ず で す 。
25. あ し た も 平 常 通 り 扱 い ま す 。

II. Fill in the blanks with appropriate kanji.

1. ゆう　びん　きょく
post office

2. きょく
| |番号
|---|
district phone number

3. き
| |る
|---|
to cut

4. きっ
| |手
|---|
postage stamp

5. そと
outside

6.
いろいろな
　　　くに
various countries

7. がい　こく
foreign country

8.
中
　　ごく
| |人
|---|
a Chinese (person)

9. そら
sky

10. こう　くう　びん
airmail

11. じょう
正| |な
|---|
normal

12.
その
　　た
the others

13.
スミス
　　さま
Mr. Smith

5 Advanced Placement Exam Practice Questions

Read the text about the postal service of Japan, and describe the postal service of your country. Please explain the differences and similarities or characteristics in Japanese in 300 to 400 characters.

郵便局のサービス

　日本には、大小あわせて24,000以上の郵便局があります。ほとんどの郵便局は平日の午前9時から午後5時までですが、夜間、休日でも開いているところもあります。

　郵便局にはいろいろなサービスがあります。手紙や[1]荷物を国内、国外へとどける郵便サービス、銀行とおなじようにお金を預かる郵便[2]貯金サービス、[3]保険会社のような保険サービスもあります。また、日本各地の[4]名物、花や食べ物なども、郵便局で申し込めば家にとどけてもらえます。

　手紙やはがきは赤いポストに入れます。外国への郵便もこのポストから送ることができます。切手やはがきは〒マークのあるお店でも買うことができます。はがきは日本国内は50円、外国へはどこの国でも70円でとどきます。手紙は重さで料金がきまります。荷物をおくるときは郵便局へもって行くか、うちにとりにきてもらうこともできます。

[1]荷物: parcel, package; baggage
[2]貯金: saving
[3]保険: insurance
[4]名物: special product

Which Way Should I Go?

どの道を通ったら いいでしょうか

Most road signs in Japan are written in kanji. The sign 立入禁止 tells you to keep out of the designated place. The sign 工事中 warns you to walk carefully, while 横断禁止 means no crossing.

It is not only helpful but fun to know the meaning of the kanji on the signs all around you. In Lessons 13 and 14, you will learn kanji that appear on different kinds of signs.

1 ▶ Introductory Quiz

Look at the map overleaf and refer to the words in **Vocabulary**. Then try the following quiz.

The arrows show the road Mr. Lee usually walks to Japanese language class. Because some construction work has just started, he is unable to take his usual route. Check the map to answer the following questions.

I. Choose the correct answers.

1. リーさんが、地下鉄を出て、歩道をみぎへ歩いて行くと、きょうから (a. こうじ　b. かじ　c. ようじ) が始まって、立入禁止になっていました。

2. ですから、(a. 取る　b. 通る　c. 立つ) ことができません。

3. それで、横断歩道を*わたって、まっすぐ歩いて行くと、こんどは通行止めでした。 そこは (a. 通れます　b. 通れません　c. 止まれません)。 (*to cross)

4. そこでみぎにまがって歩きました。つぎに、ひだりにまがると、大学の正門も (a. 通行中　b. 歩行中　c. 工事中) で、入れませんでした。

5. 正門の前では、大型トラックがこないかどうか、よく (a. 禁止　b. 注意　c. 立入) してください。

6. リーさんは、どうして地下鉄の駅を出て、すぐ道をわたらなかったのですか。

   a. そこへ自動車がきたからです。

   b. だれも歩いていなかったからです。

   c. そこで道をわたってはいけないからです。

7. 歩道というのは、どんな道ですか。

   a. 人が歩いてはいけない道です。

   b. 歩行者のための道です。

   c. 自動車が通る道です。

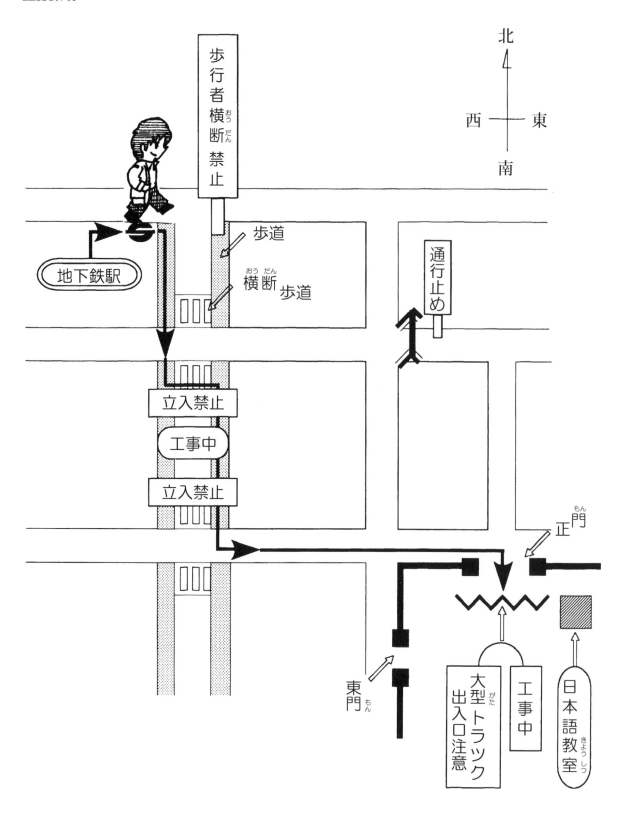

II. リーさんは、きょう東門から入って日本語教室へ行きました。駅からどの道を通ったでしょうか。
ちずに書いてください。

2 ▶ Vocabulary

Study the readings and meanings of these words to help you understand the **Introductory Quiz**.

1.	道	みち	**michi**	street, way
2.	歩道	ほどう	**hodō**	sidewalk
3.	歩く	あるく	**aruku**	to walk
4.	工事	こうじ	**kōji**	construction work
5.	火事	かじ	**kaji**	fire
6.	用事	ようじ	**yōji**	business, errand
7.	立入禁止	たちいりきんし	**tachiiri kinshi**	Keep Out
8.	工事中	こうじちゅう	**kōji chū**	Under Construction
9.	立つ	たつ	**tatsu**	to stand
10.	横断歩道	おうだんほどう	**ōdan hodō**	crosswalk
11.	通行止め	つうこうどめ	**tsūkō dome**	Closed to Traffic
12.	正門	せいもん	**seimon**	main gate
13.	通行中	つうこうちゅう	**tsūkō chū**	while passing
14.	歩行中	ほこうちゅう	**hokō chū**	while walking
15.	大型トラック	おおがたトラック	**ōgata torakku**	big truck
16.	禁止	きんし	**kinshi**	Prohibited
17.	注意	ちゅうい	**chūi**	Caution
18.	立入	たちいり	**tachiiri**	entrance
19.	歩行者	ほこうしゃ	**hokōsha**	pedestrian
20.	横断禁止	おうだんきんし	**ōdan kinshi**	No Crossing
21.	東門	ひがしもん	**higashi mon**	east gate
22.	日本語教室	にほんごきょうしつ	**nihongo kyōshitsu**	Japanese language classroom
23.	歩行者通路	ほこうしゃつうろ	**hokōsha tsūro**	pedestrian walkway

3 ▶ New Characters

Seven characters are introduced in this lesson. Use the explanations to help you understand and remember the characters. Study the compound words to increase your vocabulary.

道　歩　者　禁　立　注　意

163 道	**michi, dō** みち、ドウ street, road, path, way	丶	丷	酋	酋	产	首	首	首
		首	首	道	道				

道 combines 首 head or neck and ⻌ proceed or walk, and suggests walking down a road with head held high. An associated meaning is way.

道	みち	**michi**	road, street
車道	しゃどう	**shadō**	roadway
国道	こくどう	**kokudō**	national road
水道	すいどう	**suidō**	waterworks, tap water
片道	かたみち	**katamichi**	one-way
道路工事	どうろこうじ	**dōro kōji**	road works/repairs
高速道路	こうそくどうろ	**kōsoku dōro**	superhighway, expressway
柔道	じゅうどう	**jūdō**	judo

---

164 歩	**aru-ku, ho** ある・く、ホ walk	｜	｜	⺊	止	牛	步	歨	歩

歩 derives from a pictograph of two feet stepping right and left alternately, in other words, walking.

歩く	あるく	**aruku**	to walk
歩道	ほどう	**hodō**	sidewalk, pedestrian road
横断歩道	おうだんほどう	**ōdan hodō**	pedestrian crossing, crosswalk

---

165 者	**mono, sha** もの、シャ person	一	十	土	耂	耂	者	者	者

者 originally depicted various foods cooked on a stove, and thus became associated with various gathered things (cf. 51 都). The idea of things eventually changed to people, which gave the character its present meaning.

者	もの	**mono**	person
歩行者	ほこうしゃ	**hokōsha**	pedestrian
学者	がくしゃ	**gakusha**	scholar
記者	きしゃ	**kisha**	journalist, reporter
若者	わかもの	**wakamono**	young person, youth
歩行者天国	ほこうしゃ てんごく	**hokōsha tengoku**	street temporarily closed to vehicles (literally "pedestrian's paradise")
前者	ぜんしゃ	**zensha**	the former
後者	こうしゃ	**kōsha**	the latter

166 禁	kin キン prohibition	一	十	オ	木	朩	村	材	林
		林	埜	埜	禁	禁			

林 depicts two trees side by side, meaning wood, and 示 represents an altar (cf. 35 祝). Thus 禁 suggests a sacred wood surrounding an altar, into which entry is prohibited. (森, meaning forest, is larger than 林.)

禁止する	きんしする	**kinshi suru**	to prohibit
横断禁止	おうだんきんし	**ōdan kinshi**	No Crossing
駐車禁止	ちゅうしゃきんし	**chūsha kinshi**	No Parking
～厳禁	～げんきん	**~genkin**	~ Strictly Prohibited

---

167 立	ta-tsu, ritsu, (ri') た・つ、リツ、（リッ） stand	'	亠	亠	立	立			

立 represents a man standing on the ground. Imagine a **sumō** wrestler about to stand up for a bout.

立つ	たつ	**tatsu**	to stand
立入禁止	たちいりきんし	**tachiiri kinshi**	Keep Out
国立	こくりつ	**kokuritsu**	national
市立	しりつ	**shiritsu**	municipal
立入厳禁	たちいりげんきん	**tachiiri genkin**	Keep Out
私立	しりつ	**shiritsu**	private (school, etc.)
中立	ちゅうりつ	**chūritsu**	neutrality
立食パーティー	りっしょくパーティー	**risshoku pātī**	buffet party

---

168 注	soso-gu, chū そそ・ぐ、チュウ pour; pay attention, note	`	`	⺡	⺡	汀	汁	注	注

注 combines ⺡ water and 主 stay still (cf. 75 住). When pouring water into something, one is careful to keep the hands still. Thus 注 means pouring liquid as well as paying attention.

注文する	ちゅうもんする	**chūmon suru**	to order (a product)
注ぐ	そそぐ	**sosogu**	to pour
注目する	ちゅうもくする	**chūmoku suru**	to pay attention, to take notice
注射する	ちゅうしゃする	**chūsha suru**	to inject

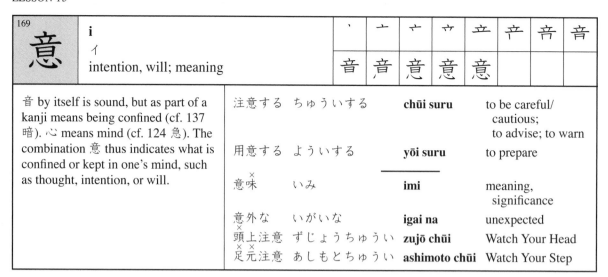

169 意	i イ intention, will; meaning	丶	亠	产	立	立	产	音	音
		音	音	意	意	意			

音 by itself is sound, but as part of a kanji means being confined (cf. 137 暗). 心 means mind (cf. 124 急). The combination 意 thus indicates what is confined or kept in one's mind, such as thought, intention, or will.	注意する ちゅういする	**chūi suru**	to be careful/ cautious; to advise; to warn
	用意する よういする	**yōi suru**	to prepare
	意味 いみ	**imi**	meaning, significance
	意外な いがいな	**igai na**	unexpected
	頭上注意 ずじょうちゅうい	**zujō chūi**	Watch Your Head
	足元注意 あしもとちゅうい	**ashimoto chūi**	Watch Your Step

4 ▶ Practice

I. Write the readings of the following kanji in hiragana.

1. 歩道   2. 用意   3. 立入禁止   4. 通行止め
5. 注意   6. 歩行者   7. 行止まり   8. 水道
9. 記者   10. 国立
11. この道は、工事中で通れません。
12. 車道は、人が歩くところではありません。
13. バスの中でずっと立っていたので、つかれました。
14. 本を注文しました。

II. Fill in the blanks with appropriate kanji.

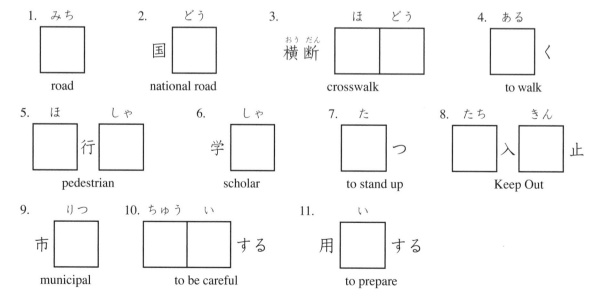

1. みち — road
2. どう — 国＿ national road
3. ほどう — 横断＿＿ (おうだん) crosswalk
4. ある — ＿く to walk
5. ほしゃ — ＿行＿ pedestrian
6. しゃ — ＿学 scholar
7. た — ＿つ to stand up
8. たちきん — ＿入＿止 Keep Out
9. りつ — 市＿ municipal
10. ちゅうい — ＿＿する to be careful
11. い — 用＿する to prepare

5 ▶ Advanced Placement Exam Practice Questions

Read this set of mobile e-mails, and choose the best answers to the questions.

☺ sender 🕓 date 📄 subject

①

☺ ゆき 🕓 5月11日　11:25
📄 おくれそう！
・・・・・・・・・・・・・・
ごめん！おくれそう！
いま、地下鉄の駅を出たところ。まち
あわせは 大学の正門前だよね。
二人はいまどこ？

②

☺ えみ 🕓 5月11日　11:27
📄 Re: おくれそう！
・・・・・・・・・・・・・・
もう、正門前でまってるよ。
まりは まだ来てない。
地下鉄の工事があるから、気をつけ
てきてね。

③

☺ ゆき 🕓 5月11日　11:30
📄 Re: Re: おくれそう！
・・・・・・・・・・・・・・
二つ目の信号から工事中で立入禁止
だけど、どうしたらいい？
むこうに通行止めって見えるんだけど。

④

☺ えみ 🕓 5月11日　11:31
📄 Re: Re: Re: おくれそう！
・・・・・・・・・・・・・・
通行止めでも、歩行者は通れるか
ら、信号をひだりにまがってもだい
じょうぶ。
道をわたって、スーパーの前を歩い
て来られるよ。

⑤

☺ まり 🕓 5月11日　11:34
📄 駅についた！
・・・・・・・・・・・・・・
いま駅についた！いそいで行くね。
三つ目の信号をひだりにまがればい
いの？スーパーの前を通って行けば
いいんだよね。 ゆきはもうついた？

⑥

☺ ゆき 🕓 5月11日　11:38
📄 Re: 駅についた！
・・・・・・・・・・・・・・
まり、二つ目の信号だから注意して
ね。わたしも ちょっとおくれたけ
ど、ついたよ。えみとまっているか
らね ☆
おいしいランチを食べにいこう〜♪

1. Where is the meeting place?
   A. the main gate of a university
   B. the corner of a street with a traffic signal
   C. in front of a restaurant
   D. in front of a supermarket

2. Where is the prohibited area?
   A. From the right of a signal
   B. From the left of a signal
   C. From the second signal
   D. From the third signal

3. Why is there a prohibited area?
   A. bridge under construction
   B. road under construction
   C. subway under construction
   D. building under construction

4. Choose the one that reflects the text.
   A. Neither a car nor a person can pass through the "Closed to Traffic" area.
   B. When you turn at a signal on the right, there is a supermarket.
   C. Emi and Yuki came to the appointed place on time.
   D. Three people are going to eat lunch now.

Where Is the Emergency Exit?

非常口はどこですか

In public places, there are many signs calling your attention to safety. Upon entering hotels, movie theaters, convention halls, buses or trains, you should locate the 非常口. A 非常電話 is installed in elevators and highway emergency parking areas. The sign 禁煙 is seen in stations, restaurants, theaters, hospitals and other public places. Learn the meanings of these signs so you can pay attention to them.

1 ▶ Introductory Quiz

Look at the illustration below and refer to the words in **Vocabulary**. Then try the following quiz.

Mr. Lee wants to smoke, but he must avoid nonsmoking areas. Read the signs below, and advise Mr. Lee.

Choose the correct answers.

1. リーさんが、大きい木の下のベンチで、たばこをすっていた時、「そこで、たばこをすわないでください。

   (a. あぶない　　b. ひじょうに　　c. しょうか) ですから。」と、そばにいる人が注意しました。

2. 「火気厳禁」のサインの前で、リーさんは道にたばこをすてました。*かみくずに火がついて、火事になりそうです。リーさんは、どうすればいいですか。　　(*waste paper)

   a. 右と左を確認する。

   b. 非常電話で電話する。

   c. 非常口に行く。

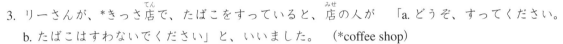

3. リーさんが、*きっさ店で、たばこをすっていると、店の人が　「a. どうぞ、すってください。

   b. たばこはすわないでください」と、いいました。　(*coffee shop)

4. それでは、リーさんは、どこでたばこをすったらいいでしょうか。

   a. 大きい木の下のベンチで　　b. きっさ店のそばのベンチで　　c. きっさ店の中で

5. リーさんが歩いて行くと、「左右確認」というサインがありました。それは、どんな*意味ですか。

   (*meaning)

   a. 右と左、どちらに行ってもいい　　b. 右にも左にも行ってはいけない　　c. 右と左をよくみてから行く

2 ▶ Vocabulary

Study the readings and meanings of these words to help you understand the **Introductory Quiz**.

1.	危険	き けん	**kiken**	Danger
2.	非常に	ひ じょう に	**hijō ni**	very, unusually
3.	消火	しょう か	**shōka**	fire extinguishing
4.	消火器	しょう か き	**shōka ki**	fire extinguisher
5.	火気厳禁	か き げん きん	**kaki genkin**	Caution: Flammables
6.	右	みぎ	**migi**	right
7.	左	ひだり	**hidari**	left
8.	非常電話	ひ じょう でん わ	**hijō denwa**	emergency telephone
9.	非常口	ひ じょう ぐち	**hijō guchi**	emergency exit
10.	禁煙	きん えん	**kin'en**	No Smoking
11.	左右確認	さ ゆう かく にん	**sayū kakunin**	Look Left and Right

3 ▶ New Characters

Eight characters are introduced in this lesson. Use the explanations to help you understand and remember the characters. Study the compound words to increase your vocabulary.

気　危　険　非　消　煙　左　右

170 気	ki キ gas; spirit, mood	ノ	⌒	⌐	气	気	気	

気 derives from 氣, which combines 气 breath coming out of a mouth and 米 rice (cf. 160 料). Thus 氣, or 気, indicates steam rising up from cooking rice, suggesting gas. An associated meaning is mood, which is as intangible as gas.

火気厳禁	かきげんきん	**kaki genkin**	Caution: Flammables
電気	でんき	**denki**	electricity
人気	にんき	**ninki**	popularity
空気	くうき	**kūki**	air
天気	てんき	**tenki**	weather
気体	きたい	**kitai**	gaseous body, gas
気分	きぶん	**kibun**	mood
気持(ち)	きもち	**kimochi**	feeling

171 危	abu-nai, ki あぶ・ない、キ dangerous	ノ	⼑	⼓	产	产	危	

厃 represents a man kneeling on the top of a cliff, and 㔾 another man at the bottom. This is dangerous, since the former may fall, and the latter may be squashed.

危ない	あぶない	**abunai**	dangerous, risky
危険な	きけんな	**kiken na**	dangerous, risky

172 険	ken ケン steep; harsh	⼄	⻆	⻏	⻏′	⻏⌒	⻏⌒	険
		险	险	険				

険 derives from 險, which combines 阝 piled-up stones (cf. 156 際), 人 cover or collect, 口口 many mouths, and 从 many people. The combination 險 or 険 suggests collecting many things and piling them up until they form a harsh, steep mountain.

危険な	きけんな	**kiken na**	dangerous, risky
高電圧危険	こうでんあつ きけん	**kō den'atsu kiken**	Danger: High Voltage

173 非	**hi** ヒ non-, un- (prefix)	ノ	ナ	ヺ	ヺ	ヺ	非	非	非	非

非 represents the two wings of a bird stretching out in opposite directions. "Not the same" and "not so" are associated meanings. 非 is often used like the prefixes non- and un-.

非常に	ひじょうに	**hijō ni**	very, unusually, greatly
非常口	ひじょうぐち	**hijō guchi**	emergency exit
非常電話	ひじょうでんわ	**hijō denwa**	emergency telephone
非常ベル	ひじょうベル	**hijō beru**	emergency bell/buzzer
非売品	ひばいひん	**hibai hin**	article not for sale

174 消	**ke-su, shō** け・す、ショウ put out, extinguish	丶	⺀	⺲	氵	氵	氵	沪	消
		消	消						

肖 was originally written 肖, which indicated cutting 月 meat (cf. 226 肉) into 小 smaller pieces. Combined with 氵 water, 消 suggests a stream of water getting smaller and finally disappearing.

消す	けす	**kesu**	to put out, to extinguish; to switch off; to erase
消しゴム	けしゴム	**keshi gomu**	pencil eraser
取(り)消(し)	とりけし	**torikeshi**	cancellation
消火器	しょうかき	**shōka ki**	fire extinguisher
消費する	しょうひする	**shōhi suru**	to consume
消防車	しょうぼうしゃ	**shōbō sha**	fire engine

175 煙	**kemuri, en** けむり、エン smoke	丶	⺀	⺲	火	炉	炉	炉	煙
		煙	煙	煙	煙	煙			

In ancient times, people lit 火 fires in the evening when the sun was just above the 土 ground or horizon in the 西 west. Fire is associated with 煙 smoke.

煙	けむり	**kemuri**	smoke
禁煙する	きんえんする	**kin'en suru**	to quit smoking
終日禁煙	しゅうじつきんえん	**shūjitsu kin'en**	No Smoking Any Time
禁煙車	きんえんしゃ	**kin'en sha**	nonsmoking car
禁煙席	きんえんせき	**kin'en seki**	nonsmoking seat/table
喫煙席	きつえんせき	**kitsuen seki**	smoking seat
喫煙室	きつえんしつ	**kitsuen shitsu**	smoking room

176 左	**hidari, sa** ひだり、サ left	一	ナ	ナ	左	左			

左 combines ナ hand (cf. 85 手) and エ carpenter's ruler (cf. 43). A carpenter usually holds a ruler with his left hand so that he can draw with his right. Thus 左 means left.

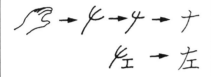

左	ひだり	**hidari**	left
左手	ひだりて	**hidarite**	left hand

左側	ひだりがわ	**hidari gawa**	the left side
左折禁止	させつきんし	**sasetsu kinshi**	No Left Turn

177 右	**migi, yū, u** みぎ、ユウ、ウ right	ノ	ナ	ナ	右	右			

右 combines ナ hand and ロ mouth (cf. 107), indicating eating with one's hand. Since most people eat with their right hands, 右 has come to mean right.

右	みぎ	**migi**	right
右手	みぎて	**migite**	right hand
左右確認	さゆうかくにん	**sayū kakunin**	Look Left and Right

右側	みぎがわ	**migi gawa**	the right side
右折禁止	うせつきんし	**usetsu kinshi**	No Right Turn

4 ▶ Practice

I. Write the readings of the following kanji in hiragana.

1. 危険 2. 非常電話 3. 消火 4. 火気厳禁
5. 禁煙 6. 左右確認 7. 電気 8. 非常に
9. 取消し 10. 煙
11. 危ないですから、気をつけてください。
12. 火事の時は、非常口から出てください。
13. 消火器で、火を消します。
14. 地下鉄の駅は、終日禁煙です。
15. 左と右をよくみてから、わたってください。

II. Fill in the blanks with appropriate kanji.

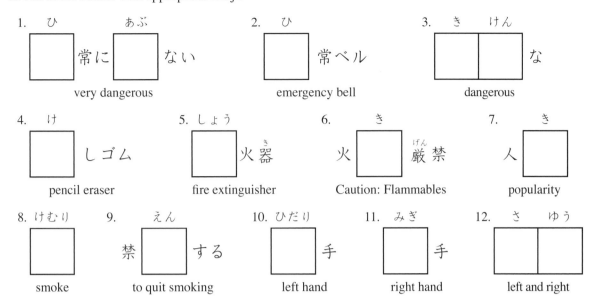

1. ひ [ ] 常に あぶ [ ] ない
very dangerous

2. ひ [ ] 常ベル
emergency bell

3. き [ ] けん [ ] な
dangerous

4. け [ ] しゴム
pencil eraser

5. しょう [ ] 火器 き
fire extinguisher

6. 火 き [ ] 厳 げん 禁
Caution: Flammables

7. 人 き [ ]
popularity

8. けむり [ ]
smoke

9. 禁 えん [ ] する
to quit smoking

10. ひだり [ ] 手
left hand

11. みぎ [ ] 手
right hand

12. さ [ ] ゆう [ ]
left and right

5 ▸ Advanced Placement Exam Practice Questions

Read the passage below and choose the best answers to the questions.

リーさんのかよっている学校で先日¹避難訓練がありました。非常ベルがなって、学校全部にアナウンスがありました。

「いまから¹避難訓練をおこないます。2かい科学室で火事が発生しました。あわてないで、まわりの火の確認をしてください。エレベーターはぜったいに使用しないでください。非常に危険です。非常かいだんを使って、正面入口にあつまってください。煙をさけるために口にハンカチやタオルをあてて、左右を確認しながら歩いてください。」

学生がみんな正面入口にあつまってから、学年ごとに分かれて、消火器を使って火を消す練習もしました。

¹避難訓練: evacuation drill, safety exercise

1. Which of the following best summarizes the text?
   A. A fire broke out at school.
   B. An emergency bell rang by accident and the students left the school building.
   C. An evacuation drill was performed throughout the entire school.
   D. The announcement system of the school was tested.

2. According to the announcement, where did the fire occur?
   A. A fire broke out on the emergency staircase.
   B. A fire broke out in the science room.
   C. A fire occurred in front of the main entrance.
   D. A fire occurred in the elevator.

3. What announcement was given?
   A. Stay away from the main entrance, because there is smoke.
   B. In order to escape quickly, students should use an elevator.
   C. Don't use the stairs, because they are very dangerous.
   D. Stay calm and walk down the stairs to the main entrance carefully.

4. Which one correctly explains the fire-fighting exercise?
   A. After verifying the departure of all students, the fire-fighting drill was performed.
   B. The fire-fighting drill was performed before the students had left the building.
   C. Instructions on how to use the fire extinguisher were given while students were escaping from the building.
   D. Instructions on how to use the fire extinguisher were given to all grades of students together.

REVIEW EXERCISE: LESSONS 11–14

I. Fill in the blanks with appropriate kanji or their corresponding letters from the list below.

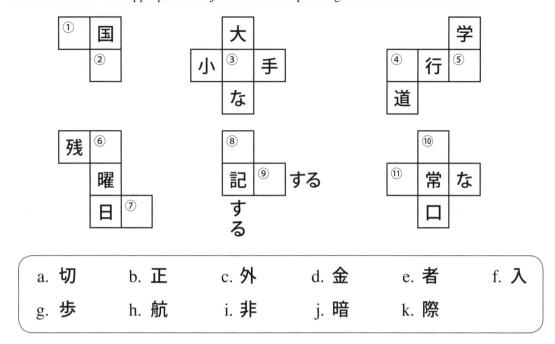

| a. 切 | b. 正 | c. 外 | d. 金 | e. 者 | f. 入 |
| g. 歩 | h. 航 | i. 非 | j. 暗 | k. 際 | |

II.   Read the following sentences and circle the correct answers.

1. (a. 郵便局   b. 電話局) へ行って、国のかぞくに速達を出しました。

2. ピーターさんは、いま (a. 外出中   b. 行き止まり) で、いません。

3. (a. 取り引き   b. 引き出し) のボタンを押します。それから、出てきたお金を取ります。

4. (a. 火気   b. 人気) のある所で、*ガソリンを扱ってはいけません。   (*gasoline)

5. 手をあげたら、タクシーが (a. 立   b. 止) まりました。

6. すみませんが、しごとの間だけ、子どもを (a. 預かって   b. 認めて) くれませんか。

137

Campus Map

キャンパス・マップ

Including junior colleges, there are approximately 1,000 universities in Japan. While mostly concentrated in large cities, some universities have recently moved their campuses into more rural areas, and a few major universities have decentralized their campuses by locating various departments in different areas. Most campus facilities include libraries, co-op stores, gymnasiums, swimming pools, and cafeterias, and some have university hospitals attached to their medical schools. Housing for faculty, staff, and students, however, tends to be very limited.

1 ▶ Introductory Quiz

Look at the illustration opposite and refer to the words in **Vocabulary**. Then try the following quiz.

Opposite is a campus map of Mr. Lee's university and a photograph of a sign showing the main gate's opening and closing times. While looking at the map and sign, choose the correct answers for the following questions.

1. これは大学の地図です。リーさんは、まい日（a. せいもん　b. なかもん）から入ります。そして、自分のけんきゅうしつのある（a. 1号館　b. 11号館）へ行きます。それから、（a. 1号館　b. 11号館）へ行って、日本語をべんきょうします。

2. ひるごはんは、大講堂の地下にある（a. ちゅうおうしょくどう　b. せいきょう）でたべます。午後は、本部の（a. 西　b. 東）にあるとしょかんへ行って、本やざっしをよみます。

3. グラウンドの南には（a. 大学病院　b. 学生会館）があって、ここでは、よく留学生のパーティーがあります。

4. 西門のそばにある（a. 国際交流室　b. 留学生センター）でも、いろいろな国の留学生が日本語をべんきょうしています。

5. 本やノートをかうときは、（a. 生協　b. 食堂）へ行きます。

6. びょうきになった時は、（a. 大学病院　b. 大講堂）へ行きます。それは、グラウンドの（a. 北　b. 南）にある大きなたてものです。

7. 正門は、（a. 10時半　b. 0時半）にしまりますから、それまでに大学を出ます。

138

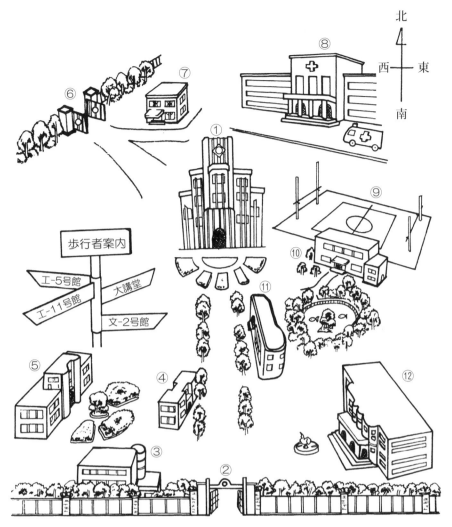

① 大講堂（中央食堂）

② 正門

③ 工学部11号館（日本語教室）

④ 本部（国際交流室）

⑤ 工学部1号館（リーさんの研究室）

⑥ 西門

⑦ 留学生センター

⑧ 大学病院

⑨ グラウンド

⑩ 学生会館

⑪ 文学部2号館（生協）

⑫ 図書館

The parentheses indicate places in the buildings.

2 ▶ Vocabulary

Study the readings and meanings of these words to help you understand the **Introductory Quiz**.

1. 地図 　　　　　 ち　ず　　　　　　　　　 **chizu** 　　　　　 map
2. 正門 　　　　　 せい　もん　　　　　　　 **seimon** 　　　　 main gate
3. 中門 　　　　　 なか　もん　　　　　　　 **nakamon** 　　　 middle gate
4. 西門 　　　　　 にし　もん　　　　　　　 **nishimon** 　　　 west gate
5. ～号館 　　　　 ～ ごう　かん　　　　　 **~gō kan** 　　　 Building no. ~
6. 研究室 　　　　 けん　きゅう　しつ　　　 **kenkyū shitsu** 　 research laboratory
7. 日本語教室 　　 に　ほん　ご　きょう　しつ 　**nihongo kyōshitsu** 　Japanese language classroom
8. 大講堂 　　　　 だい　こう　どう　　　　 **daikōdō** 　　　 large auditorium
9. 地下 　　　　　 ち　か　　　　　　　　 **chika** 　　　　　 underground
10. 中央食堂 　　　 ちゅう　おう　しょく　どう 　**chūō shokudō** 　 main cafeteria
11. 生協 　　　　　 せい　きょう　　　　　　 **seikyō** 　　　　 co-op
12. 本部 　　　　　 ほん　ぶ　　　　　　　 **hombu** 　　　　 headquarters
13. 図書館 　　　　 と　しょ　かん　　　　　 **toshokan** 　　　 library
14. グラウンド　　　　　　　　　　　　　 **guraundo** 　　　 athletic field
15. 大学病院 　　　 だい　がく　びょう　いん 　**daigaku byōin** 　 university hospital
16. 学生会館 　　　 がく　せい　かい　かん　 **gakusei kaikan** 　 student hall
17. 国際交流室 　　 こく　さい　こう　りゅう　しつ 　**kokusai kōryū shitsu** 　International Exchange Office
18. 留学生センター りゅう　がく　せい　センター 　**ryūgakusei sentā** 　Foreign Students' Center
19. 開門 　　　　　 かい　もん　　　　　　　 **kaimon** 　　　　 gate opening
20. 閉門 　　　　　 へい　もん　　　　　　　 **heimon** 　　　　 gate closing

3 ▶ New Characters

Nine characters are introduced in this lesson. Use the explanations to help you understand and remember the characters. Study the compound words to increase your vocabulary.

講 堂 食 門 館 会 協 図 閉

178 講 — kō / コウ — lecture, study

ヽ	二	ニ	言	言	言	言	言	計
計	詳	講	諅	講	講	講	講	

講 combines 言 speak and 冓, which represents two identical wooden frames and indicates shared common elements. Thus 講 means lecture, during which someone speaks to listeners about a subject of common interest.

開講する	かいこうする	**kaikō suru**	to open/begin a new course
休講	きゅうこう	**kyūkō**	no lecture
講師	こうし	**kōshi**	lecturer
講演する	こうえんする	**kōen suru**	to give a lecture, to deliver an address
講座	こうざ	**kōza**	lecture course; professorial chair
講習会	こうしゅうかい	**kōshū kai**	short training course

179 堂 — dō / ドウ — big building, hall

ﾉ	ﾘ	ﾂ	ﾟ	严	労	芦	兴
堂	堂	堂					

堂 combines 尚 smoke rising up high above a stove (cf. 159 常) and 土 ground. Thus 堂 means tall building on the ground.

講堂	こうどう	**kōdō**	auditorium
公会堂	こうかいどう	**kōkaidō**	public/town hall
国会議事堂	こっかいぎじどう	**kokkai gijidō**	the Diet Building

180 食 — ta-beru, shoku, (sho') / た・べる、ショク、（ショッ） — eat, meal

ノ	八	八	今	今	全	負	食
食							

食 depicts a bowl of cooked rice (cf. 11 百) resting on a stand with a lid on top, and suggests meal and eating.

食べる	たべる	**taberu**	to eat
食堂	しょくどう	**shokudō**	dining room, cafeteria
食事する	しょくじする	**shokuji suru**	to have a meal
定食	ていしょく	**teishoku**	set meal
食券	しょっけん	**shokken**	meal ticket/coupon
外食する	がいしょくする	**gaishoku suru**	to eat out, to eat at a restaurant
食前	しょくぜん	**shokuzen**	before meals
食後	しょくご	**shokugo**	after meals
食間	しょっかん	**shokkan**	between meals

141

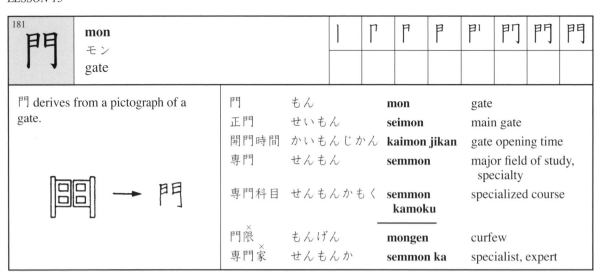

181 門	**mon** モン gate	｜	｢	｢	｢	｢¹	門	門	門

門 derives from a pictograph of a gate.	門	もん	**mon**	gate
	正門	せいもん	**seimon**	main gate
	開門時間	かいもんじかん	**kaimon jikan**	gate opening time
	専門	せんもん	**semmon**	major field of study, specialty
	専門科目	せんもんかもく	**semmon kamoku**	specialized course
	×門限	もんげん	**mongen**	curfew
	専門×家	せんもんか	**semmon ka**	specialist, expert

182 館	**kan** カン building, hall	ノ	入	仒	今	今	今	飠	食
		食'	食'	飦	飦	飵	飵	館	館

館 combines 飠 (a variation of 食) eat, and 官, a rich bureaucrat with a puffed-up stomach in a house. 館 formerly meant a building where bureaucrats ate, and now has come to mean public building or hall.	一号館	いちごうかん	**ichigō kan**	Building no. 1
	大使館	たいしかん	**taishi kan**	embassy
	本館	ほんかん	**honkan**	main building
	分館	ぶんかん	**bunkan**	branch building, annex
	×別館	べっかん	**bekkan**	annex
	×旅館	りょかん	**ryokan**	Japanese-style inn
	×映画×館	えいがかん	**eiga kan**	movie theater
	×美術×館	びじゅつかん	**bijutsu kan**	art museum/gallery

183 会	**a-u, kai** あ・う、カイ meet, meeting, association	ノ	入	스	숙	会	会		

会 combines 스 collect or gather, and 云 being surrounded on all four sides. From these concepts, 会 has come to mean meet, meeting, or association.	会う	あう	**au**	to meet/see
	学会	がっかい	**gakkai**	academic meeting; academic society
	国会	こっかい	**kokkai**	the Diet
	学生会館	がくせいかいかん	**gakusei kaikan**	student hall
	×講演会	こうえんかい	**kōen kai**	lecture meeting
	会社	かいしゃ	**kaisha**	company, firm
	社会	しゃかい	**shakai**	society
	会×員	かいいん	**kaiin**	member of a society/association/club

184 協	**kyō** キョウ cooperation	丨	十	忄	忭	协	协	協	協

十 ten suggests adding five and five, and 力 indicates power or force (cf. 67 男). Thus 協 can be thought of as combining three forces together in an act of cooperation.

生協	せいきょう	**seikyō**	co-op
協会	きょうかい	**kyōkai**	society, association
アジア学生 協会	アジアがくせい きょうかい	**Ajia Gakusei Kyōkai**	Asian Students' Association
協力する	きょうりょく する	**kyōryoku suru**	to cooperate
国際協力	こくさい きょうりょく	**kokusai kyōryoku**	international cooperation

185 図	**zu, to** ズ、ト drawing, diagram	丨	冂	冂	冂	図	図	図	

図 derives from 圖, which combines 啚 a grain storehouse and farm land, and 囗 paper. 圖, or 図, originally indicated a map drawn on a sheet of paper, and came to mean drawing or diagram in general.

図	ず	**zu**	figure, diagram
図-3	ずーさん	**zu-san**	Figure 3
地図	ちず	**chizu**	map
案内図	あんないず	**annaizu**	guide/information map
図書館	としょかん	**tosho kan**	library
図表	ずひょう	**zuhyō**	charts, figures, and tables
図面	ずめん	**zumen**	drawing

186 閉	**shi-maru, shi-meru, hei** し・まる、し・める、ヘイ close, shut	丨	冂	冂	冃	冃	門	門	門
		門	閉	閉					

閉 represents a gate with a cross bar that closes to prevent people from entering.

閉まる	しまる	**shimaru**	to close (vi.)
閉める	しめる	**shimeru**	to close (vt.)
閉会する	へいかい する	**heikai suru**	to close a meeting; for a meeting to close
閉門時間	へいもん じかん	**heimon jikan**	gate closing time
閉館する	へいかん する	**heikan suru**	to close (a library, hall, etc.)
開閉	かいへい	**kaihei**	opening and shutting
閉会式	へいかいしき	**heikai shiki**	closing ceremony

4 ▶ Practice

I. Write the readings of the following kanji in hiragana.

1. 地 図　　　　　2. 西 門　　　　　3. ～ 号 館　　　　4. 大 講 堂
5. 中 央 食 堂　　6. 生 協　　　　　7. 図 書 館　　　　8. 学 生 会 館
9. 閉 門　　　　　10. 休 講　　　　11. 食 事　　　　　12. 食 券
13. 専 門　　　　14. 本 館　　　　15. 国 会　　　　　16. 協 会
17. 案 内 図　　　18. 閉 会 す る
19. まい 日 、 生 協 の 食 堂 で 、 ひ る ご は ん を 食 べ ま す 。
20. よ る は 、 門 を か な ら ず 閉 め て く だ さ い 。
21. 正 門 は 、 午 後 十 時 に 閉 ま り ま す 。
22. で は あ し た 、 大 使 館 で 会 い ま し ょ う 。

II. Fill in the blanks with appropriate kanji.

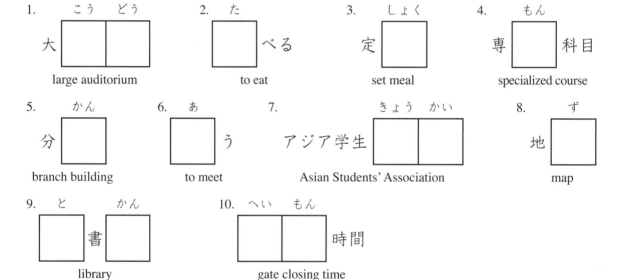

1. こう どう
大 ☐ ☐
large auditorium

2. た
☐ べる
to eat

3. しょく
定 ☐
set meal

4. もん
専 ☐ 科目
specialized course

5. かん
分 ☐
branch building

6. あ
☐ う
to meet

7. きょう かい
アジア学生 ☐ ☐
Asian Students' Association

8. ず
地 ☐
map

9. と かん
☐ 書 ☐
library

10. へい もん
☐ ☐ 時間
gate closing time

5 ▶ Advanced Placement Exam Practice Questions

A Japanese tutor is showing new students around the campus of a university. Read the passage and choose the best answers to the questions.

　ここが大講堂です。この地下には中央食堂と生協があります。とてもやすいので、学生はよく食べにきます。食堂と生協は文学部二号館にもあります。生協もあとで行きましょう。いろいろなものがあるので、便利ですよ。大講堂の東にグラウンドがあって、[1]体育館やプールもあります。グラウンドの南にある学生会館では、よく留学生のパーティーがあります。あしたのパーティーも学生会館ですから、いっしょに行きましょう。

大講堂の西にある西門のちかくに留学生センターがあります。そこでいろいろな国の留学生が勉強しています。もちろん、図書館でも勉強できます。図書館は正門の東にあります。正門は午前七時に開きます。

みなさんの日本語クラスは工学部一号館にありますから、これから行ってみましょう。工学部一号館は正門の西にあります。大きないちょうの木が一号館の前にあるので、すぐにわかりますよ。

¹体育館: gymnasium

1. There is one more co-op other than at the large auditorium. Where is the other?
   A. the basement of a student hall
   B. the back of the library
   C. near the west gate
   D. the Department of Literature, Building no. 2

2. Where is the library?
   A. south of the sports ground
   B. east of the main gate
   C. behind a student hall
   D. near the west gate

3. Which is the nearest to their Japanese classroom?
   A. a big tree
   B. the west gate
   C. sports field
   D. the co-op

4. Choose the item that reflects the text.
   A. Tomorrow's party will be held at the foreign students' center.
   B. The main gate is opened at 6:00 A.M.
   C. There is a main cafeteria in the basement of a large auditorium.
   D. A Japanese class is in the building of the Department of Literature.

5. Choose the item that is not stated in the text.
   A. The main cafeteria is popular among students.
   B. New students also attend a party on the next day.
   C. Now students are in front of a large auditorium, and next they'll go to a Japanese class.
   D. There is a big swimming pool in front of the Department of Engineering, Building no.1.

At the University

大学のたてものの中

As you'd expect, many kinds of rooms are found in Japanese university buildings; for example, lecture rooms, conference rooms, study rooms and offices. The names of the rooms are often written on signs in kanji. This lesson will help you recognize kanji for these rooms.

1 ▶ Introductory Quiz

Look at the illustration below and refer to the words in **Vocabulary**. Then try the following quiz.

I.   Here is the first floor layout of a university building where Mr. Lee studies. While looking at the floor plan, choose the correct answers to the questions at the top of the facing page.

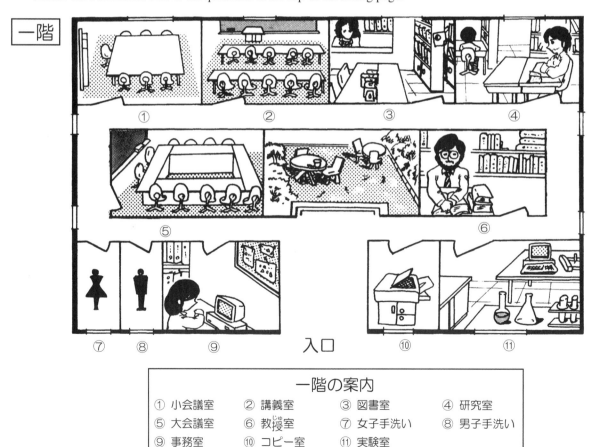

一階

入口

一階の案内

① 小会議室	② 講義室	③ 図書室	④ 研究室
⑤ 大会議室	⑥ 教授室	⑦ 女子手洗い	⑧ 男子手洗い
⑨ 事務室	⑩ コピー室	⑪ 実験室	

1. 入口の左には、（a. じむ室　b. じっけん室）があります。

2. しょうかいぎ室のとなりは、（a. としょ室　b. こうぎ室）です。

3. 一階には、（a. けんきゅう室　b. しょくどう）はありません。

4. 学生は、（a. 大会議室　b. 研究室）でべんきょうします。

5. 専門のクラスは、（a. 講義室　b. 事務室）であります。

6. 本やざっしがよみたい時は、（a. 実験室　b. 図書室）へ行けばいいです。

II. Room names are usually posted over doors. The signs hanging on the doors show whether each room is vacant or occupied. Look at the picture below and choose the correct answers to the following questions.

1. 講義室と研究室の間に、（a. としょ室　　b. しょうかいぎ室）があります。

2. 小会議室は、いま（a. 使えます。　　b. 使えません。）

3. 講義室は、いま（a. あいています。　　b. 使っています。）

III. Combine these kanji to make compounds, and then write the kanji in the spaces below.

A.
会　休　講
館　議　義
事　務　室

A.　1. Ex. 会議室 _____

　　2. _____

　　3. _____

　　4. _____

　　5. _____

B.
一　番　研
階　号　究
実　験　室

B.　1. _____

　　2. _____

　　3. _____

　　4. _____

　　5. _____

2 ▶ Vocabulary

Study the readings and meanings of these words to help you understand the **Introductory Quiz**.

1. 一階	いっかい	**ikkai**	the 1st floor
2. 研究室	けんきゅうしつ	**kenkyū shitsu**	research laboratory, research unit
3. 事務室	じむしつ	**jimu shitsu**	administrative office
4. 実験室	じっけんしつ	**jikken shitsu**	laboratory for experiments
5. 会議室	かいぎしつ	**kaigi shitsu**	conference room
6. 図書室	としょしつ	**tosho shitsu**	library room
7. 講義室	こうぎしつ	**kōgi shitsu**	lecture room
8. 教授室	きょうじゅしつ	**kyōju shitsu**	professor's office
9. 空室	くうしつ	**kūshitsu**	Vacant Room
10. 使用中	しようちゅう	**shiyō chū**	Occupied
11. コピー室	コピーしつ	**kopī shitsu**	photocopy room

3 ▶ New Characters

Nine characters are introduced in this lesson. Use the explanations to help you understand and remember the characters. Study the compound words to increase your vocabulary.

階　義　議　室　研　究　務　実　験

187 階	**kai, (gai)** カイ、（ガイ） stair, story; rank	７	３	阝	阝¯	阝ヒ	阝ヒ˙	阝比	阝比
		陟	階	階	階				

階 combines 阝 stone hedge, 比 two men lined up, and 白 modified from 自 oneself (cf. 99). In ancient times, people piled up stones to make stairs. Rank is an associated meaning. By itself 皆 means everybody.

四階	よんかい	**yonkai**	the 4th floor
地下一階	ちかいっかい	**chika ikkai**	the 1st basement
三階	さんがい	**sangai**	the 3rd floor
階段	かいだん	**kaidan**	staircase, stairs
地階	ちかい	**chikai**	basement

188 義

gi
ギ
justice, righteousness

丶	`	⺷	⺷	羊	羊	差
羊	美	義	義	義		

義 combines 羊 beautiful or right (cf. 130 着), and 我, a hand holding a weapon to protect oneself, meaning I. Thus 義 means a right way of doing something, which is related to the idea of justice.

講義する	こうぎする	**kōgi suru**	to give a lecture
主義	しゅぎ	**shugi**	principle, -ism
定義する	ていぎする	**teigi suru**	to define
意義	いぎ	**igi**	meaning, significance
正義	せいぎ	**seigi**	justice
義理	ぎり	**giri**	social duty, obligation; in-law

189 議

gi
ギ
deliberate, discuss

丶	亠	言	言	言	言	言	言	言	誩
詳	詳	誩	議	議	議	議	議	議	議

議, which combines 言 speak and 義 justice or righteousness, means discussing and deliberating to come to right conclusions.

会議	かいぎ	**kaigi**	meeting, conference
国際会議	こくさい かいぎ	**kokusai kaigi**	international conference
議論する	ぎろんする	**giron suru**	to argue, to discuss
議題	ぎだい	**gidai**	subject for discussion, agenda
議長	ぎちょう	**gichō**	chairperson
議会	ぎかい	**gikai**	assembly, the Diet, Congress, Parliament
議員	ぎいん	**giin**	member of an assembly/ the Diet/Congress/ Parliament

190 室

shitsu
シツ
room

丶	⸍	宀	宀	宏	宏	宏	室
室							

室 combines 宀 house and 至 bird diving down to the ground, meaning reaching a goal. Thus 室 means room, which can be thought of as the goal to reach in a house.

会議室	かいぎしつ	**kaigi shitsu**	conference room
図書室	としょしつ	**tosho shitsu**	library room
講義室	こうぎしつ	**kōgi shitsu**	lecture room
空室	くうしつ	**kūshitsu**	vacant room
地下室	ちかしつ	**chika shitsu**	basement
五号室	ごごうしつ	**gogō shitsu**	room no. 5
室内	しつない	**shitsunai**	indoor, inside the room
浴室	よくしつ	**yokushitsu**	bathroom

191 研	ken ケン polish, sharpen	一	丁	石	石	石	石	矴	研
		研							

研, which combines 石 stone (cf. 139 確) and 幵 make things even, indicates making something smooth with a stone, namely, polishing or sharpening.

羊羊 → 开 → 开

~研	~けん	**~ken**	abbreviation for ~研究所/室 (~ Research Institute/ Laboratory)
研修生	けんしゅうせい	**kenshū sei**	trainee

---

192 究	kyū キュウ investigate	'	''	宀	宀	究	究	究

究 combines 宀 hole (cf. 158 空) and 九 nine, the number that ends the series of single digits. Thus 究 means searching or investigating an unknown space to its end.

研究する	けんきゅうする	**kenkyū suru**	to research, to investigate
研究室	けんきゅうしつ	**kenkyū shitsu**	research laboratory; research unit
研究生	けんきゅうせい	**kenkyū sei**	research student
研究所	けんきゅうじょ	**kenkyū jo**	research institute
研究会	けんきゅうかい	**kenkyū kai**	research society/ meeting
研究員	けんきゅういん	**kenkyū in**	research fellow

---

193 務	mu ム work; serve	フ	マ	ヌ	予	矛	矛	矛	矛
		務	務	務					

務 combines 矛 halberd, 力 power (cf. 67 男), and 夂, indicating an action (cf. 47 攻). Fighting powerfully with a halberd was an important duty of warriors. From this association, 務 came to mean work in general.

事務室	じむしつ	**jimu shitsu**	office, administrative office
事務所	じむしょ	**jimu sho**	office
義務教育	ぎむきょういく	**gimu kyōiku**	compulsory education
公務員	こうむいん	**kōmuin**	government employee, public servant
外務省	がいむしょう	**gaimushō**	Ministry of Foreign Affairs
法務省	ほうむしょう	**hōmushō**	Ministry of Justice
勤務先	きんむさき	**kimmu saki**	one's place of work

194 実	**mi, jitsu, (ji')** み、ジツ、（ジッ） fruit; truth, actuality	`	`	宀	宀	宇	宇	宇	実

実 derives from 實, which combines 宀 house, 毌 or 田 rice paddy (cf. 88), and 貝 money (cf. 200 費). Thus 實 or 実 implies a fruitful harvest, which means fruit or nuts as well as actual money for a household. Truth is an associated meaning.

事実	じじつ	**jijitsu**	fact
実際	じっさい	**jissai**	fact, reality; actually
木の実	きのみ	**kinomi**	nut
実物	じつぶつ	**jitsubutsu**	real/actual thing
実用	じつよう	**jitsuyō**	practical use
×実習する	じっしゅう する	**jisshū suru**	to have practical training
実行する	じっこう する	**jikkō suru**	to execute, to implement

195 験	**ken** ケン test, examine	❘	厂	Π	厈	厍	馬	馬	馬	馬
		馬	馭	駖	駖	駖	験	験	験	験

験 derives from 驗, which combines 馬 horse (cf. 70 駅) and 僉 collect many things (cf. 172 険). The ancient Chinese examined and tested many horses before buying one.

実験する	じっけん する	**jikken suru**	to conduct an experiment
実験室	じっけん しつ	**jikken shitsu**	laboratory for experiments
×試験	しけん	**shiken**	text, examination
×経験する	けいけん する	**keiken suru**	to experience, to go through
×体験する	たいけん する	**taiken suru**	to experience personally, to go through

4 ▶ Practice

I. Write the readings of the following kanji in hiragana.

1. 事 務 室   2. 実 験 室   3. 講 義 室   4. 一 階

5. 研 究 室   6. 三 階   7. 研 究 生   8. 事 実

9. 実 験 す る   10. 食 堂 は 、 地 下 二 階 に あ り ま す 。

11. 来 月 、 京 都 で 国 際 会 議 が あ り ま す 。

12. い ま 、 大 会 議 室 は 使 用 中 で す が 、 小 会 議 室 は 空 室 で す 。

13. そ れ は 、 実 際 に あ っ た こ と で す 。

II. Fill in the blanks with appropriate kanji.

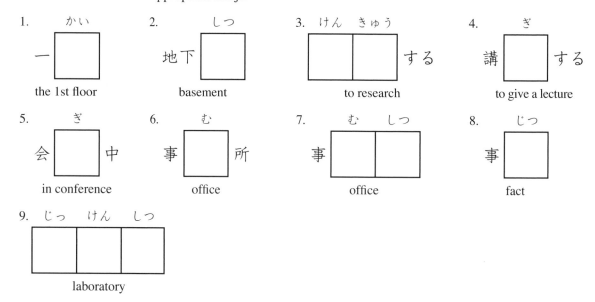

1. かい
一☐
the 1st floor

2. しつ
地下☐
basement

3. けん きゅう
☐☐する
to research

4. ぎ
講☐する
to give a lecture

5. ぎ
会☐中
in conference

6. む
事☐所
office

7. む しつ
事☐☐
office

8. じつ
事☐
fact

9. じっ けん しつ
☐☐☐
laboratory

5 ▸ Advanced Placement Exam Practice Questions

Read the conversation that the professor's secretary had with a university staff member, first on the phone and then in a room. Then answer the following questions.

（電話で）

[1]秘書： はい、田中研究室です。

大木： 事務の大木です。こちらは二階の第二会議室から電話しているんですが、田中教授はいらっしゃいますか。

秘書： 教授は3時間目の講義からまだもどりませんが …

大木： 3時間目は2時50分に終わりますよね、講義はどちらで？

秘書： 講義室です。

大木： 講義室ならこの階ですよね、会議が3時からなのですが、まだいらっしゃらないんです。

秘書： ちょっとおまちください。スケジュールを確認します。

教授もわかっているはずです。会議の [2]資料もコピーしましたし …

あ、実験室のつくえのことで、事務室へ行かなければといっていたわ。

大木： え、そうですか。じゃ、おなじ階だから事務室からそのまま第一会議室へ行かれたのかなあ。

秘書： わたし第一会議室をみてきます。

大木： はい、おねがいします。

（第二会議室で）

秘書：教授はまだいらっしゃいませんか。

第一会議室は空室になっていました。

大木：どうしたんだろう。じゃ、30分まではまちましょう。

秘書：もうしわけありません。

¹秘書: secretary
²資料: documents

1. Professor Tanaka's research laboratory
    A. is on the first floor.
    B. is on the second floor.
    C. is on the same floor as conference room #2.
    D. We don't know what floor it is on.

2. Where was Professor Tanaka supposed to go after the lecture, according to the understanding of the secretary?
    A. the laboratory for experiments.
    B. the library room.
    C. the administrative office.
    D. the photocopy room.

3. The administrative office is
    A. next door to the laboratory for experiments.
    B. on the same floor as conference room #1.
    C. next door to the photocopy room.
    D. on the same floor as conference room #2.

4. When the secretary went to conference room #1,
    A. it was occupied.
    B. Professor Tanaka was there.
    C. a "vacant room" sign was on the door.
    D. it was locked.

5. What can be said about the meeting?
    A. It started as soon as they knew the Professor was missing.
    B. Even though Professor Tanaka hadn't come, it started at 3:00.
    C. It was cancelled because Professor Tanaka didn't show up at all.
    D. Whether Professor Tanaka comes or not, it starts at 3:30.

Announcements

何のお知らせですか

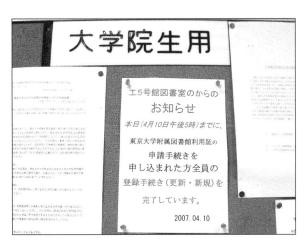

Bulletin boards contain a lot of useful information. Campus bulletin boards offer announcements like dates of final exams, when new courses start, names of scholarship recipients, and so on. Municipal offices, supermarkets, banks, and other public places also use bulletin boards for official notices and personal advertisements. Thanks to ads on bulletin boards, you can find anything from part-time jobs to bicycles at discount prices. Sometimes if you are lucky, you can even get things such as used furniture or electrical appliances for free. The community bulletin boards give you the latest news in your neighborhood and the schedules of local events.

In this lesson, you will learn how to read bulletin boards and, in the process, you may even find some useful information on the bulletin boards where you work or study.

1 ▶ Introductory Quiz

Look at the illustrations, and refer to the words in **Vocabulary**. Then try the following quiz.

I. Posted below is a notice about a lecture by Professor Brown of London University. Read the notice carefully and write the correct answers in the spaces provided.

1. ブラウン教授は、何について話しますか。

 ＿＿＿＿＿＿＿＿＿＿＿＿＿ について話します。

2. 講演をききたいのですが、どのたてものに行けばいいですか。

 ＿＿＿＿＿＿＿＿＿＿＿＿＿ に行けばよいです。

3. 四階のどのへやに行けばいいですか。

 ＿＿＿＿＿＿＿＿＿＿＿＿＿ に行けばいいです。

4. ブラウン教授の講演は何日ですか。

 ＿＿＿＿＿＿＿＿＿＿＿＿＿ です。

II. Below is a notice about a field trip to the Yokohama Bay Bridge. To join the trip you must fill in the application form. Read the notice and write the correct answers in the spaces provided.

横浜ベイブリッジ見学ツアー

日時: 3月7日（火）★ 9時出発
費用: 3,000円

行く人は申込書に記入して、
山本研究室に出して下さい。

しめ切り: 3月1日(水)

見学ツアー申込書

見学ツアーに行きます。
大学院　修士（　　　）年
　　　　博士（　　　）年

名前 _____

1. 見学ツアーは何日ですか。

_____ です。

2. お金はいくらかかりますか。

_____ かかります。

3. 見学ツアーに行きたい人はどうすればいいですか。

_____ に記入して、 _____ に出します。

4. いつまでに出さなければなりませんか。

_____ までに出さなければなりません。

5. しゅうしコースの学生も、はかせコースの学生も行けますか。

_____ 。

III. Practice filling in these forms.

Application Form for a Certificate of Student Status or Proof of Graduation

証明書交付願				
			請求年月日　平成　　年　　月　　日	
入　　　学 年　月　日	平成　　年　　月　　日 　　　　　　　　入　学	修了（見込） 年　　　月	平成　　年　　月　　修　了 　　　　　　　　　修了見込	
専　　攻	専　攻	ローマ字		
課　　程	修士　・　博士	氏　　名		印
学生証番号			年　　　　月　　　　日生	
住　　　所	（〒　　　）			
			電話　　　（　　）	
使用目的				
提　出　先				

Course Registration Form

履修科目届	
	平成　　年度　　学期
科目担当者名	
科　目　番　号	
科　目　名	単位
上記科目を申告します。	
所　　属	専　攻 修士　・　博士
学　生　証　番　号	
氏　　名	

2 ▶ Vocabulary

Study the readings and meanings of these words to help you understand the **Introductory Quiz**.

1. お知らせ	おしらせ	**oshirase**	notice
2. 教授	きょう じゅ	**kyōju**	professor
3. 講師	こう し	**kōshi**	lecturer
4. ロンドン大学	ロンドン だい がく	**Rondon daigaku**	London University
5. 講演会	こう えん かい	**kōen kai**	lecture
6. 会場	かい じょう	**kaijō**	lecture hall
7. ~番教室	~ばん きょう しつ	**~ban kyōshitsu**	classroom no. ~
8. 講演する	こう えん する	**kōen suru**	to give a lecture
9. 見学ツアー	けん がく ツアー	**kengaku tsuā**	field trip
10. 横浜ベイブリッジ	よこ はま ベイブリッジ	**Yokohama Beiburijji**	Yokohama Bay Bridge
11. 費用	ひ よう	**hiyō**	cost
12. 出発	しゅっ ぱつ	**shuppatsu**	departure
13. 山本研究室	やま もと けん きゅう しつ	**Yamamoto kenkyū shitsu**	Yamamoto Research Laboratory
14. しめ切り	しめ きり	**shimekiri**	deadline
15. 大学院	だい がく いん	**daigakuin**	graduate school
16. 修士	しゅう し	**shūshi**	master degree
17. 博士	はく し	**hakushi**	doctoral degree
18. ~証明書交付願	~しょう めい しょ こう ふ ねがい	**~shōmeisho kōfu negai**	application for ~ certificate
19. 学生証	がく せい しょう	**gakusei shō**	student ID card
20. 履修科目届	り しゅう か もく とどけ	**rishū kamoku todoke**	course registration

3 ▶ New Characters

Eleven characters are introduced in this lesson. Use the explanations to help you understand and remember the characters. Study the compound words to increase your vocabulary.

知 場 教 見 費 院 修 士 博 明 届

196 知	shi-ru, chi し・る、チ know	ノ	⺊	⻧	午	矢	矢	知	知

知, which combines 矢 arrow and 口 mouth, suggests speaking straight and accurately. In order to do so, knowledge of the subject is required.

知る	しる	**shiru**	to know
お知らせ	おしらせ	**oshirase**	information, notice
通知する	つうちする	**tsūchi suru**	to notify, to inform
知事	ちじ	**chiji**	prefectural governor
知(り)合い	しりあい	**shiriai**	acquaintance
知識	ちしき	**chishiki**	knowledge
知人	ちじん	**chijin**	acquaintance

197 場	ba, jō ば、ジョウ place	一	十	土	坿	圹	圹	垣	垣
		坦	場	場	場				

場 combines 扌(土) ground and 昜 sun rising high and shining brightly. From indicating a place where the sun shines on the ground, 場 has come to mean place in general.

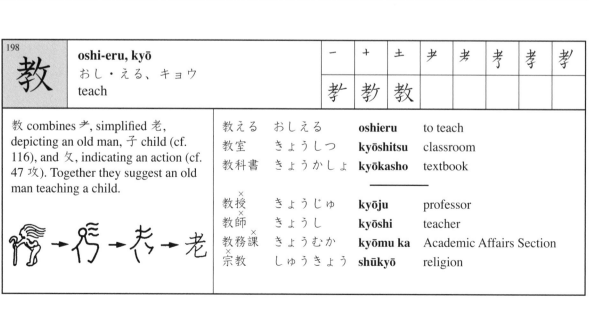

場所	ばしょ	**basho**	place, location
工場	こうじょう	**kōjō**	factory
会場	かいじょう	**kaijō**	meeting/party/lecture/ exhibition place
入場券	にゅうじょうけん	**nyūjō ken**	admission/platform ticket
場合	ばあい	**baai**	case, occasion
現場	げんば	**gemba**	the scene (of accident, etc.); work site
場内	じょうない	**jōnai**	inside the place
駐車場	ちゅうしゃじょう	**chūsha jō**	parking lot

198 教	oshi-eru, kyō おし・える、キョウ teach	一	十	土	尹	耂	考	孝	孝
		孝	教	教					

教 combines 耂, simplified 老, depicting an old man, 子 child (cf. 116), and 攵, indicating an action (cf. 47 攻). Together they suggest an old man teaching a child.

教える	おしえる	**oshieru**	to teach
教室	きょうしつ	**kyōshitsu**	classroom
教科書	きょうかしょ	**kyōkasho**	textbook
教授	きょうじゅ	**kyōju**	professor
教師	きょうし	**kyōshi**	teacher
教務課	きょうむか	**kyōmu ka**	Academic Affairs Section
宗教	しゅうきょう	**shūkyō**	religion

158

199 見

mi-ru, ken
み・る、ケン
see, watch

| 丨 | 冂 | 冂 | 月 | 目 | 貝 | 見 | |

見 combines 目 eye and 儿 legs, a reference to man. A man's eyes enable him to see.

見る	みる	**miru**	to see, to watch
見本	みほん	**mihon**	sample
見学する	けんがくする	**kengaku suru**	to visit (a factory, etc.) for study
意見	いけん	**iken**	opinion
見出し	みだし	**midashi**	headline
発見する	はっけんする	**hakken suru**	to discover
記者会見	きしゃ かいけん	**kisha kaiken**	press conference

200 費

tsui-yasu, hi, (pi)
つい・やす、ヒ、（ピ）
cost, extend; spend

| 一 | 二 | 弓 | 弔 | 弗 | 弗 | 弗 | 弗 |
| 費 | 費 | 費 | 費 | | | | |

費 combines 弗, a vine being untangled by two sticks, meaning split, and 貝 shell, which was formerly used as money. Money being split up to cover various expenses has given 費 the meaning of spend or expense.

費用	ひよう	**hiyō**	expense, cost
食費	しょくひ	**shoku hi**	food expenses
学費	がくひ	**gaku hi**	school expenses
会費	かいひ	**kai hi**	membership fee
交通費	こうつうひ	**kōtsū hi**	transportation expenses
費やす	ついやす	**tsuiyasu**	to spend
国費	こくひ	**koku hi**	national expenditure
私費	しひ	**shihi**	private expense
実費	じっぴ	**jippi**	actual expense
消費者	しょうひしゃ	**shōhi sha**	consumer

201 院

in
イン
institution

| ⁊ | 孑 | 阝 | 阝' | 阝' | 阝宀 | 阝宀 | 阝宀 |
| 阰 | 院 | | | | | | |

院 represents a building 宀 surrounded by a stone wall 阝 where bald men 元 such as priests or scholars used to work. Thus 院 stands for temples, hospitals, and other institutions.

大学院	だいがくいん	**daigakuin**	graduate school
大学院生	だいがくいんせい	**daigakuin sei**	graduate student
入院する	にゅういんする	**nyūin suru**	to be hospitalized
美容院	びよういん	**biyōin**	beauty parlor
退院する	たいいんする	**taiin suru**	to be discharged from a hospital
寺院	じいん	**jiin**	temple

202 修

shū
シュウ
master, mend

ノ	イ	化	仏	攸	攸	攸	修
修	修						

修 combines 彡 hair ornament and 攸 pouring water on someone's back, both suggesting putting something into good shape. From this 修 has come to mean master something.

研修	けんしゅう	**kenshū**	on-the-job training
研修生	けんしゅうせい	**kenshū sei**	trainee
修了証書	しゅうりょう しょうしょ	**shūryō shōsho**	certificate of completion
修学旅行	しゅうがく りょこう	**shūgaku ryokō**	school excursion
修理する	しゅうりする	**shūri suru**	to mend, to repair
修正する	しゅうせいする	**shūsei suru**	to amend, to correct

203 士

shi
シ
man; scholar

一	十	士					

士 depicts a man standing upright.

修士	しゅうし	**shūshi**	master degree
学士	がくし	**gakushi**	bachelor degree
力士	りきし	**rikishi**	sumo wrestler
代議士	だいぎし	**daigishi**	member of the Diet (usually House of Representatives)

204 博

haku, (paku)
ハク、（パク）
broad, extensive

一	十	十	忄	忛	恒	恒	博
博	博	博	博				

博, which combines 十 add (cf. 184 協), 尃 specialize (cf. 46), and 、 point, suggests broadening one's specialization by adding various points to one's knowledge. From this 博 has come to mean broad or extensive.

博士	はくし／*はかせ	**hakushi/hakase**	doctoral degree; doctor
工学博士	こうがくはくし／ *はかせ	**kōgaku hakushi/ hakase**	Doctor of Engineering
博物館	はくぶつかん	**hakubutsu kan**	museum of history and culture
万博	ばんぱく	**bampaku**	abbreviation for 万国博覧会 (world exposition)

205 明	aka-rui, mei あか・るい、メイ bright, clear; next	丨	冂	月	日	旧	明	明	明

When the sun 日 and the moon 月 come together, everything becomes bright.	明るい	あかるい	**akarui**	bright
	証明する	しょうめいする	**shōmei suru**	to prove, to certify
	証明書	しょうめいしょ	**shōmei sho**	certificate
	証明証	しょうめいしょう	**shōmei shō**	certificate
	×説明書	せつめいしょ	**setsumei sho**	explanatory booklet, manual
	文明	ぶんめい	**bummei**	civilization
	明日	*あす／*あした	**asu/ashita**	tomorrow

206 届	todo-ku, todo-keru とど・く、とど・ける reach; deliver; notify	⁀	⁀	尸	尸	尼	届	届	届

届 combines 尸 reclining man and 由 bottle of wine. From the idea of delivering wine to a sick person, 届 has come to mean deliver. Reach is an associated meaning.	届く	とどく	**todoku**	(a letter, etc.) to reach/arrive
	届ける	とどける	**todokeru**	to deliver; to notify
	届(け)	とどけ	**todoke**	notification
	×履修 科目届	りしゅうかもく とどけ	**rishū kamoku todoke**	course registration
	受講届	じゅこうとどけ	**jukō todoke**	course registration
	××変更届	へんこうとどけ	**henkō todoke**	notice of change of ~
	×欠席届	けっせきとどけ	**kesseki todoke**	absentee notice
	届け先	とどけさき	**todoke saki**	delivery destination

▶4 Practice

I. Write the readings of the following kanji in hiragana.

1. お知らせ
2. 教授
3. 会場
4. 見学ツアー
5. 費用
6. 大学院
7. 修士
8. 博士
9. 証明書
10. 届ける
11. 通知する
12. 履修科目届
13. 教科書
14. 工場
15. 食費
16. 入院する
17. 講演会の場所を教えて下さい。
18. 工場で、研修します。
19. この教室は、明るいですね。
20. 交通費は、自分で出さなければなりません。

II. Fill in the blanks with appropriate kanji.

1. し
□る
to know

2. おし
□える
to teach

3. ブラウン □ 授
きょう
じゅ
Professor Brown

4. み
□る
to see

5. けん
□意
opinion

6. ば
□所
place

7. じょう
入□券
admission ticket

8. ひ
学□
school expenses

9. しゅう し
□□
master degree

10. しゅう
研□生
trainee

11. はく し
文学□□
Doctor of Literature

12. いん
大学□生
postgraduate student

13. めい
証□する
to prove

14. とど
□く
to reach

---

5 ▶ Advanced Placement Exam Practice Questions

Below is a notice about a concert. Read the notice and choose the best answers to the questions.

コンサートのお知らせ

日時: 10月10日（土）
午前の部: 10時から11時半まで
午後の部: 3時から4時半まで
場所: 午前、午後ともに大講堂

東京大学生5人によるピアノコンサートです。
午後はピアノといっしょに大学院生3人がバイオリンをひきます。
※15分前までに会場に入ってください。

Autumn Piano concert

©naoko nakajima

※ 入場料（む）は無料です。
メンバーを募集（ぼ しゅう）しています。

水曜と土曜の午後、三番教室で練習（れん しゅう）しています。いつでも見学に来てください。

1. If you want to go to this concert in the afternoon, what time do you have to enter the concert hall?
   A. 2:45 P.M.
   B. 3:00 P.M.
   C. 3:45 P.M.
   D. 4:15 P.M.

2. Who will play in this concert in the afternoon?
   A. 5 university students
   B. 3 graduate students and 3 professors
   C. 5 university students and 3 graduate students
   D. 5 university students and 3 professors

3. On what day of the week does this group practice?
   A. Monday and Thursday
   B. Tuesday and Friday
   C. Wednesday and Saturday
   D. Thursday and Sunday

4. If you want to visit them, what should you do?
   A. First you have to ask when you can visit them.
   B. You can visit them at any time, if it is a practice day.
   C. You have to make a reservation.
   D. You're not allowed to visit their practices.

5. Which of the following statements about this notice is not true?
   A. Date: 10th Oct. (Sunday)
   B. Morning concert: 10:00 A.M.–11:30 A.M.
   C. Entrance fee: free
   D. Concert hall: large auditorium

Going to the Hospital

病院へ行きます

I f you become ill, you may decide to visit either a small neighborhood clinic or a big hospital. One convenient aspect of a small clinic is that you can make an appointment to see a doctor, receive medicine, and make payments all at one window. Larger hospitals are more bureaucratic and each window has a different function. In this lesson, you will study some kanji frequently seen in hospitals, as well as kanji found in instructions for taking medicine.

1 ▶ Introductory Quiz

Look at the illustration below, and refer to the words in **Vocabulary**. Then try the following quiz.

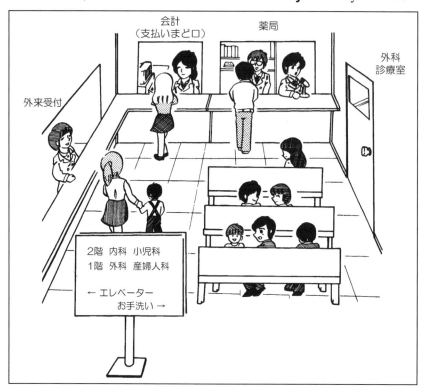

I. Match the right and left phrases. Write the correct letters (a ~ d) in the spaces provided.

1. Mr. Lee has come to the hospital. Help him out by telling him what to do at each window.
   1) 外来受付 （　　　） a. お医者さんにみてもらう
   2) 会計（支払いまど口） （　　　） b. くすりをもらう
   3) 薬局 （　　　） c. お金をはらう
   4) 診療室 （　　　） d. 保険証や診察券を出す

2. Which medical departments should he go to for the following complaints?
   1) *かぜをひいた時 (*a cold) （　　　） a. 外科
   2) *はがいたい時 (*a toothache) （　　　） b. 内科
   3) 子どもが病気になった時 （　　　） c. 歯科
   4) *けがをした時 (*an injury) （　　　） d. 小児科

II. Mr. Lee has received his medicine. Refer to the instructions on the prescription envelope, and then choose the correct answers to the questions below.

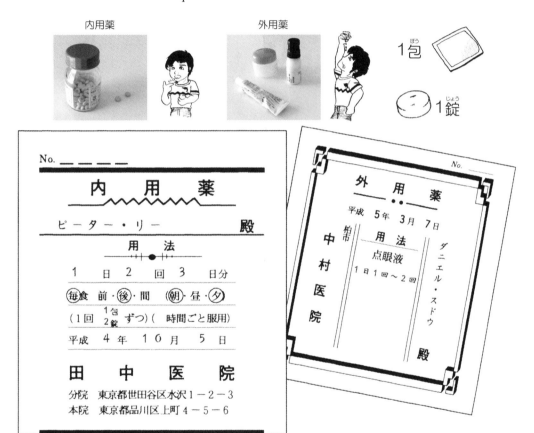

1. のむ薬はどちらですか。 　　　 a. 外用薬　　 b. 内用薬

2. リーさんはどのぐらい薬をもらいましたか。 （a. 二　　 b. 三　　 c. 四）　か分

3. 一日、何回のみますか。 （a. 一　　 b. 二　　 c. 三）　回

4. いつ、のみますか。 　 a. 朝食と夕食のあと、ときどき
   　　 b. 朝食と夕食のあと、いつも
   　　 c. 朝食か夕食のあと、どちらか

5. 毎回、いくつ、のみますか。 （a. 一　　 b. 二　　 c. 三）　包
   （a. 一　　 b. 二　　 c. 三）　錠

2 ▶ **Vocabulary**

Study the readings and meanings of these words to help you understand the **Introductory Quiz**.

1. 病院	びょう いん	**byōin**	hospital
2. 病気	びょう き	**byōki**	sickness
3. 外来受付	がい らい うけ つけ	**gairai uketsuke**	outpatient reception
4. 会計	かい けい	**kaikei**	bill, payment
5. 支払いまど口	し はらい まど ぐち	**shiharai madoguchi**	payment window
6. 薬局	やっ きょく	**yakkyoku**	pharmacy
7. 診察室	しん さつ しつ	**shinsatsu shitsu**	examination room
8. 医者	い しゃ	**isha**	medical doctor
9. 診察券	しん さつ けん	**shinsatsu ken**	patient's card
10. 保険証	ほ けん しょう	**hoken shō**	health insurance certificate
11. 外科	げ か	**geka**	surgery
12. 内科	ない か	**naika**	internal medicine unit
13. 産婦人科	さん ふ じん か	**sanfujinka**	obstetrics and gynecology
14. 歯科	し か	**shika**	dentistry
15. 小児科	しょう に か	**shōnika**	pediatrics
16. 内用薬	ない よう やく	**naiyō yaku**	medicine for internal use
17. 外用薬	がい よう やく	**gaiyō yaku**	medicine for external use
18. 用法	よう ほう	**yōhō**	instructions for use
19. 毎食	まい しょく	**maishoku**	every meal
20. 毎回	まい かい	**maikai**	every time
21. 朝食	ちょう しょく	**chōshoku**	breakfast
22. 夕食	ゆう しょく	**yūshoku**	supper
23. 3日分	みっ か ぶん	**mikka bun**	3 days' worth
24. ～包	～ ほう	**~hō**	~ pack(s)
25. ～錠	～ じょう	**~jō**	~ tablet(s)

3 ▶ **New Characters**

Seventeen characters are introduced in this lesson. Use the explanations to help you understand and remember the characters. Study the compound words to increase your vocabulary.

病 医 歯 児 産 保 受 付 来 薬 診 察 計 支 払 法 毎

207 病

byō
ビョウ
sickness, illness

Stroke order: 丶 亠 广 疒 疒 疒 疒 病 病 病

病, which combines 疒 man in bed and 丙 stiff legs, means sickness. 疒 is used as a radical to refer to sickness.

病院	びょういん	**byōin**	hospital
病気	びょうき	**byōki**	sickness, disease
病室	びょうしつ	**byōshitsu**	sickroom
病人	びょうにん	**byōnin**	sick person
急病	きゅうびょう	**kyūbyō**	sudden illness
病名	びょうめい	**byōmei**	the name of a disease
大学病院	だいがく びょういん	**daigaku byōin**	university hospital
成人病	せいじん びょう	**seijin byō**	adult disease

208 医

i
イ
medicine; healing

Stroke order: 一 丆 匚 三 壬 矢 医

医 combines 匚 box and 矢 arrow (cf. 196 知), referring here to fine needles used in acupuncture. Originally indicating a doctor's box of needles, 医 has come to mean medical science, healing, or medical doctor.

医者	いしゃ	**isha**	medical doctor
医院	いいん	**iin**	clinic, doctor's office
医学	いがく	**igaku**	medical science
外科医	げかい	**gekai**	surgeon
内科医	ないかい	**naikai**	physician, internist
医療費	いりょうひ	**iryō hi**	medical expenses

209 歯

ha, (ba), shi
は、（ば）、シ
tooth

Stroke order: 丨 卜 止 止 芷 芷 歩 歩 歩 歩 歯 歯

Formerly written 齒, 歯 combines 止 stop (cf. 149) and a pictograph of the front teeth. Thus 齒 originally suggested stopping food in the mouth by biting it with one's teeth, and now simply means tooth.

歯医者	はいしゃ	**haisha**	dentist
歯科	しか	**shika**	dental surgery, dentistry
歯科医	しかい	**shikai**	dentist
虫歯	むしば	**mushiba**	decayed tooth
前歯	まえば	**maeba**	front tooth
入(れ)歯	いれば	**ireba**	dentures
義歯	ぎし	**gishi**	artificial tooth, dentures

167

210 児	ji, ni ジ、ニ infant, child	l	ll	lⁿ	lⱝ	lⱝ	lⱝ児	児	

児 was originally written 兒, which derived from a pictograph of an infant whose head is large and whose skull bones have not yet joined completely.

小児科	しょうにか	**shōnika**	pediatrics
小児科医	しょうにかい	**shōnika i**	pediatrician
児童	じどう	**jidō**	child

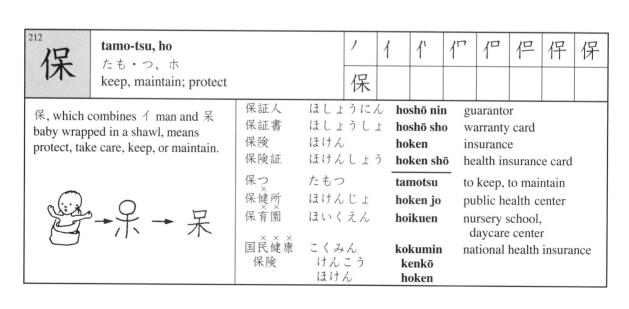

---

211 産	u-mu, san う・む、サン give birth; produce	'	亠	产	宀	立	产	产	产
		产	产	産					

産 combines life 生 (cf. 42) and 产 becoming obvious and visible, which comes from a man standing 立 (cf. 167) on a cliff 厂. Thus 産 suggests new life becoming visible, such as giving birth or producing.

産む	うむ	**umu**	to give birth
産婦人科	さんふじんか	**sanfujinka**	obstetrics and gynecology
生産する	せいさんする	**seisan suru**	to produce
特産品	とくさんひん	**tokusan hin**	special product
土産	*みやげ	**miyage**	souvenir

---

212 保	tamo-tsu, ho たも・つ、ホ keep, maintain; protect	ノ	イ	イ	伫	伫	伫	伫	保
		保							

保, which combines イ man and 呆 baby wrapped in a shawl, means protect, take care, keep, or maintain.

保証人	ほしょうにん	**hoshō nin**	guarantor
保証書	ほしょうしょ	**hoshō sho**	warranty card
保険	ほけん	**hoken**	insurance
保険証	ほけんしょう	**hoken shō**	health insurance card
保つ	たもつ	**tamotsu**	to keep, to maintain
保健所	ほけんじょ	**hoken jo**	public health center
保育園	ほいくえん	**hoikuen**	nursery school, daycare center
国民健康保険	こくみん けんこう ほけん	**kokumin kenkō hoken**	national health insurance

168

213 受 — u-keru, ju / う・ける、ジュ / receive

Stroke order: 一 ⺈ ⺈ ⻖ ⻖ ⼜ 受 受

受 combines ⺈ hand, 冖 ship, and 又 another hand. Goods carried by ships were received by one person from another, hand to hand, at a port.

受ける	うける	**ukeru**	to receive; to take (a test); to have (an operation)
受(け)取る	うけとる	**uketoru**	to receive, to get
受(け)身	うけみ	**ukemi**	passive voice
郵便受け	ゆうびんうけ	**yūbin'uke**	mail box
受験する	じゅけんする	**juken suru**	to take an examination

214 付 — tsu-ku, tsu-keru, fu / つ・く、つ・ける、フ / attach

Stroke order: ノ イ 仁 付 付

付 represents a hand 寸 attaching a stick 丶 to a man イ.

付く	つく	**tsuku**	to stick
付ける	つける	**tsukeru**	to attach, to put, to stick
時間外受付	じかんがい うけつけ	**jikan gai uketsuke**	reception before and after office hours
付録	ふろく	**furoku**	supplement, appendix
付属病院	ふぞく びょういん	**fuzoku byōin**	hospital attached to ~
交付する	こうふする	**kōfu suru**	to deliver/issue (a certificate, etc.)

215 来 — ku-ru, rai / く・る、ライ / come

Stroke order: 一 ⼀ 口 立 平 来 来

来 derives from a pictograph of ripe grain ready to be harvested. Since harvest suggests the coming of new crops, 来 means come or coming.

来る	くる	**kuru**	to come
来週	らいしゅう	**raishū**	next week
来月	らいげつ	**raigetsu**	next month
外来受付	がいらい うけつけ	**gairai uketsuke**	outpatient reception
外来語	がいらいご	**gairai go**	foreign loanword
将来	しょうらい	**shōrai**	future
来年	らいねん	**rainen**	next year

169

216 薬	**kusuri, (gusuri), yaku, (ya')** くすり、（ぐすり）、ヤク、（ヤッ） medicine	一	十	艹	芢	艹	苩	苩	苩
		苩	茞	薝	薝	薝	薅	薬	薬

薬 combines the radical 艹 plant and 楽, a tree laden with nuts that makes a pleasant sound when shaken. Thus 薬 suggests plants used to make sick people feel better, a form of medicine.

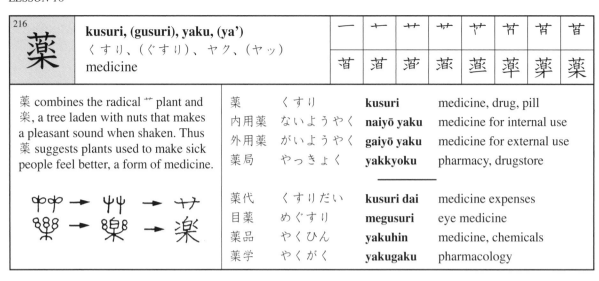

薬	くすり	**kusuri**	medicine, drug, pill
内用薬	ないようやく	**naiyō yaku**	medicine for internal use
外用薬	がいようやく	**gaiyō yaku**	medicine for external use
薬局	やっきょく	**yakkyoku**	pharmacy, drugstore
———			
薬代	くすりだい	**kusuri dai**	medicine expenses
目薬	めぐすり	**megusuri**	eye medicine
薬品	やくひん	**yakuhin**	medicine, chemicals
薬学	やくがく	**yakugaku**	pharmacology

217 診	**shin** シン diagnose, examine	、	二	三	言	言	言	言	言
		診	診	診	診				

診 combines 言 speak (cf. 78 話) and 彡 lots of hair covering 个 a head. Thus 診 suggests a doctor asking a patient lots of questions to cover all his symptoms, in other words, diagnosing him.

休診日	きゅうしんび	**kyūshin bi**	vacation day for clinic
受診	じゅしん	**jushin**	having medical examination
———			
×初診	しょしん	**shoshin**	the first medical examination
×再診	さいしん	**saishin**	medical re-examination
×検診	けんしん	**kenshin**	medical examination
×診療時間	しんりょうじかん	**shinryō jikan**	consultation/surgery hours

218 察	**satsu** サツ investigate; judge; guess	、	丷	宀	宀	灾	灾	灾	灾
		灾	灾	宓	宓	察	察		

察, which combines 宀 house and 祭 festival (cf. 36), suggests purifying a house thoroughly. By extension, 察 now means investigate thoroughly and judge based on investigation. An associated meaning is guess.

診察する	しんさつする	**shinsatsu suru**	to examine/see a patient
診察室	しんさつしつ	**shinsatsu shitsu**	examination/consultation room
診察券	しんさつけん	**shinsatsu ken**	patient's card
診察日	しんさつび	**shinsatsu bi**	consultation/surgery day
診察料	しんさつりょう	**shinsatsu ryō**	doctor's fee
×警察	けいさつ	**keisatsu**	police

170

219 計

kei
ケイ
measure; total; plan

丶	亠	言	言	言	言	言	言
計							

計, which combines 言 speak (cf. 78 話) and 十 add (cf. 184 協), suggests adding up the number of words that a person speaks. From this, 計 has come to mean measure or total.

会計	かいけい	**kaikei**	accounts, bill; cashier
時計	*とけい	**tokei**	watch, clock
		———	
計算する	けいさんする	**keisan suru**	to calculate, to compute
小計	しょうけい	**shōkei**	subtotal
合計する	ごうけいする	**gōkei suru**	to total, to add up
計画する	けいかくする	**keikaku suru**	to plan

220 支

sasa-eru, shi
ささ・える、シ
branch; support

一	十	步	支				

支 represents a branch that is held in a hand.

支出	ししゅつ	**shishutsu**	expenses, expenditure
		———	
支える	ささえる	**sasaeru**	to support
支部	しぶ	**shibu**	branch (of a union, association, etc.)
支社	ししゃ	**shisha**	branch office of a company
支持する	しじする	**shiji suru**	to support

221 払

hara-u, (bara-i)
はら・う、（ばら・い）
pay; sweep off

一	十	扌	払	払			

払 derives from 拂, which combines 扌 hand and 弗 vine being untangled by two sticks (cf. 200 費). Thus 払 suggests sweeping and, by extension, pay (an act of clearing up debts).

払う	はらう	**harau**	to pay; to sweep off
支払う	しはらう	**shiharau**	to pay
支払(い)窓口	しはらい まどぐち	**shiharai madoguchi**	payment window, cashier
払(い)込み	はらいこみ	**harai komi**	payment
払(い)戻し	はらい もどし	**harai modoshi**	refund, repayment
現金払い	げんきん ばらい	**genkin barai**	cash payment
分割払い	ぶんかつ ばらい	**bunkatsu barai**	payment in installments

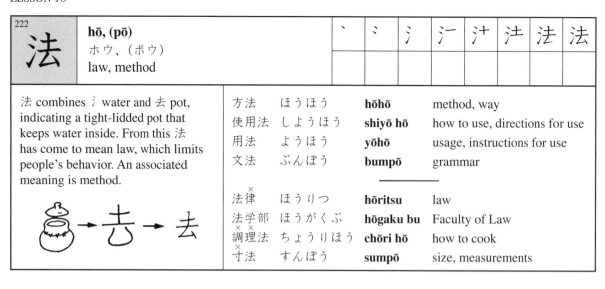

222	**hō, (pō)**	`	ミ	ミ	氵	汁	汁	法	法
法	ホウ、（ポウ） law, method								

法 combines 氵 water and 去 pot, indicating a tight-lidded pot that keeps water inside. From this 法 has come to mean law, which limits people's behavior. An associated meaning is method.

方法	ほうほう	**hōhō**	method, way
使用法	しようほう	**shiyō hō**	how to use, directions for use
用法	ようほう	**yōhō**	usage, instructions for use
文法	ぶんぽう	**bumpō**	grammar
法律	ほうりつ	**hōritsu**	law
法学部	ほうがくぶ	**hōgaku bu**	Faculty of Law
調理法	ちょうりほう	**chōri hō**	how to cook
寸法	すんぽう	**sumpō**	size, measurements

223	**mai**	ノ	㇉	匕	匂	匃	毎		
毎	マイ every, each								

毎 combines 亠 hair pin and 母, a derivation of 母, which is composed of 女 woman and two dots for breasts and means mother. 母, which originally also represented mother, has come to mean every, because every mother has a child.

毎日	まいにち	**mainichi**	every day
毎回	まいかい	**maikai**	every time
毎食	まいしょく	**maishoku**	each/every meal
毎日新聞	まいにち しんぶん	**Mainichi shimbun**	Mainichi Daily News
毎週	まいしゅう	**maishū**	every week
毎月	まいつき	**maitsuki**	every month
毎年	まいとし／ まいねん	**maitoshi/ mainen**	every year

▶4 Practice

I. Write the readings of the following kanji in hiragana.

1. 病 院　　　2. 病 気　　　3. 外 来 受 付　　　4. 会 計
5. 支 払 い　　6. 薬 局　　　7. 診 察 室　　　8. 医 者
9. 保 険 証　　10. 外 科　　11. 内 科　　　12. 産 婦 人 科
13. 歯 科　　　14. 小 児 科　　15. 外 用 薬　　16. 内 用 薬
17. 用 法　　　18. 毎 食　　19. 毎 回　　　20. 医 院
21. 医 学　　　22. 歯 科 医　　23. 保 証 人　　24. 外 来 語
25. 使 用 法　　26. 歯 医 者 さ ん に 行 っ た ら 、 き ょ う は 、 休 診 日 で し た 。
27. 受 付 で 、 診 察 券 を 受 け 取 っ て く だ さ い 。

172

28. 来週、国のともだちが日本へ来ます。

29. この薬を毎日三回のみなさい。

30. さいごに、会計の窓口^{まど}でお金を払います。

II. Fill in the blanks with appropriate kanji.

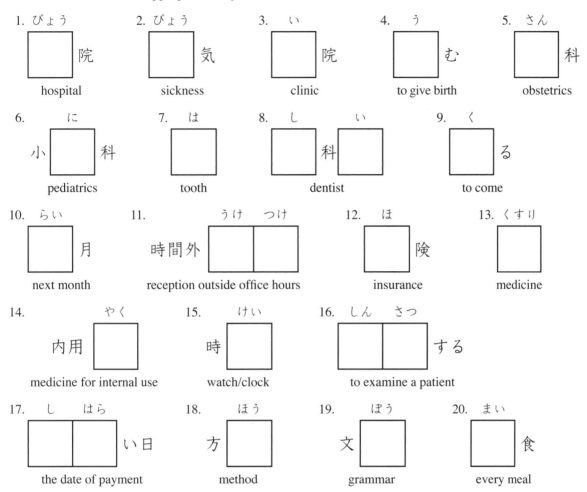

1. びょう ☐院 hospital

2. びょう ☐気 sickness

3. い ☐院 clinic

4. う ☐む to give birth

5. さん ☐科 obstetrics

6. に 小☐科 pediatrics

7. は ☐ tooth

8. し い ☐科☐ dentist

9. く ☐る to come

10. らい ☐月 next month

11. うけ つけ 時間外☐☐ reception outside office hours

12. ほ ☐険 insurance

13. くすり ☐ medicine

14. やく 内用☐ medicine for internal use

15. けい 時☐ watch/clock

16. しん さつ ☐☐する to examine a patient

17. し はら ☐☐い日 the date of payment

18. ほう 方☐ method

19. ぽう 文☐ grammar

20. まい ☐食 every meal

▶ 5 Advanced Placement Exam Practice Questions

Read the explanation below and then study the hospital sign board overleaf. Use this information to choose the correct answer to the questions that follow.

ジョンさんは大学生です。きのうから頭^{あたま}がいたくて、高いねつがあります。ひとりでアパートのちかくの大きな病院へ来ました。ここははじめてです。いま病院の前にいます。

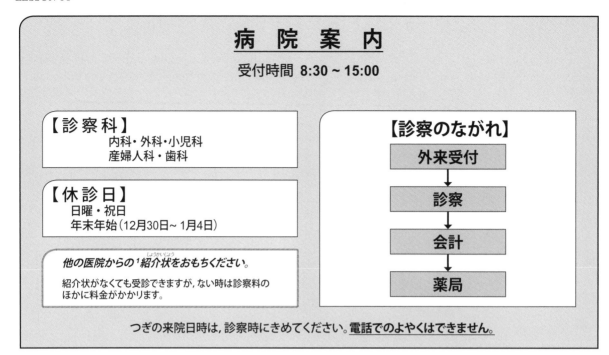

病　院　案　内

受付時間 8:30 ～ 15:00

【診察科】
　　内科・外科・小児科
　　産婦人科・歯科

【休診日】
　　日曜・祝日
　　年末年始（12月30日～ 1月4日）

他の医院からの¹紹介状をおもちください。

紹介状がなくても受診できますが, ない時は診察料の
ほかに料金がかかります。

【診察のながれ】
外来受付
　↓
診察
　↓
会計
　↓
薬局

つぎの来院日時は, 診察時にきめてください。電話でのよやくはできません。

1 紹介状 : referral form

1. John came alone to this hospital for the first time, without any referral form. Can he get a medical examination?
   A. Since he does not have a referral form, he cannot consult a doctor.
   B. In order to see a doctor, he has to come with someone to introduce him.
   C. Even if he has no referral form, he can get a medical exam. But he has to pay money for that.
   D. It is not clear whether he can see the doctor, because it depends on the number of patients there.

2. There are many medical examination departments in this hospital. To which department should John go?
   A. 外科
   B. 内科
   C. 産婦人科
   D. 小児科

3. In which order should John go to the necessary places?
   A. outpatient reception → examination room → pharmacy → payment
   B. outpatient reception → payment → examination room → pharmacy
   C. outpatient reception → pharmacy → examination room → payment
   D. outpatient reception → examination room → payment → pharmacy

4. According to this notice, what can be said about John's next visit to see the doctor?
   A. If he has a fever again, he can visit the hospital without making an appointment.
   B. Being a university student, he will be accepted even if he comes late in the evening.
   C. He has to make an appointment for the next visit during the medical examination today.
   D. He can make an appointment on the telephone if he has taken all the medicine.

REVIEW EXERCISE: LESSONS 15–18

I. The words listed below relate to one of three places: A) in the university building, B) on the university campus, or C) in the hospital. Group them appropriately and write their letters in the spaces provided.

A) 大学の建物の中

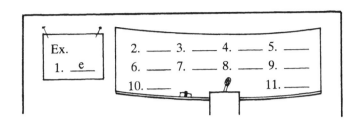

Ex.
1. _e_
2. ___ 3. ___ 4. ___ 5. ___
6. ___ 7. ___ 8. ___ 9. ___
10. ___ 11. ___

B) 大学のキャンパス

12. ___ 13. ___ 14. ___
15. ___ 16. ___
17. ___ 18. ___

C) 病院

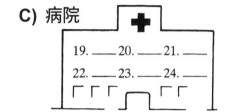

19. ___ 20. ___ 21. ___
22. ___ 23. ___ 24. ___

a. 図書館	b. 研究室	c. 支払い窓口	d. 文学部教授
e. 開講する	f. 入院費用	g. 教科書	h. 外来受付
i. 講義	j. 生協	k. 工学博士	l. 学生食堂
m. 小児科医	n. 会議	o. 診察日	p. 講堂
q. 学生会館	r. 研修生	s. 留学生センター	t. 図書室
u. 専門科目	v. 工学部一号館	w. 実験室	x. 急病

II. Find the missing kanji and write them or their corresponding letters in the spaces below.

1. ☐ 局
2. ☐ 験
3. 使 用 ☐
4. 会 ☐
5. ☐ 科
6. 証 ☐ 書
7. ☐ 協
8. ☐ 険
9. 事 ☐ 室
10. 開 ☐
11. ☐ 所
12. 交 通 ☐

a. 疾 b. 歯 c. 明 d. 費 e. 計 f. 門 g. 療 h. 生 i. 保 j. 務 k. 場 l. 法

Shopping at the Supermarket

スーパーでセールがあります

Department stores in Japan carry a wide variety of products, while supermarkets stock mainly food and other daily necessities. For people who prefer smaller, specialized stores, there are butcher shops, fish markets, vegetable shops, and so on. Although bargaining is not encouraged, stores do occasionally hold sales. Especially at the end of the season, stores carry lots of discount merchandise to attract customers. To save money, look for advertising leaflets in newspapers.

1 ▸ Introductory Quiz

I. Decide which characters represent the following pictures, and then circle the correct answers.

1
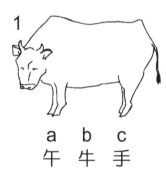
```
a   b   c
午  牛  手
```

2
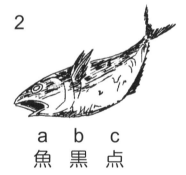
```
a   b   c
魚  黒  点
```

3
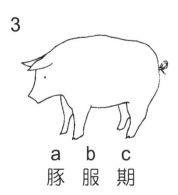
```
a   b   c
豚  服  期
```

4
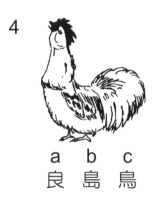
```
a   b   c
良  島  鳥
```

II. Read the following advertisement for a supermarket sale, and refer to the words in **Vocabulary**. Then try the following quiz.

スーパー　大京ストア　〈北山店〉

大特売！

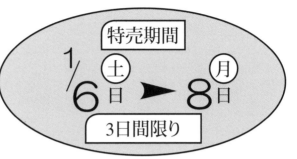

特売期間

1/6（土）日 ▶ 8（月）日

3日間限り

牛肉、豚肉、鳥肉、ハム 1割引
魚、さしみ................. 3割引
やさい、くだもの.......... 2割引

このほか食料品は、全品お安くなつて
おります。きょうのお買い物は、ぜひ
大京ストア　食料品売り場へ！

営業時間　　10:00A.M. ~ 7:00P.M.

定休日　　　第1、3水曜日

1. この店は、大京ストアの（a. きたやまみせ　　b. きたやまてん）です。

2. 6日から8日までは、（a. 高く　　b. 安く）売ります。

3. 肉、魚、*やさいの中で、一番安くなる物は（a. 肉　　b. 魚　　c. やさい）です。(*vegetables)

4. さしみは（a. 肉　　b. 魚）売り場で買います。

5. *ハムは（a. 魚　　b. 肉）売り場で買います。　(*ham)

6. （a. くつした　　b. コーヒー）も安くなります。

7. いま、午後5時です。店は（a. 開いています。　　b. 閉まっています。）

8. 毎月、第2、第4水曜日は（a. 休みです。　　b. 開いています。）

2 ► Vocabulary

1. スーパー		**sūpā**	supermarket
2. 店	みせ	**mise**	store
3. 北山店	きた やま てん	**kitayama ten**	Kitayama store
4. 大特売	だい とく ばい	**dai tokubai**	super sale
5. 高い	たか い	**takai**	expensive
6. 安い	やす い	**yasui**	cheap
7. 売る	うる	**uru**	to sell
8. 肉	にく	**niku**	meat
9. 牛肉	ぎゅう にく	**gyūniku**	beef
10. 豚肉	ぶた にく	**butaniku**	pork
11. 鳥肉	とり にく	**toriniku**	chicken
12. 魚	さかな	**sakana**	fish
13. 1割引	いち わり びき	**ichi waribiki**	10% discount
14. 一番	いち ばん	**ichi ban**	the most
15. 安くなる	やす くなる	**yasuku naru**	to be discounted
16. 物	もの	**mono**	thing
17. 売り場	うり ば	**uriba**	counter in a shop
18. 買う	かう	**kau**	to buy
19. 食料品	しょく りょう ひん	**shokuryō hin**	groceries, provisions
20. 全品	ぜん ぴん	**zempin**	all items
21. (お)買い物	(お)か い もの	**(o)kaimono**	shopping
22. 営業時間	えい ぎょう じ かん	**eigyō jikan**	business hours
23. 開く	あ く	**aku**	to open
24. 閉まる	し まる	**shimaru**	to close
25. 第1水曜日	だい いち すい よう び	**daiichi sui yōbi**	the first Wednesday
26. 定休日	てい きゅう び	**teikyū bi**	Shop Holiday, regular holiday

3 ► New Characters

Thirteen characters are introduced in this lesson. Use the explanations to help you understand and remember the characters. Study the compound words to increase your vocabulary.

店 売 肉 牛 豚 鳥 魚 割 品 安 買 物 業

178

224 店 mise, ten / みせ、テン / shop, store

		ヽ	亠	广	庁	庐	店	店	店

店 combines 广 roof or house, 卜 fortuneteller's stick (cf. 154 外), and 口 space or place. 占 formerly meant selecting and occupying a good place according to the advice of a fortuneteller. 店 thus came to mean a house set up in a place good for business, that is, a shop or store.

店	みせ	**mise**	shop, store
書店	しょてん	**shoten**	bookstore
開店時間	かいてんじかん	**kaiten jikan**	store opening time
閉店時間	へいてんじかん	**heiten jikan**	store closing time
本店	ほんてん	**honten**	main store, head office
支店	してん	**shiten**	branch store/office
百貨店	ひゃっかてん	**hyakka ten**	department store
専門店	せんもんてん	**semmon ten**	specialty store, store specializing in ~

225 売 u-ru, bai / う・る、バイ / sell

		一	十	士	产	壱	声	売	

売 derives from 賣, which combines 士, a simplified form of 出 take out or show (cf. 108), and 買, which usually means buying (cf. 234), but here means something to do with business. Thus 売 suggests selling. (Imagine a man 士 standing 儿 behind a showcase in a shop 冖.)

売る	うる	**uru**	to sell
売場	うりば	**uriba**	counter in a shop, vending area
特売	とくばい	**tokubai**	special/bargain sale
売店	ばいてん	**baiten**	stand, stall
大売(り)出し	おおうりだし	**ōuridashi**	big sale
発売日	はつばいび	**hatsubai bi**	the day of release for sale
新発売	しんはつばい	**shin hatsubai**	newly on sale

226 肉 niku / ニク / meat

		丨	冂	内	内	肉	肉		

肉 derives from a pictograph of meat. When 肉 is used as a part of other kanji, it is written 月.

肉	にく	**niku**	meat
挽(き)肉	ひきにく	**hiki niku**	minced/ground meat
肉料理	にくりょうり	**niku ryōri**	meat dishes
焼肉	やきにく	**yakiniku**	grilled meat

179

| 227 牛 | **ushi, gyū**
うし、ギュウ
cow, bull | ノ | ⺊ | 二 | 牛 | | | | |

牛 derives from a pictograph of a cow or bull's head.

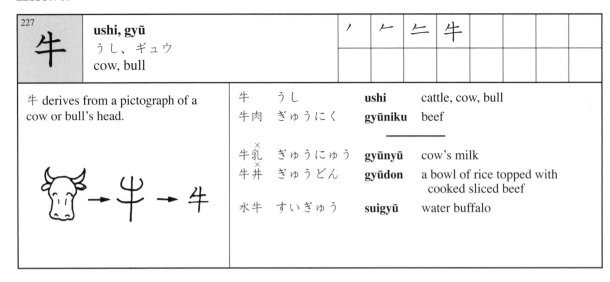

牛	うし	**ushi**	cattle, cow, bull
牛肉	ぎゅうにく	**gyūniku**	beef
―――			
牛乳	ぎゅうにゅう	**gyūnyū**	cow's milk
牛丼	ぎゅうどん	**gyūdon**	a bowl of rice topped with cooked sliced beef
水牛	すいぎゅう	**suigyū**	water buffalo

| 228 豚 | **buta, ton**
ぶた、トン
pig | ノ | 刀 | 月 | 月 | 胪 | 肜 | 肸 | 肦 |
| | | 肠 | 豚 | 豚 | | | | | |

豕 derives from a pictograph of a pig. 月 meat (cf. 226 肉) was added in order to specify a pig which is eaten, namely, pork.

豚	ぶた	**buta**	pig
豚肉	ぶたにく	**butaniku**	pork
豚カツ	とんカツ	**tonkatsu**	breaded pork cutlet
―――			
焼豚	やきぶた	**yakibuta**	roast pork
酢豚	すぶた	**subuta**	sweet-and-sour pork

| 229 鳥 | **tori, chō**
とり、チョウ
bird; chicken | ′ | ⺅ | ⼴ | 户 | 户 | 自 | 鸟 | 鳥 |
| | | 鳥 | 鳥 | 鳥 | | | | | |

鳥 derives from a pictograph of a bird.

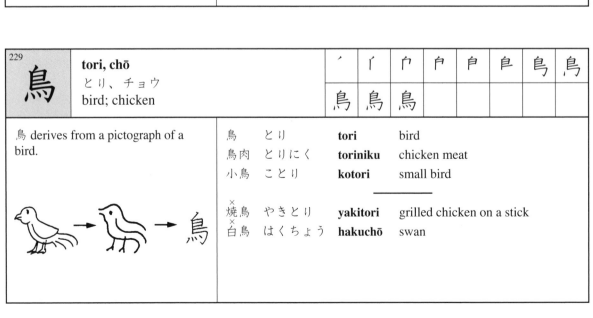

鳥	とり	**tori**	bird
鳥肉	とりにく	**toriniku**	chicken meat
小鳥	ことり	**kotori**	small bird
―――			
焼鳥	やきとり	**yakitori**	grilled chicken on a stick
白鳥	はくちょう	**hakuchō**	swan

230 魚

sakana, (zakana), uo, gyo
さかな、（ざかな）、うお、ギョ
fish

ノ	ク	ク	宀	角	角	角	魚
魚	魚	魚					

魚 derives from a pictograph of a fish.

魚	さかな	**sakana**	fish
魚つり	さかなつり	**sakana tsuri**	fishing
焼魚	やきざかな	**yakizakana**	grilled fish
魚屋	さかなや	**sakana ya**	fish store
魚市場	うおいちば	**uo ichiba**	fish market
金魚	きんぎょ	**kingyo**	goldfish

231 割

wa-ru, katsu
わ・る、カツ
divide; proportion

'	'	宀	宀	中	宇	宝	害
害	害	割	割				

割 combines 刂 sword and 害, a basketlike mask over a mouth, indicating an obstacle. 割 formerly meant cutting an obstacle, and then came to mean divide and proportion. 害 by itself means harm.

割る	わる	**waru**	to divide, to break, to split
二割	にわり	**ni wari**	20%
割 (り) 引き	わりびき	**waribiki**	discount
学割	がくわり	**gaku wari**	student discount
割合	わりあい	**wariai**	rate, ratio; comparatively
分割する	ぶんかつする	**bunkatsu suru**	to divide, to partition

232 品

shina, hin, (pin)
しな、ヒン、（ピン）
goods, article; quality

`	口	口	口	吕	吕	品	品
品							

品 derives from a pictograph of goods piled up.

品	しな	**shina**	goods; quality
品川	しながわ	**Shinagawa**	Shinagawa (place)
食料品	しょくりょうひん	**shokuryō hin**	foodstuff, groceries
スポーツ用品	スポーツようひん	**supōtsu yōhin**	sporting goods
全品	ぜんぴん	**zempin**	all items/goods
品切れ	しなぎれ	**shinagire**	out of stock, sold out
食品	しょくひん	**shokuhin**	food, foodstuff
作品	さくひん	**sakuhin**	piece of work, product
日用品	にちようひん	**nichiyō hin**	daily necessities
電気製品	でんきせいひん	**denki seihin**	electrical appliance

233

yasu-i, an
やす・い、アン
peaceful; inexpensive, cheap

`	`	宀	宀	安	安		

安 represents a woman 女 in a house 宀, which suggests a peaceful household. Inexpensive is an associated meaning, perhaps coming from the idea of staying at home and making things oneself.

 → 宀 → 安

安い	やすい	**yasui**	inexpensive, cheap
安売り	やすうり	**yasuuri**	bargain sale
円安	えんやす	**en'yasu**	low value of the yen
安全な	あんぜんな	**anzen na**	safe, secure
安心する	あんしんする	**anshin suru**	to feel easy/relieved
不安な	ふあんな	**fuan na**	uneasy, restless

234

ka-u, bai
か・う、バイ
buy

`	冂	冂	罒	罒	罒	罒	買
買	買	買	買				

買 combines 罒 net and 貝 money (cf. 200 費). In old times, people used net bags when buying goods.

買う	かう	**kau**	to buy
購買部	こうばいぶ	**kōbai bu**	cooperative store
売買する	ばいばいする	**baibai suru**	to buy and sell, to deal, to trade

235

mono, butsu, motsu
もの、ブツ、モツ
object, thing

ノ	牛	牛	牛	牛	物	物	物

物 combines 牛 or 牛 cattle (cf. 227) and 勿 elephant's tusks and trunk. The Chinese chose these animals to represent the concept of things.

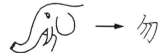 → 勿

物	もの	**mono**	thing
品物	しなもの	**shinamono**	goods, article
買(い)物する	かいものする	**kaimono suru**	to shop
見物する	けんぶつする	**kembutsu suru**	to sightsee
忘れ物	わすれもの	**wasuremono**	things left behind, lost property
動物	どうぶつ	**dōbutsu**	animal
荷物	にもつ	**nimotsu**	baggage, cargo

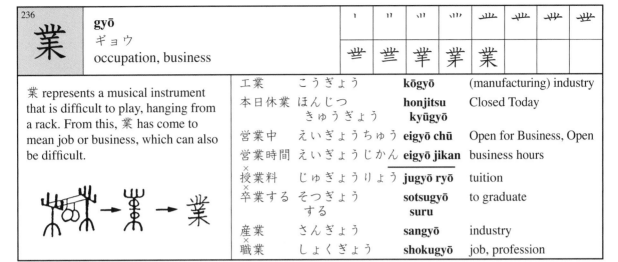

236 業	**gyō** ギョウ occupation, business	⟍	⟍⟍	⟍⟍⟍	⟍⟍⟍⟍	⟍⟍⟍⟍⟍	⟍⟍⟍⟍⟍⟍	⟍⟍⟍⟍⟍⟍⟍	⟍⟍⟍⟍⟍⟍⟍⟍
		丵	丵	業	業	業			

業 represents a musical instrument that is difficult to play, hanging from a rack. From this, 業 has come to mean job or business, which can also be difficult.

工業	こうぎょう	**kōgyō**	(manufacturing) industry
本日休業	ほんじつ きゅうぎょう	**honjitsu kyūgyō**	Closed Today
営業中	えいぎょうちゅう	**eigyō chū**	Open for Business, Open
営業時間	えいぎょうじかん	**eigyō jikan**	business hours
授業料	じゅぎょうりょう	**jugyō ryō**	tuition
卒業する	そつぎょう する	**sotsugyō suru**	to graduate
産業	さんぎょう	**sangyō**	industry
職業	しょくぎょう	**shokugyō**	job, profession

4 ▶ Practice

I. Write the readings of the following kanji in hiragana.

1. 北山店   2. 大特売   3. 牛肉   4. 豚肉

5. 鳥肉   6. 魚   7. 一割引   8. 売場

9. 食料品   10. 全品   11. お買い物   12. 営業時間

13. 定休日   14. 書店   15. 特売   16. 焼肉

17. 牛   18. 豚カツ   19. 学割   20. 品川

21. 安全な   22. 休業

23. あの店には、品物がたくさんあります。

24. ケーキをつくりますから、たまごを三つ、割ってください。

25. 安くてよいセーターが買えて、うれしいです。

II. Fill in the blanks with appropriate kanji.

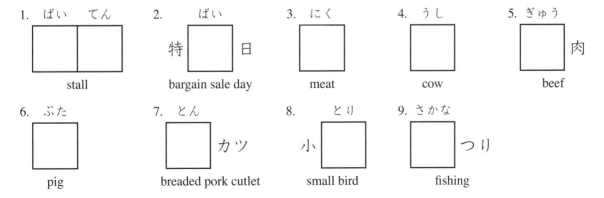

1. ばい てん
□□
stall

2. ばい
特 □ 日
bargain sale day

3. にく
□
meat

4. うし
□
cow

5. ぎゅう
□ 肉
beef

6. ぶた
□
pig

7. とん
□ カツ
breaded pork cutlet

8. とり
小 □
small bird

9. さかな
□ つり
fishing

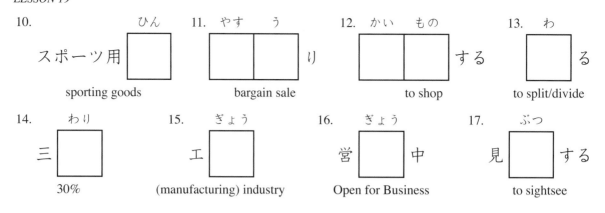

10. スポーツ用〔 ひん 〕
sporting goods

11. 〔 やす 〕〔 う 〕り
bargain sale

12. 〔 かい 〕〔 もの 〕する
to shop

13. 〔 わ 〕る
to split/divide

14. 三〔 わり 〕
30%

15. 工〔 ぎょう 〕
(manufacturing) industry

16. 営〔 ぎょう 〕中
Open for Business

17. 見〔 ぶつ 〕する
to sightsee

---

5 ▶ Advanced Placement Exam Practice Question

When you went into a supermarket, you heard the following announcement. Read the below, and answer the questions.

いらっしゃいませ、いらっしゃいませ！ 文京スーパー、三丁目店へようこそ！
本日は大特売！
肉売り場では、牛肉、鳥肉は2割引、豚肉、ソーセージはなんと3割引！
魚売り場では、お魚が安いよ！4割引！
やさい、くだものも今日は全品1割引！
ほかの食料品も、大特売！
食料品は、みんなまとめて文京スーパー三丁目店でどうぞ！
本日、営業時間はいつもより1時間ながく、午後10時まで！
お買い物は文京スーパー、三丁目店で！！
明日、第3月曜日は、定休日だよ、お買い物は今日のうちに！！

1. Which has the biggest discount?
   A. beef
   B. pork
   C. fish
   D. tomatoes

2. How much is an apple discounted?
   A. 40% discount
   B. 30% discount
   C. 20% discount
   D. 10% discount

3. Which one is not discounted?
   A. さしみ
   B. コーヒー
   C. くすり
   D. ハム

4. What time does this supermarket usually close?
   A. 9:00 P.M.
   B. 10:00 P.M.
   C. 10:30 P.M.
   D. 11:00 P.M.

5. What day of the week is it today?
   A. Saturday
   B. Sunday
   C. Monday
   D. Tuesday

Eating Out

食堂に入りましょう

At lunch time many restaurants offer low-priced set meals. Japanese noodles or rice dishes served in bowls are an even cheaper and simpler alternative. Japanese tea and water are served free of charge, and in many company and university cafeterias, self-serve machines for cold water, hot water, and tea are available. In this lesson, you will learn how to read words commonly used in cafeterias, in restaurants, and on menus.

1 ▶ Introductory Quiz

Look at the illustrations below and refer to the words in **Vocabulary**. Then try the following quiz.

I. Which of the following signs means the restaurant is open?

a. 　b. 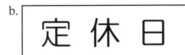　c.

II. Read the signs on the tables below, and then choose the correct answers.

1. よやくしてあります。　　　　（ a.　　b.　　c. ）
2. たばこをすってもいいです。　（ a.　　b.　　c. ）
3. たばこをすってはいけません。（ a.　　b.　　c. ）

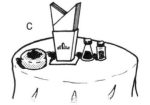

185

III.Read the menu then write T if the statement is true and F if the statement is false.

1. (   ) この店の焼肉は牛肉です。
2. (   ) 牛丼は定食です。
3. (   ) 豚汁は和食です。
4. (   ) みそ汁は洋食です。
5. (   ) 鳥肉からあげは飲み物です。
6. (   ) 紅茶は飲み物です。
7. (   ) おゆは350円です。

********** *MENU* **********

お食事

焼肉定食（豚焼肉、サラダ、みそ汁、ごはん、つけもの）	1000円
和定食（焼魚、煮もの、豚汁、ごはん、つけもの）	980円
中華定食（鳥肉からあげ、マーボどうふ、サラダ、ごはん）	850円
洋食弁当（エビフライ、コロッケ、サラダ、ライス）	950円
牛丼	450円
天ぷらそば	650円
スパゲッティ	500円

お飲み物

ビール（大）	500円
ビール（小）	300円
紅茶	350円
コーヒー	350円
ジュース	300円

*パーティーのご予約お受けいたします。

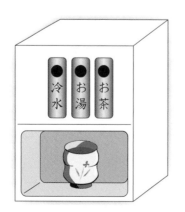

In university cafeterias and other less expensive restaurants, you will often find self-service tea, hot water, or ice water free of charge.

Samples from the menu

煮物　　焼魚

豚汁

和定食　９８０円

洋食弁当　９５０円

牛丼　４５０円

つけもの

サラダ

焼肉

ごはん

みそ汁

焼肉定食　１，０００円

Vocabulary

Study the readings and meanings of these words to help you understand the **Introductory Quiz**.

1.	食堂	しょく どう	**shokudō**	restaurant/cafeteria
2.	準備中	じゅん び ちゅう	**jumbi chū**	Preparing to Open
3.	定休日	てい きゅう び	**teikyū bi**	Shop Holiday, regular holiday
4.	営業中	えい ぎょう ちゅう	**eigyō chū**	Open for Business
5.	予約席	よ やく せき	**yoyaku seki**	reserved table
6.	禁煙席	きん えん せき	**kin'en seki**	nonsmoking table
7.	(お)食事	(お)しょく じ	**(o)shokuji**	meal
8.	焼肉	やき にく	**yakiniku**	grilled meat
9.	定食	てい しょく	**teishoku**	set meal
10.	みそ汁	みそ しる	**misoshiru**	miso soup
11.	つけもの		**tsukemono**	pickles
12.	牛丼	ぎゅう どん	**gyūdon**	a bowl of rice topped with sliced beef
13.	天ぷらそば	てん ぷら そば	**tempura soba**	soba with tempura
14.	鳥肉からあげ	とり にく からあげ	**toriniku karaage**	fried chicken
15.	(お)飲み物	(お)の み もの	**(o)nomimono**	beverage
16.	中華	ちゅう か	**chūka**	Chinese style
17.	マーボどうふ		**mābo dōfu**	tofu with chili pepper
18.	紅茶	こう ちゃ	**kōcha**	black tea
19.	(お)湯	(お)ゆ	**(o)yu**	hot water
20.	(お)茶	(お)ちゃ	**(o)cha**	Japanese tea
21.	冷水	れい すい	**reisui**	ice water
22.	(ご)予約	(ご)よ やく	**(go)yoyaku**	reservation
23.	受ける	う ける	**ukeru**	to receive
24.	豚汁	ぶたじる／とんじる	**butajiru/tonjiru**	miso soup with pork and vegetables
25.	和食	わ しょく	**washoku**	Japanese food/meal
26.	和定食	わ てい しょく	**wa teishoku**	Japanese-style set meal
27.	焼魚	やき ざかな	**yaki zakana**	grilled fish
28.	煮物	に もの	**nimono**	cooked vegetables seasoned with soy sauce
29.	洋食	よう しょく	**yōshoku**	Western food/meal
30.	弁当	べん とう	**bentō**	meal in a box
31.	エビフライ		**ebifurai**	fried prawns
32.	コロッケ		**korokke**	croquette

3 New Characters

Ten characters are introduced in this lesson. Use the explanations to help you understand and remember the characters. Study the compound words to increase your vocabulary.

和 洋 汁 飲 茶 湯 予 約 席 備

237 和	**wa** ワ peace, harmony; Japan	ノ	二	千	千	禾	禾	和	和

和, which combines 禾 grain (cf. 45 科) and 口 mouth, indicates peace, because eating makes people happy and peaceful. In addition, 和 is often used to mean Japan, because ancient Japan was called 倭, pronounced **wa**.	平和	へいわ	**heiwa**	peace
	和室	わしつ	**washitsu**	Japanese-style room
	和食	わしょく	**washoku**	Japanese food/meal
	和定食	わていしょく	**wa teishoku**	Japanese-style set meal
	和風	わふう	**wafū**	Japanese style
	和英辞典	わえいじてん	**waei jiten**	Japanese-English dictionary
	漢和辞典	かんわ じてん	**kanwa jiten**	dictionary of kanji in Japanese

238 洋	**yō** ヨウ ocean; foreign, Western	丶	丷	シ	ジ	ジ	洋	洋	洋
		洋							

洋 combines 氵 water and 羊 sheep's head, meaning beautiful or correct and by extension, splendid and big (cf. 130 着; 188 義). A big, splendid body of water is an ocean. Beyond the ocean, there are foreign lands.	東洋	とうよう	**tōyō**	the East, the Orient
	西洋	せいよう	**seiyō**	the West
	洋食	ようしょく	**yōshoku**	Western food/meal
	洋室	ようしつ	**yōshitsu**	Western-style room
	太平洋	たいへいよう	**taiheiyō**	the Pacific Ocean
	洋書	ようしょ	**yōsho**	Western book
	洋式	ようしき	**yōshiki**	Western style
	洋服	ようふく	**yōfuku**	Western clothes

239 汁　shiru, (jiru)　しる、（じる）　soup

` ｀ 丶 ｀ シ- 汁

汁 combines 氵 water and 十 add (cf. 184 協). In order to cook soup, various ingredients are added to water.

みそ汁	みそしる	**misoshiru**	miso soup
豚汁	ぶたじる/とんじる	**butajiru/tonjiru**	miso soup with pork and vegetables

---

240 飲　no-mu, in　の・む、イン　drink

ノ 八 父 今 今 今 食 食
飠 飲 飲 飲

飲 combines 飠 eat or meal (cf. 180 食) and 欠 wide open mouth, and refers to opening one's mouth wide to drink. 欠 by itself means lack or absence.

飲む	のむ	**nomu**	to drink
飲（み）物	のみもの	**nomi mono**	beverage
飲（み）水	のみみず	**nomi mizu**	drinking water
飲料水	いんりょうすい	**inryō sui**	drinking water (formal)
飲食店	いんしょくてん	**inshoku ten**	eating house, restaurant

---

241 茶　cha, sa　チャ、サ　tea

一 十 サ ｻ 茶 芝 苳 苶
茶

茶 derives from 荼. The radical ⺾ represents plant, and 余 indicates dividing 八 a piled up 十 mound 亼 to make space, implying extra space, time, etc. 茶 thus means tea (the plant for brewing the drink, or the drink itself), which people enjoy in their spare time.

（お）茶	（お）ちゃ	**(o)cha**	(Japanese) tea
紅茶	こうちゃ	**kōcha**	black tea
茶色	ちゃいろ	**chairo**	brown color
茶道	さどう	**sadō**	art of tea ceremony
喫茶店	きっさてん	**kissa ten**	tearoom, coffee shop

242	**yu, tō** ゆ、トウ hot water	丶	冫	氵	汀	沪	沪	沪	浔
湯		渇	湯	湯	湯				

湯, which combines 氵 water and 昜 sun rising up high (cf. 197 場), indicates hot water with steam rising up out of it.

（お）湯	（お）ゆ	**(o)yu**	hot water
		—	
〜湯	〜ゆ	**〜yu**	suffix for bathhouses or hot springs
銭湯	せんとう	**sentō**	public bathhouse
給湯	きゅうとう	**kyūtō**	hot water supply
熱湯	ねっとう	**nettō**	boiling water

243	**yo** ヨ in advance, beforehand	フ	マ	ヱ	予				
予									

予 combines ㄱ crouching man, and 了 (or 了) which resembles a hanging string tied up with a knot and means complete or finish. From the idea of crouching just before leaping toward a goal, 予 has come to mean in advance.

予定	よてい	**yotei**	schedule, plan
予定表	よていひょう	**yotei hyō**	timetable, written schedule
		—	
予習する	よしゅうする	**yoshū suru**	to prepare one's lessons
天気予報	てんきよほう	**tenki yohō**	weather forecast
予算	よさん	**yosan**	budget, estimate of income and expenses

244	**yaku** ヤク appointment, promise; approximately	乚	幺	幺	糸	糸	糸	糹	約
約		約							

約 combines 糸 thread and 勺 large spoon. When the ancient Chinese made an appointment, they carved a spoonlike shape into a tree and tied a thread there to mark the place. Thus 約 came to mean appointment.

約〜	やく〜	**yaku〜**	about, approximately
予約する	よやくする	**yoyaku suru**	to reserve, to book, to subscribe
先約	せんやく	**sen'yaku**	previous appointment
		—	
約束する	やくそくする	**yakusoku suru**	to promise, to make an appointment
契約書	けいやくしょ	**keiyaku sho**	written contract

245 席	**seki** セキ seat, place	丶	亠	广	户	庐	庐	庐	庐
		席	席						

席 combines 巾 cloth (cf. 146 帳) and 产, simplified from 庶, which here indicates warm because of 灬 fire (cf. 250 無). Together they suggest a cushion, a place for sitting, or seat.	席	せき	**seki**	seat
	出席する	しゅっせきする	**shusseki suru**	to attend
	予約席	よやくせき	**yoyaku seki**	reserved seat/table
	禁煙席	きんえんせき	**kin'en seki**	nonsmoking seat/table
	欠席する	けっせきする	**kesseki suru**	to be absent from
	優先席	ゆうせんせき	**yūsen seki**	priority seat (for the aged or handicapped, etc.)
	自由席	じゆうせき	**jiyū seki**	unreserved seat
	指定席	していせき	**shitei seki**	reserved seat
	座席	ざせき	**zaseki**	seat

246 備	**bi** ビ prepare, furnish	ノ	イ	亻	亻	伫	倅	伊	伊
		俻	俻	備	備				

備 combines 亻 man and 𦥑, a container in which arrows are placed before being used, and suggests preparing or furnishing something.	準備する	じゅんびする	**jumbi suru**	to prepare
	準備中	じゅんびちゅう	**jumbi chū**	in preparation, Preparing to Open
	設備	せつび	**setsubi**	facility, equipment
	備考	びこう	**bikō**	remark, note
	予備	よび	**yobi**	spare; preparatory, preliminary
	予備校	よびこう	**yobi kō**	cram school

備 → 俻 → 𦥑

4 ▶ Practice

I. Write the readings of the following kanji in hiragana.

1. 準 備 中　　　　2. 営 業 中　　　　3. 予 約 席　　　　4. 禁 煙 席
5. 焼 肉 定 食　　　6. み そ 汁　　　　7. 牛 丼　　　　　8. お 飲 み 物
9. 紅 茶　　　　　10. お 湯　　　　　11. 豚 汁　　　　　12. 和 食
13. 焼 魚　　　　　14. 洋 食　　　　　15. 平 和　　　　　16. 西 洋
17. 飲 料 水　　　　18. 予 定　　　　　19. 先 約
20. 東 洋 医 学 は 、 な か な か よ さ そ う で す ね 。
21. お 茶 を 飲 み ま し ょ う 。
22. パ ー テ ィ ー を す る 時 は 、 予 約 し て く だ さ い 。
23. こ の 席 は 、 あ い て い ま す か 。
24. 約 ５ ０ 名 が 会 議 に 出 席 し ま し た 。

II. Fill in the blanks with appropriate kanji.

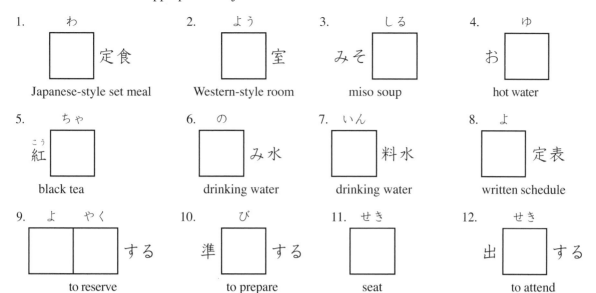

1. わ ☐ 定食
Japanese-style set meal

2. よう ☐ 室
Western-style room

3. しる みそ ☐
miso soup

4. ゆ お ☐
hot water

5. ちゃ 紅(こう)☐
black tea

6. の ☐ み水
drinking water

7. いん ☐ 料水
drinking water

8. よ ☐ 定表
written schedule

9. よ やく ☐☐ する
to reserve

10. び 準 ☐ する
to prepare

11. せき ☐
seat

12. せき 出 ☐ する
to attend

5 ▶ Advanced Placement Exam Practice Questions

Read the e-mail below, and answer the following questions. Note that the e-mail continues overleaf.

From　：マリー
To　　：Class II
Subject：パーティーのお知らせ

Hi, everybody,

わたしたちの日本語のクラスも来週で終わります。金曜日の勉強(べんきょう)のあと、　12時半からみんなでパーティーをしませんか。先生がたにも来てもらおうとおもっています。わたしとポールさんで学校の前のお店に行って、どんなパーティーができるか、料金やメニューをしらべました。時間は2時間です。プランが3つあります。みんなの意見をきいて、きめたいとおもいます。

A 洋食 レストラン本郷	**B** 和食 東大前食堂	**C** 中華(かべきんはんてん)北京飯店
1600円(料理のみ)	1800円(料理のみ)	2500円(料理 ＋ 飲み物)
料理(り)	**料理**	**料理 ＋ 飲み物**
サンドイッチ、サラダ	和風(ふう)サラダ、さしみ	中華(か)サラダ、ぎょうざ
フライドチキン、ピザ	天(てん)ぷら、煮物	鳥肉からあげ、チャーハン
エビフライ、スパゲティ	ごはん、みそ汁	マーボどうふ、やきそば
フルーツ	くだもの	スープ
飲み物		中国酒、ビール、
ワイン、ビール、ジュース	**飲み物**	ワイン、ジュース
コーヒー、紅(こう)茶	日本酒(しゅ)、ビール、ワイン、	
(180円から)	ジュース	
	※プラス 700円で ¹飲みほうだい	※²食べほうだい 　飲みほうだい

¹飲みほうだい: you can drink as much as you want for a certain amount of money
²食べほうだい: you can eat as much as you want for a certain amount of money

出席できますか？　　　　　　（　出席します　出席しません　）
どのプランがいいですか。　　（　A　B　C　）
予約をするので、今週中にわたしにメールしてください。
マリー　Mary@abcd.ac.jp

1. What kind of party is described in this e-mail?
    A. A party to celebrate Paul's graduation.
    B. A party to celebrate the starting of the Japanese language class.
    C. A party to celebrate the completion of the Japanese language class.
    D. A party to celebrate the birthday of the Japanese language teacher.

2. Which of the following statements about plan A is correct?
    A. It is simply the cheapest plan of the three.
    B. We do not know whether it is cheap, because we only get the price for food.
    C. Only this plan serves fruit.
    D. You can drink as much as you want for 180 yen.

3. Which of the following statements about plan B is correct?
    A. You can eat or drink as much as you want for 1800 yen.
    B. You can have as much as you want of any kind of drink for 700 yen.
    C. This is the cheapest plan of the three.
    D. This plan is for Japanese-style food, so only Japanese sake is served.

4. Which of the following statements about plan C is correct?
    A. You can eat or drink as much as you want for 2500 yen.
    B. You can eat as much food as you want for 2500 yen, but drinks are not included.
    C. This plan also serves fruit.
    D. You can drink as much as you want for 2500 yen, but food is not included.

5. What should the person who got this e-mail do?
    A. Inform Mary of his or her attendance at the party.
    B. Tell Mary about other plans.
    C. Tell Mary which plan he or she chooses, and about his/her attendance.
    D. Call the restaurant directly and make a reservation by the end of this week.

At the Real Estate Agency

不動産屋で

When looking for a place to live, try visiting a real estate company or looking over a real estate rental magazine. If you have already chosen a location, it will be helpful to visit a local real estate agent in that district. Agents typically hang house and apartment listings in the window.

Some terms commonly used when searching for housing are technical but important to know. So, in this lesson, you will have an opportunity to learn some kanji outside of the 250 basic characters taught in this book.

1 ▶ Introductory Quiz

After signing a contract, you usually pay your first month's rent, a nominal administrative fee, a security deposit (usually 2 to 3 months' rent), a gift payment to the landlord (usually 2 to 3 months' rent), and an agent's fee (usually 1 month's rent).

Normal leases are for a period of two years, but it is possible to leave before that time by notifying the landlord and paying a penalty, usually 1 month's rent. Contracts can be renewed after the initial two-year period by making another payment to the landlord, usually 1 to 2 months' rent.

Look at the illustrations on the next page, and refer to the words in **Vocabulary**. Then try the following quiz.

A real estate agent offers information on two apartments, A and B (overleaf). Compare the two in detail. Which do you prefer? Why?

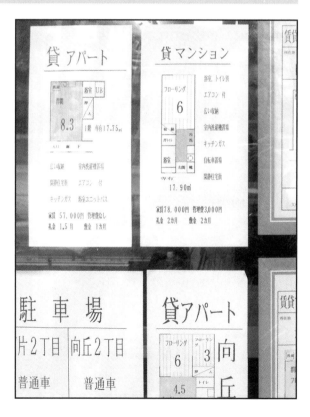

195

Apartment A

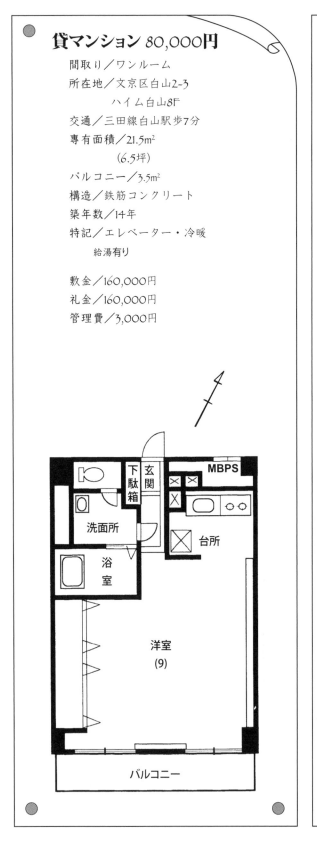

貸マンション 80,000円

間取り／ワンルーム

所在地／文京区白山2-3

　　　　ハイム白山8F

交通／三田線白山駅歩7分

専有面積／21.5m²

　　　　(6.5坪)

バルコニー／3.5m²

構造／鉄筋コンクリート

築年数／14年

特記／エレベーター・冷暖

　　　給湯有り

敷金／160,000円

礼金／160,000円

管理費／3,000円

Apartment B

貸アパート 98,000円

間取り／2K

所在地／足立区千住元町

　　　　5—13

　　　　北都ハウス2F

交通／千代田線・日比谷線

　　　　北千住駅バス10分

　　　　歩1分

専有面積／25.5m²

　　　　(7.7坪)

バルコニー／3.9m²

構造／木造モルタル

築年数／7年

特記／給湯・シャワー有り

敷金／1ケ月

礼金／2ケ月

管理費／無し

2 ► Vocabulary

Study the readings and meanings of these words to help you understand the **Introductory Quiz**.

1. 不動産屋	ふ どう さん や	**fudōsan ya**	real estate agency/agent
2. 貸	かし	**kashi**	for rent, for lease
3. ～有り	～あ り	**~ari**	with ~, ~ available
4. ～無し	～な し	**~nashi**	without ~, no ~
5. 間取り	ま ど り	**madori**	arrangement of rooms, floor plan
6. 洋室	よう しつ	**yōshitsu**	Western-style room
7. 和室	わ しつ	**washitsu**	Japanese-style room
8. 玄関	げん かん	**genkan**	entry hall
9. 台所	だい どころ	**daidokoro**	kitchen
10. 浴室	よく しつ	**yokushitsu**	bathroom
11. 洗面所	せん めん じょ	**semmen jo**	washroom
12. 押入	おし いれ	**oshiire**	closet
13. ～畳／帖	～じょう	**~jō**	counter for tatami mats
14. 交通	こう つう	**kōtsū**	transportation
15. 歩～分	ほ～ふん	**ho~fun**	~ minutes on foot
16. 専有面積	せん ゆう めん せき	**sen'yū menseki**	privately owned area
17. ～坪	～つぼ	**~tsubo**	counter for 3.3m^3 area
18. 構造	こう ぞう	**kōzō**	structure
19. 鉄筋コンクリート	てっ きん コンクリート	**tekkin konkurīto**	reinforced concrete
20. 木造モルタル	もく ぞう モルタル	**mokuzō morutaru**	wood and mortar
21. 築年数	ちく ねん すう	**chiku nensū**	years since constructed
22. 冷暖（房）	れい だん （ぼう）	**reidam(bō)**	air-conditioner and heater
23. 給湯	きゅう とう	**kyūtō**	hot water supply
24. 敷金	しき きん	**shikikin**	deposit money
25. 礼金	れい きん	**reikin**	gift money to landlord
26. 管理費	かん り ひ	**kanri hi**	administrative fee

3 ► New Characters

Four characters are introduced in this lesson. Use the explanations to help you understand and remember the characters. Study the compound words to increase your vocabulary.

屋　貸　有　無

247 屋 — ya, oku / や、オク / roof; house; shop

ᄀ	ᄀ	尸	尸	屋	层	屋	屋
屋							

屋 combines 尸 cloth covering something and 至 reaching a goal or dead end (cf. 190 室). Thus 屋 suggests a cover for shutting something out, meaning roof or house. An associated meaning is a house of business, namely, a shop.

不動産屋	ふどうさんや	**fudōsan ya**	real estate agency/agent
部屋	へや	**heya**	room
肉屋	にくや	**nikuya**	meat shop
屋上	おくじょう	**okujō**	housetop, roof
八百屋	やおや	**yaoya**	vegetable store, greengrocery
屋外	おくがい	**okugai**	outdoor
屋内	おくない	**okunai**	indoor

248 貸 — ka-su / か・す / lend, rent out

ノ	イ	仁	代	代	代	伐	貸
貸	貸	貸	貸				

貸 combines 代 replace or substitute (cf. 89) and 貝 money (cf. 200 費). When lending or renting something, one receives money in substitution for what is lent.

貸す	かす	**kasu**	to lend, to rent out
貸室	かししつ	**kashi shitsu**	room for rent
貸出期間	かしだし きかん	**kashidashi kikan**	lending period
貸マンション	かしマンション	**kashi manshon**	apartment for rent
貸切りバス	かしきりバス	**kashikiri basu**	chartered bus

249 有 — a-ru, yū / あ・る、ユウ / exist

ノ	ナ	才	右	有	有		

有, which combines 手 hand (cf. 85 手) and 月 meat (cf. 226 肉), indicates a hand holding meat to show proof of its existence.

有る	ある	**aru**	to exist; to have
〜有り	〜あり	**~ari**	with ~, ~ available
有名な	ゆうめいな	**yūmei na**	famous, well-known
有料	ゆうりょう	**yūryō**	payment required
有楽町線	ゆうらくちょう せん	**Yūrakuchō sen**	Yurakucho Line
有効期間	ゆうこう きかん	**yūkō kikan**	the term/period of validity
有効期限	ゆうこう きげん	**yūkō kigen**	the deadline for validity

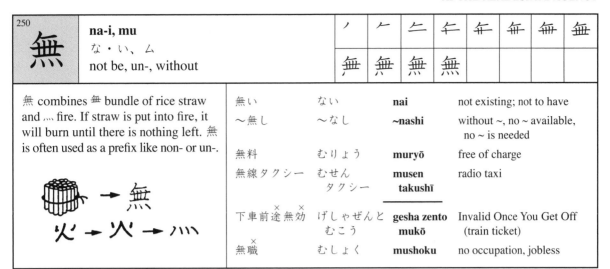

| 250 無 | **na-i, mu**
な・い、ム
not be, un-, without | ノ | ㇗ | ㇗ | 仁 | 𠂉 | 無 | 無 | 無 |
| | | 無 | 無 | 無 | 無 | | | | |

無 combines 𣜄 bundle of rice straw and 灬 fire. If straw is put into fire, it will burn until there is nothing left. 無 is often used as a prefix like non- or un-.

無い	ない	**nai**	not existing; not to have
～無し	～なし	**~nashi**	without ~, no ~ available, no ~ is needed
無料	むりょう	**muryō**	free of charge
無線タクシー	むせん タクシー	**musen takushī**	radio taxi
下車前途無効	げしゃぜんと むこう	**gesha zento mukō**	Invalid Once You Get Off (train ticket)
無職	むしょく	**mushoku**	no occupation, jobless

---

4 ▶ Practice

I. Write the readings of the following kanji in hiragana.

1. 不動産屋   2. 貸室   3. ～有り   4. ～無し
5. 台所   6. 浴室   7. 押入   8. 交通
9. 屋上   10. 無料   11. 貸出期間
12. この部屋には、シャワーは有りますが、ふろは無いです。
13. ともだちにお金を貸してあげました。
14. あの方が、有名なブラウン博士です。

II. Fill in the blanks with appropriate kanji.

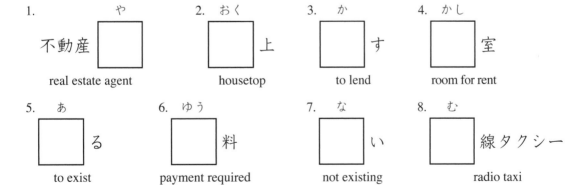

1. や　　不動産 ☐ 　real estate agent
2. おく　☐ 上 　housetop
3. か　☐ す 　to lend
4. かし　☐ 室 　room for rent
5. あ　☐ る 　to exist
6. ゆう　☐ 料 　payment required
7. な　☐ い 　not existing
8. む　☐ 線タクシー 　radio taxi

199

5 ▶ Advanced Placement Exam Practice Questions

You have been looking for an apartment, and are visiting a real estate company. You're talking to the agent, Mr. Yasuda, about an apartment you want to rent. Answer in Japanese.

1. Respond.

   Yasuda: 部屋をきめるとき、何が一番、大切ですか。

   You:

2. Respond.

   Yasuda: どうしてですか。

   You:

3. Respond.

   Yasuda: 駅から歩いて、何分までならいいですか。

   You:

4. Respond.

   Yasuda: どんな間取りがいいですか。

   You:

5. Respond.

   Yasuda: 和室でもいいですか。

   You:

6. Respond.

   Yasuda: では、いい部屋が二つあります。ひとつは、大きなバルコニーがあります。もうひとつは、押入がたくさんあって便利です。どうでしょう。

   You:

   Yasuda: これから部屋を見に行きましょう。

REVIEW EXERCISE: LESSONS 19–21

I. Find the correct words from the box below and write their corresponding letters in the parentheses.

1. (　　) で、いいアパートを見つけました。

2. とんカツは、牛肉ではなく（　　）でつくるんです。

3. 日本のお金がよわくなることを（　　）といいます。

4. もう（　　）なので、買い物をやめなくてはいけません。

5. この道路は（　　）ですから、お金を払ってください。

6. デパートに行けば、いろいろな（　　）が買えます。

7. (　　) にはたいてい、たたみがあります。

8. (　　) で定期券を買ったほうが安くなります。

```
a. 物      b. 閉店時間    c. 学割    d. 豚肉

e. 有料    f. 和室        g. 円安    h. 不動産屋
```

II. Many of the 250 kanji you have learned in this book have pronunciations in common. Shown below are compound words that include examples of this. Write these kanji in the blanks.

1. よう

東 [　] the East

専 [　] for exclusive use

水 [　] Wednesday

2. あん

[　] 内所 information center

[　] 全な safe

[　] 証番号 Personal Identification Number

3. どう

自 [　] automatic

水 [　] tap water

食 [　] dining room

4. かい

[　] 場 meeting place

[　] 速 semi-express train

[　] 始 start

5. こう

[　] 学部 Faculty of Engineering

[　] 空便 airmail

[　] 義室 lecture room

6. けん

危 [　] danger

実 [　] experiment

意 [　] opinion

201

7. じ

故　accident
間　time
分　oneself

8. きゅう

研　research
特　special express train
連　consecutive holidays

9. きょう

都　Kyoto
室　classroom
会　association

10. き

電　electricity
日　diary
定　regular

11. しょう

火器　fire extinguisher
学生　primary school children
月　the New Year

12. せん

週　last week
門　major field
面所　wash room

13. ふ

通　stoppage of traffic
通　ordinary

14. ぎょう

三　目　the third line
営　中　Open

15. よ

定　schedule
金　money deposited

16. せい

学　student
平　the Heisei era

17. しん

入生　new student
察券　patient's card

18. ぶん

半　half
学　literature

19. し

休　pause
都　city

20. ぽう

文　grammar
一　通行　one way traffic

21. かん

図書　library
五日　five days

22. やく

予　席　reserved seat
内用　internal medicine

23. む

事　所　office
料　free of charge

24. いん

入　hospitalization
料水　drinking water

APPENDIX A

Japanese Names

Below are some Japanese names using the 250 kanji in this book.

Family Names

平山	大山	中山	本山	丸山	西山	東山
小山	北山	内山	水田	平田	大田	前田
金田	土田	本田	上田	山田	中田	小田
西田	北田	南田	高田	内田	安田	和田
水口	田口	山口	山本	中本	木下	山下
田中	山中	金子	土屋	大平	本間	田代

ひらやま	おおやま	なかやま	もとやま	まるやま	にしやま	ひがしやま
こやま	きたやま	うちやま	みずた	ひらた	おおた	まえだ
かねだ	つちだ	ほんだ	うえだ	やまだ	なかた／だ	おだ
にしだ	きただ	みなみだ	たかだ	うちだ	やすだ	わだ
みずぐち	たぐち	やまぐち	やまもと	なかもと	きのした	やました
たなか	やまなか	かねこ	つちや	おおひら	ほんま	たしろ

First Names

(Male)

学	正	修	博	洋	明	正一
義一	研二	洋三	文男	正男	和男	安男

まなぶ	ただし	おさむ	ひろし	ひろし	あきら	しょういち
よしかず	けんじ	ようぞう	ふみお	まさお	かずお	やすお

(Female)

曜子	京子	文子	博子	正子	道子
明子	保子	洋子	和代	安代	

ようこ	きょうこ	ふみこ	ひろこ	まさこ	みちこ
あきこ	やすこ	ようこ	かずよ	やすよ	

APPENDIX B

Main Radicals

Below are the main radicals presented in this book, and some examples.

I.   へん (left part) ◼️◻️
   1.   イ   man, people   休、使、住、何、代、(人)、停、便、他、修、保、付、備
   2.   言   word, speak   語、話、証、認、訂、記、講、議、診、計
   3.   日   sun   (日)、時、曜、暗、明、普、(cf. 間)
   4.   糸   thread   線、絡、終、約
   5.   氵   water   (水)、洗、準、注、消、法、洋、汁、湯
   6.   金   metal, gold   (金)、鉄、銀
   7.   扌   hand   (手)、押、扱、払
   8.   阝   wall, hill   際、険、階、院

II. つくり (right part) ◻️◼️
   1.   攵   strike, hit   攻、故、務、教
   2.   阝   village   部、都、郵

III. かんむり (top part) ◻️
   1.   艹   plant   薬、茶
   2.   宀   roof, house   定、室、実、察、安、(cf. 案、空)

IV. あし (bottom part) ◼️
   1.   儿   legs   先、児、(cf. 洗、祝、院、売、見)
   2.   心   mind   急、意、(cf. 認、快)

V.   かまえ (enclosing part) ◼️ ◼️
   1.   門   gate   間、開、(門)、閉
   2.   囗   enclosure   四、回、国、図

VI. にょう (left and bottom part) ◻️
   1.   辶   proceed   週、込、通、連、速、道

VII. たれ (top and left part) ◻️
   1.   尸   corpse   局、届、屋
   2.   疒   sickness   病

VIII. その他 (miscellaneous)
   1.   木   tree   (木)、本、東、案、業、様、(cf. 休)
   2.   土   earth   (土)、地、堂、場、(cf. 煙)
   3.   十   add, many   (十)、千、協、博、(cf. 準、計、汁)
   4.   口   mouth, box   名、(口)、各、号、右、品、和、(cf. 語、故、知)

APPENDIX C

Kanji Compounds

I. Main Types of Compounds and Some Examples

Type I. Adjective + Noun
正門、正面、前者、後半、外国、内線、東口、西洋、洋服、和食、全国、全部、各地、各駅、大会、大型、小包、本館、本店、分館、支店、先週、現代、次回、新年、故人、他人、若者、国道、実費、私費、実物、空車、定食、近所、急用、終電、初診、紅茶、冷水、暗室、金魚

Type 2. Verb (Modifier) + Noun
学者、歩行者、講師、歌手、引力、保証人、証明書、洗濯機、入口、出口、住所、案内所、教室、食堂、会議室、売店、会場、学会、講演会、連絡先、入場券、用法、記事、着物、食品、送料、運賃、来月

Type 3. Adverb + Verb
外出、外食、予約、予定、予習、予報、中止、中立、代表、実験、実習、実行、厳禁、公認、右折、専用、始発、急行

Type 4. Verb + Noun (Objective)
入国、出国、入学、休講、授業、卒業、入院、退院、開門、開店、閉店、閉館、発音、発車、停車、下車、駐車、見物、買物、読書、禁煙、給湯、消火、預金

Type 5. Pair of Synonyms
都市、道路、場所、階段、中央、方向、品物、職業、書状、出発、到着、開始、停止、禁止、使用、分割、研究、確認、故障、議論、変更、訂正、正確、平和、平常、危険、部分

Type 6. Pair of Antonyms
大小、前後、左右、上下、出入、東西、南北、男女、売買、終始、発着、開閉

II. Kanji Commonly Used in Compounds and Some Examples

部: 部分、部屋、全部、本部、支部、北部、工学部、文学部

書: 書状、読書、洋書、辞書、教科書、参考書、申込書、証明書、保証書、説明書、案内書、契約書、修了証書

用: 用事、用紙、用法、用意、使用、利用、専用、学生用、外用薬

券: 食券、入場券、乗車券、定期券、回数券、急行券、特急券、指定券、診察券

所: 住所、所在地、現住所、洗面所、案内所、停留所、市役所、区役所、保健所、研究所、事務所、発電所、近所

内: 内科、案内、都内、車内、学内、室内、屋内、年内、家内

線: 東京メトロ線、都営線、山手線、新幹線、国内線、国際線、内線、無線

代: 代表、代金、代理人、電気代、薬代、時代、世代、現代

中: 中立、中止、中学、中心、準備中、工事中、会議中、営業中、使用中、一日中

全: 全国、全線、全品、全学、全体、全員、全部、全快

車: 車内、電車、発車、停車、下車、駐車、自動車、自転車、普通車、空車

口: 口座、入口、出口、東口、西口、北口、南口、非常口、連絡口、窓口、人口

出: 出席、出発、出国、出口、出前、提出、輸出

便: 便利、郵便、航空便、船便、宅急便、学内便、定期便、不便

事: 事実、事件、事務、事故、火事、工事、用事、大事、記事、知事

不: 不安、不通、不用、不便、不可、不足、不明、不動産

急: 急行、急用、急病、急停車、準急、特急、救急車

発: 発車、発音、発表、発電所、始発、終発、開発

正: 正式、正門、正義、正常、正確、正解、正月、正面、訂正、修正

記: 記入、記号、記事、記念、記者、日記、暗記、左記

外: 外国、外出、外来、外用薬、外務省、外科、海外、市外、屋外、時間外、意外

常: 通常、平常、正常、日常、非常口

料: 料金、料理、有料、無料、授業料、送料、手数料、資料、調味料

道: 道路、車道、歩道、鉄道、国道、水道、柔道、茶道、片道

者: 学者、医者、記者、歩行者、消費者、経営者、前者、後者

気: 気体、気分、天気、電気、火気、人気、空気

講: 講義、講演、講堂、講師、講座、講習会、開講、休講、受講届

食: 食堂、食事、食券、食前、食後、食間、定食、外食、立食

館: 大使館、本館、分館、別館、学生会館、図書館、一号館、映画館、美術館、博物館、旅館、閉館

会: 会話、会社、会場、会議、会員、会費、会計、会館、社会、大会、学会、国会、講演会、忘年会、研究会、協会、閉会、面会、入会金、記者会見

義: 義理、義務教育、講義、主義、定義、正義、意義

議: 議論、議題、議長、議会、議員、会議、国会議事堂

室: 教室、講義室、五号室、研究室、実験室、図書室、会議室、事務室、診察室、喫煙室、室内、浴室、洋室、地下室、暗室、空室

実: 実物、実用、実習、実行、実験、実際、事実

場: 場内、場合、工場、会場、市場、駐車場、入場券

費: 費用、食費、学費、会費、交通費、医療費、実費、国費、私費

法: 法律、法人、法学部、文法、用法、使用法、調理法、寸法

店: 書店、開店、閉店、本店、支店、売店、百貨店、専門店、飲食店、喫茶店

品: 品物、全品、食品、食料品、用品、作品、日用品、電気製品、非売品、特産品、薬品

洋: 洋食、洋室、洋書、洋式、洋服、東洋、西洋

予: 予約、予定、予備、予習、予報、予算

席: 出席、欠席、座席、空席、予約席、自由席、指定席、優先席、禁煙席、喫煙席

屋: 屋上、屋外、屋内、部屋、肉屋、八百屋、魚屋、不動産屋

ANSWERS TO THE INTRODUCTORY QUIZZES, REVIEW EXERCISES, AND ADVANCED PLACEMENT EXAM PRACTICE QUESTIONS

Answers to the Introductory Quizzes

Lesson 1
1. 460
2. 930
3. 500
4. (5437) 0171
5. 省略 (omitted)
6. 省略 (omitted)

Lesson 2
I. 1. c
    2. b
    3. b
    4. b
    5. b
    6. b
    7. c
II. 1. 12がつ25にち
    2. 1がつなのか
    3. 2しゅうかん
    4. 12がつ15にち、4がつ ついたち

Lesson 3
1. へいせい
2. よっか、いつか
3. もく、きん、ど
4. 5
5. 4
6. げつ
7. か
8. 10
9. げつ、きん

Lesson 4
1. a
2. a, b
3. b
4. b
5. a
6. b, a

Lesson 5
I. 1. 六本木、東京
    2. 9, 5, 12, 4
    3. 8,900
    4. スミス
    5. a

II. 省略 (omitted)

Lesson 6
I. 1. f
    2. c
    3. d
    4. a
    5. b
    6. e
II. 1. c, d, e, f
    2. a
    3. b, e
    4. e
III. c, d

Lesson 7
I. 1. a. 190; b. 130; c. 160; d. 150
    2. a, d
II. 1. a, b
    2. c
    3. e

Lesson 8
1. a
2. a
3. b
4. a

Lesson 9
I. 1. c
    2. f
    3. e
    4. a
II. 1. b
    2. a
    3. b
    4. b
    5. a

Lesson 10
I. 1. a, e, g
    2. b
    3. f
    4. d
    5. c

II. 1. 5:00
    2. 0:03
III. 1. a
     2. b
     3. b
     4. a

Lesson 11
I. b, a
II. 1. C
    2. A
    3. E
    4. D
    5. B

Lesson 12
1. a
2. c, g
3. f
4. e
5. b

Lesson 13
I. 1. a
    2. b
    3. b
    4. c
    5. b
    6. c
    7. b
II. 省略 (omitted)

Lesson 14
1. a
2. b
3. b
4. b
5. c

Lesson 15
1. a, a, b
2. a, b
3. b
4. b
5. a
6. a, a
7. b

207

Lesson 16
I. 1. a
    2. b
    3. b
    4. b
    5. a
    6. b
II. 1. a
    2. a
    3. b
III. A. 講義室、事務室、会館、休講
     B. 研究室、実験室、番号、一
        番、
          一階、一号室

Lesson 17
I. 1. 新しい都市
    2. 工学部11号館
    3. 二番教室
    4. 2月24日
II. 1. 3月7日
    2. 3,000円

    3. 申込書 、山本研究室
    4. 3月1日
    5. はい、行けます。
III. 省略 (Omitted)

Lesson 18
I. 1. 1) d, 2) c, 3) b, 4) a
    2. 1) b, 2) c, 3) d, 4) a
II. 1. b
    2. b
    3. b
    4. b
    5. a, b

Lesson 19
I. 1. b
    2. a
    3. a
    4. c
II. 1. b
    2. b
    3. b

    4. b
    5. b
    6. b
    7. a
    8. b

Lesson 20
I. c
II. 1. a
    2. a, c
    3. b
III. 1. F
     2. F
     3. T
     4. F
     5. F
     6. T
     7. F

Lesson 21
省略 (Omitted)

Answers to the Review Exercises

Review Exercise, Lessons 1–5
I. 1. d
    2. e
    3. b
    4. k
    5. i
    6. g
    7. o
    8. l
    9. c
    10. f
    11. a
    12. h
    13. p
    14. n
    15. j
    16. m
II. 1. b
    2. a
    3. b
    4. a
    5. a
    6. b
    7. b
    8. b
    9. a

Review Exercise, Lessons 6–10
I. 1. a
    2. h
    3. j
    4. e
    5. b
    6. c
    7. i, n
    8. f, k
    9. d, g, l, m
    10. s
    11. r
    12. t
    13. q
    14. o
II. 1. e
    2. c
    3. i
    4. b
    5. j
    6. g
    7. a

Review Exercise, Lessons 11–14
I. 1. c
    2. k
    3. a
    4. g
    5. e
    6. d
    7. h
    8. j
    9. f
    10. i
    11. b
II. 1. a
    2. a
    3. b
    4. a
    5. b
    6. a

Review Exercise, Lessons 15–18
I. 1. e A. 2–11: b, d, g, i, k, n,
               r, t, u, w
        B. 12–18: a, j, l, p, q, s, v
        C. 19–24: c, f, h, m, o, x

Review Exercise, Lessons 15–18 (continued)

II.
1. g
2. a
3. l
4. e
5. b
6. c
7. h
8. i
9. j
10. f
11. k
12. d

Review Exercise, Lessons 19–21

I.
1. h
2. d
3. g
4. b
5. e
6. a
7. f
8. c

II.
1. 洋、用、曜
2. 案、安、暗
3. 動、道、堂
4. 会、快、開
5. 工、航、講
6. 険、験、見
7. 事、時、自
8. 究、急、休
9. 京、教、協
10. 気、記、期
11. 消、小、正
12. 先、専、洗
13. 不、普
14. 行、業
15. 予、預
16. 生、成
17. 新、診
18. 分、文
19. 止、市
20. 法、方
21. 館、間
22. 約、薬
23. 務、無
24. 院、飲

Answers to the Advanced Placement Exam Practice Questions

Lesson 1
1. B
2. A
3. C
4. D

Lesson 2
1. C
2. B
3. D
4. C
5. B

Lesson 3
1. B
2. A
3. B
4. D
5. B

Lesson 4
1. D
2. C
3. D
4. A
5. B

Lesson 5
Omitted

Lesson 6
1. A
2. B
3. A
4. A
5. B

Lesson 7
1. D
2. C
3. B
4. D

Lesson 8
1. D
2. A
3. B
4. B

Lesson 9
1. A
2. C
3. C
4. D
5. C

Lesson 10
1. A
2. D
3. A
4. B
5. C

Lesson 11
1. B
2. B
3. A
4. C
5. D

Lesson 12
Omitted

Lesson 13
1. A
2. C
3. C
4. D

Lesson 14
1. C
2. B
3. D
4. A

Lesson 15
1. D
2. B
3. A
4. C
5. D

Lesson 16
1. D
2. C
3. B
4. C
5. D

Lesson 17
1. A
2. C
3. C
4. B
5. A

Lesson 18
1. C
2. B
3. D
4. C

Lesson 19
1. C
2. D
3. C
4. A
5. B

Lesson 20
1. C
2. B
3. B
4. A
5. C

Lesson 21
Omitted

ON-KUN INDEX

The words in this index are taken from the kanji charts. **On-yomi** in katakana and **kun-yomi** in hiragana are followed by the kanji, the lesson number where it's found, and its serial number in this book. Hiragana after "•" indicates **okurigana**. Modified readings, enclosed in ( ), follow after original readings.

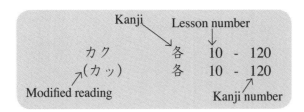

VOCABULARY INDEX

The words in this index are taken from the vocabulary lists and kanji charts in Lessons 1 through 21.